Environmental Justice
as Social Work Practice

Environmental Justice as Social Work Practice

CHRISTINA L. ERICKSON

OXFORD
UNIVERSITY PRESS

OXFORD
UNIVERSITY PRESS

Oxford University Press is a department of the University of Oxford. It furthers
the University's objective of excellence in research, scholarship, and education
by publishing worldwide. Oxford is a registered trade mark of Oxford University
Press in the UK and certain other countries.

Published in the United States of America by Oxford University Press
198 Madison Avenue, New York, NY 10016, United States of America.

© Oxford University Press 2018

Library of Congress Cataloging-in-Publication Data
Names: Erickson, Christina L., author.
Title: Environmental justice as social work practice /
Christina L. Erickson.
Description: New York: Oxford University Press, 2018. |
Includes bibliographical references and index.
Identifiers: LCCN 2017055366 (print) | LCCN 2018010980 (ebook) |
ISBN 9780190871062 (updf) | ISBN 9780190871079 (epub) | ISBN 9780190871055 (paperback)
Subjects: LCSH: Social service. | Environmental justice. | BISAC: SOCIAL SCIENCE / Social Work.
Classification: LCC HV40 (ebook) | LCC HV40.E6685 2018 (print) | DDC 361.3/201—dc23
LC record available at https://lccn.loc.gov/2017055366

9 8 7 6 5 4 3 2 1

Printed by WebCom, Inc., Canada

I dedicate this book to the purest joys of my life, Todd, Mia, and Sonja.

To my Mom, who in 1974 said to me, "You can be anything you want to be."

CONTENTS

CHAPTER 3. Theoretical Foundations: Systems, Narrative, and Structural Theories   43

CHAPTER 4. Ethics for Environmental Justice   56

CHAPTER 5. Understanding Yourself and the Natural Environment   71

PREFACE

To the Student:

Welcome to the world of environmental justice and social work practice!

Solving environmental concerns cannot be the sole call of one discipline. It requires multidisciplinary perspectives, theories, and applications from a wide range of thinkers and problem-solvers. Social workers have worked for decades toward justice for all people; we now recognize that the natural environment is a crucial element in securing justice for current and future generations. Environmental justice is the newest area in efforts for justice-making in social work—but we know it is deeply intertwined with our long-standing work for social and economic justice. I hope you will find ways to consistently integrate environmental justice into all phases of your social work practice. Onward with joy!

To the Teacher:

I hope this book meets the needs of a growing area of social work teaching. The book is built to be the main text in a specialized course on social work and the environment, but it can be a text in any generalist practice course as a stand-alone or supplemental text. The book contains several key components that will aid you in planning and teaching your course:

- Critical thinking questions and additional learning activities at the end of each chapter provide ready assignment activities.
- A stand-alone section on ethics connects to the practice chapters and incorporates social work and other ethical principle statements.
- Theories are presented early on and are threaded throughout the chapters, encouraging students to understand the theory underlying the skills they are learning.

- Diversity (human and other) is threaded intentionally within each chapter of the text.
- Stories, applications, and descriptions bring content to life in every chapter.
- Key terms highlight the main elements of each chapter.
- Educational competencies of the Council on Social Work Education are embedded in each chapter, highlighted in a chart.
- The 10 chapters are ready to map to a course syllabus, allowing time for dense material and local readings and events.

It can be daunting to teach about environmental justice. The complexity of the issues makes it difficult to detangle them from the many pressing problems social workers face. This book will help you do that. I encourage you to jump in. The world needs us. Keep talking, writing, thinking, teaching. We have so many good environmental social workers who have laid the foundation. Social workers already know so much about the systems that hold privilege and oppression in place. Apply the practice wisdom of social work to the growing understanding of environmental justice to assure its centrality to social work and the environmental movement. I hope you find this book helpful. More importantly, I look forward to the future of environmental justice and the social work voice within it. All the best!

ACKNOWLEDGMENTS

The writing of this book grew out of reading the work of many intellectually stimulating social work authors and practitioners. I am indebted to social work pioneers who have focused on justice, decolonizing social work, radical social work, structural social work, and environmental social work. Their work helped me be brave enough to develop and offer a course on environmental justice and social change. That course eventually led me to recognize that a practice-focused text for social workers could be a useful contribution. It has been suggested that the writing of textbooks is a political practice in addition to an intellectual exercise. I fully agree. Not all stories and perspectives can be included in one book. Where I have left gaps, I look forward to learning from other social work and environmental justice advocates who will grow and challenge and enlarge this dialogue. Thank you in advance.

Council on Social Work Education Competencies

	Competency 1 Demonstrate Ethical and Professional Behavior	Competency 2 Engage Diversity and Difference in Practice	Competency 3 Advance Human Rights and Social, Economic, and Environmental Justice	Competency 4 Engage in Practice-Informed Research and Research-Informed Practice	Competency 5 Engage in Policy Practice	Competency 6 Engage with Individuals, Families, Groups, Organizations, and Communities	Competency 7 Assess Individuals, Families, Groups, Organizations, and Communities	Competency 8 Intervene with Individuals, Families, Groups, Organizations, and Communities	Competency 9 Evaluate Practice with Individuals, Families, Groups, Organizations, and Communities
Chapter 1 History					✓				
Chapter 2 Foundational Concepts			✓						
Chapter 3 Theories			✓	✓					
Chapter 4 Ethics	✓	✓							
Chapter 5 Self & Environment		✓							
Chapter 6 Phases of Social Work Practice				✓		✓	✓	✓	✓
Chapter 7 Individuals & Families						✓	✓	✓	✓
Chapter 8 Groups & Communities						✓	✓	✓	✓
Chapter 9 Organizations & Policies					✓	✓	✓	✓	✓
Chapter 10 Holistic Practice	✓								

CHAPTER 1

Environmental Justice and Social Work Practice

HISTORICAL ROOTS

Indigenous philosophies are premised on the belief that the human relationship to the earth is primarily one of partnership. The land was created by a power outside of human beings, and a just relationship to that power must respect the fact that human beings did not have a hand in making the earth; therefore, they have no right to dispose of it as they see fit. —Taiaiake Alfred, from Taiaiake.net

Humans and nature influence each other in ways we do not yet fully understand. Choices we make as individuals, and as communal groups, impact our natural world in ways we see and others we don't. Over the last few decades, scientists, spiritual leaders, and scholars have described the consequences of human modernization and its impact on nature. However, for a very long time, indigenous cultures around the world were able to live with a significant measure of harmony between human needs and the resources of Earth. While we have made great strides in increasing the human lifespan, developed medical and technological discoveries, and expanded our economies, the current modern era in industrialized nations has largely stripped humans from their natural connection to Earth and burdened the planet with nearly irreversible damage. The modern currency of relationship between humans and nature is built not on respect for Earth but on securing resources for economic gain, often for a small percentage of people at the top of an economic hierarchy.

Human experiences of nature today reflect burdens for those who are marginalized and benefits for those who are privileged. People who live near available green space have several benefits, including lower rates of poor mental health and cardiovascular disease (Richardson, Pearce, Mitchell, & Kingham, 2013). Walking in nature or even viewing pictures of nature can improve attention abilities (Berman, Jonides, & Kaplan, 2006); increased vegetation around apartment buildings leads to reductions in property and violent crimes (Kuo & Sullivan, 2001). On the other

1

hand, exposure to pesticides has been shown to harm developing children's lungs (Raanan et al., 2016), access to healthy food is unavailable to economically poor communities (Bell, Mora, Hagan, Rubin, & Karpyn, 2013), and clean water security is threatened all over the world as rain patterns change and underwater reserves decline (Friends of the Earth, 2007).

Due to social work's unique dual focus on persons and their environment, we are in a position to influence our human relationships and experiences with the natural world. Social work's interest emerges out of the disproportionality reflected in humans' experiences of the environment; and our contribution is to work across social and economic divides to bring social work's specialized knowledge, values, and skills to address the challenges of humans in the environment.

Environmental Justice Is Social Work Practice

Justice has long been at center stage for social work practice. It is the heart of the work that social workers do on the micro and macro levels, and it is the essential, organizing value of all we do (Marsh, 2005). Having attended to social and economic justice for decades, including environmental justice is a natural extension of the knowledge, values, and skills social workers already employ. In addition, our foremother, Jane Addams, taught us well with her efforts to establish city parks, her understanding of the need for recreation and art, her emphasis on welcoming human diversity, as well as her success at increasing sanitation and garbage removal in an effort to improve public health (Bryan & Davis, 1990). Mary Richmond, our other foremother, was eloquent for the time in her efforts to explore and explain how environmental variables affect individual well-being (Marx, 2004). Embracing and engaging the natural environmental components of justice work threads neatly into social and economic justice. As social workers we are already attending to the social environment of the clients we serve, and turning our attention to the natural environment is an obvious extension: "communities most affected by environmental injustices are often the same communities where social workers are entrenched in service provision at the individual, family, and community level" (Teixeira & Krings, 2015, p. 513). Over the past few decades our conceptual recognition of environmental justice as part of social work has grown. In 2015, the Council on Social Work Education included environmental justice in the competencies and practice behaviors of social work education, cementing our ongoing commitment to growing and understanding social work and environmental justice. And while our history edifies our place in environmental justice work, recent research shows that the need for these skills is strong. Nesmith and Smyth (2015) found that 71% of social workers in one Midwest US state have clients facing an environmental justice challenge. Their top concerns were food deserts, safe play spaces, and lead poisoning (Nesmith & Smyth, 2015).

For years social work has worked to improve the human condition through work in the social and economic spheres and ignored the physical environment, despite our dependence (McKinnon, 2008). In fact, "social work discourse has considered the physical environment to be, for the most part, an endless resource and inconsequential background for human concerns and activities" (Coates, 2003, p. 58). Social workers, like many others, fled the natural world and embraced contemporary standards of living, without realizing we were paying a price. In many ways, we have lost our connection to the natural world—and in doing so we lost parts of our human diversity. Winona LaDuke (1999, p. 1) put it aptly, "There is a direct relationship between the loss of cultural diversity and the loss of biodiversity. Wherever Indigenous peoples still remain, there is also a corresponding enclave of biodiversity." To save, respect, and elevate our human diversity, we must do the same for our natural and nonhuman diversity.

One of the ways that social work is unique is its attention to the intersections of the social, political, economic, and natural environments that surround the person(s) we are helping with a focus on their strengths. "Wicked problems like climate change, the death of nature in key locales . . . and the need for a different socio-economic-political order are problems that cannot be solved with the same means and ways of life that created them" (Rasmussen, 2013, p. 5). In fact, social workers frequently target these arenas for their interventions. Skills that are used to intervene in the social, political, and economic environment are transferable to the natural environment. Social work is uniquely situated to respond to and collaborate at the intersections of these varied points of intervention.

In 2016, 12 grand challenges for the social work profession were identified. The grand challenges and initiative, led by the American Academy of Social Work and Social Welfare, aim to support initiatives that advance social progress informed by science. One of the grand challenges is related to the natural environment. These challenges call on social work to create social responses to a changing environment, including climate change, urbanization, population displacement, and natural disasters. These global issues threaten health, undermine coping, and deepen existing social and environmental inequities (Kemp & Palinkas, 2015). The Ecological Credo for Social Workers explicates the ways social workers can view and imagine work that includes the natural environment and the social, economic, and political spheres. Developed and published in 1993 (Berger & Kelly, 1993), the credo has staying power and still provides guidance in our work. Most important, it is a hopeful and strengths-based credo reflecting social work values. Review Box 1.1 to read the entire credo.

Social work has been accused of coming late to the game of environmental action. Social work thinkers have identified ways that the profession of social work has been slow to see the connections between our clients' lives and the natural environment in which we live, despite our long-standing perspective of a person in the environment (Coates, 2003). Part of the reason for social work's slow response is that we

Box 1.1 **More to Explore—Ecological Credo for Social Workers**

1. Social work is concerned not only with the interactions between people and their social environments but with the full range of interconnectedness among all systems within Earth's biosphere.
2. Social work promotes self-determination and respect for individuals within the context of individual and community respect for nature. Self-respect and respect for nature are inseparable.
3. Social work believes in global equality, that is, in the right of all people of the world to share equally in Earth's bounty. It recognizes that global harmony cannot exist when a minority of people in developed nations consumes a disproportionate share of global resources.
4. Social work seeks the establishment of social and economic policies that promote human welfare. Human welfare is understood to include not only short-term needs for consumption but also the needs of future generations. Therefore, social work supports only those social and economic policies that promote sustainable use of Earth's resources.
5. Social work has the responsibility to promote social, political, and economic systems that respect the integrity of the biosphere. This support extends to the new means of economic, social, and political organization that will reverse current practices of ecological damage and resource depletion.
6. Social work is confident of the integrity of the natural ecosystem. At the same time, social work acknowledges the carrying capacity of the biosphere and respects the limits of that capacity.
7. Social work values the principle of diversity. The diversity of ecological niches and life forms that form the biosphere is reflected in the diverse races, ethnic groups, cultures, and values of people. Such diversity is valued for the resilience it brings to all systems.
8. Social work assumes a global and universal perspective. Humans are not separate from or superior to other parts of the biosphere. Rather, humans are both one aspect of a vast universe in which every aspect is interconnected.
9. Social work promotes stewardship of the Earth's resources by its human inhabitants.
10. Social work acknowledges the obligation of its professionals to speak out when they have knowledge of damage to the environment that will adversely affect the quality or sustainability of life for current or future generations of living systems.

11. Social work believes that humans have the moral capacity to apply their intelligence and technology to create ecologically sound, humane, and sustainable lifestyles.

12. Social work believes in the essential goodness of people. The people of Earth will voluntarily live in harmony with Earth's resources when afforded the opportunity to assume ecologically responsible lifestyles.

_____

(Berger & Kelly, 1993, pp. 524–525)

did not see ourselves as leaders in the environmental movement but as outsiders—a movement that had excluded financially poor people and people of color (Agyeman, 2005). At the realization of the environmental injustices some groups face, social workers have gained an understanding that our contribution to the environmental movement is unique and that we are needed as leaders in addressing environmental injustices. Recognition of that leadership role, and claiming our knowledge base in assessing and intervening in these areas, is the next step for social work.

Environmental issues are relevant for all social work students. In fact, our profession must recognize that all social work practice methods—whether with individuals, groups, or organizations—have an environmental impact and cost. This rendering of the environmental costs of our work must become part of our analysis of our practice methods, including the social groups affected by these decisions. To help us begin this work, we'll review a short history of environmentalism. This chapter will then explore definitions of environmental justice and some of the experiences that shape our understanding of the problems. We will end the chapter by exploring social work and environmental justice terminology.

Four Waves of Environmentalism

In the history of the organized environmental movement, there have been multiple waves, or areas of focus, in which the movement has turned its attention. Reviewing these waves shows how environmentalism and environmental justice have emerged and merged over the years. Each wave is significant, reflects the time period in which it developed, and provides a foundation for where we are today. Environmental justice was not at the forefront of the environmental movement for many years. The early thrust of the environmental movement was the preservation of natural spaces. "The relationship between environmental justice and sustainability groups has traditionally been uneasy" (Agyeman, 2005, p. 1). However, the evolution of the environmental movement is rapidly opening space for a broader and deeper involvement of human interests. The following descriptions of these waves are based on a dominant middle-class and white narrative of the movement. It does provide major points of progress and contention during the historical movement. Taylor (2002) has developed a full and thoughtful review of the environmental movement and participation based on race, class, and gender during these time periods. We cover major points of interest here and refer to Jones (2008) for an accessible review of the four waves, with some additions noted.

FIRST WAVE OF ENVIRONMENTALISM

In the late 1800s, this first wave of environmental activists began to view the wilderness as precious and finite and recognized that preservation of natural beauty was an important component of national identity. The leaders of this first wave of environmentalism were often white men such as Henry David Thoreau and John Muir. President Theodore Roosevelt, who served from 1901 to 1909, was an avid lover of the outdoors and was influential in conservation efforts to maintain grand landscapes within the borders of the United States. These men viewed nature as a remedy to the chaotic life of the city and believed that preservation of the land was part of preserving the history and beauty of our nation for centuries to come. This first wave, which continued through the mid-1900s, started the traditional environmental movement focused on preservation (see Box 1.2). During this wave of environmentalism, social work was just beginning as a profession; and while our focus was on the important social and economic issues of the time, there are threads of environmental social work from these early days. Jane Addams worked in sanitation and garbage pickup to remove trash from the most destitute of communities as a starting point for her community work. The Association for the Prevention of Cruelty to Animals, a precursor to child welfare, also developed during this time.

THE SECOND WAVE OF ENVIRONMENTALISM

The second wave of environmentalism began in the mid-1900s. People began to reconsider progress and questioned the consumption and environmental output of some modern conveniences. There began to be a sense of danger and even risk as people considered the impact of human progress on the environment. Rachel Carson is recognized as having noted one of the potential dangers of modern society during this time. In her book *Silent Spring* (1962), she carefully documented the impact of agricultural pesticides and herbicides on the natural environment. The book's title refers to the frightening possibility that springtime could be silent without the sounds of birds, bees, and other insects so vital to the maintenance of our plant diversity. Rachel Carson was a harbinger of the current crisis of pollinator reduction, in which bee colony loss poses a danger to our pollination and

---

Box 1.2 **Organizations in Action—The Sierra Club**

The year 1892 brought the beginning of one of the most influential nature conservation societies in the United States, the Sierra Club. It was started by John Muir, a man who loved wild and beautiful spaces and was a writer, traveler, and naturalist. The Sierra Club began by advocating for saving some of the most iconic places in the United States, such as Yosemite and the Sierra Nevada mountains, from the impact of modern development and resource depletion. This early activism secured these places as part of the U.S. federal government and created their status as a shared, common good for all citizens. During the 1900s, the Sierra Club experienced multiple successes in saving wild spaces and supporting laws to protect the environment. In 2000, the Sierra Club formed the Environmental Justice Program as it began to recognize the human disparities in natural experiences. The solutions to save the environment actually reside in our human endeavors. The executive director of the Sierra Club stated the following:

> Racism in our society—and the fear, ignorance, and misunderstanding that accompanies it—is a direct threat to our environmental progress. The Sierra Club's mission is to "enlist humanity" to protect the planet. To combat climate change, we need to build an economy powered by 100 percent clean energy for everyone. But how can we come together to do this when racism threatens to tear us apart? How can we rise to the challenge of creating clean energy prosperity—where communities of color, which have suffered the heaviest burden of carbon pollution, really benefit—when we're sinking to our deepest fears about each other? (Brune, 2016)

---

food production systems (Neumann & Carreck, 2010). During the mid-1900s social work was beholden to the psychotherapeutic method and advancing the profession (Marx, 2004), distancing itself from the environment and systems around people, preferring explanations of human suffering that were within the individual. This turning inward to psychological and emotional methods to assist people would soon be shed as public attention to civil rights, nature, war, and poverty was beginning to blossom. "The Wilderness Act and the Civil Rights Act are two of our most enduring and powerful pieces of legislation in the United States. Both legislative acts were passed in 1964" (Finney, 2014, p. 43). The Wilderness Act preserves designated land as wild and not to be changed or modified through human intervention. The Civil Rights Act forbids discrimination in hiring, firing, or promoting on the basis of race or gender. These two acts lay the groundwork for contentious contemporary issues we still see in the news today: the right to a livable-wage job and the need for natural spaces that are untouched by human endeavors. During this time leaders for social justice and environmental preservation gathered momentum in identifying and educating about the inequities of the time; but a shared vision of advocating for human and natural spaces is yet to emerge.

THE THIRD WAVE OF ENVIRONMENTALISM

In the third wave of environmentalism, there began a radical rethinking of how culture and environment intersect to impact the lives of people and nature. Beginning in the 1970s, several events occurred. The civil rights movement had laid seeds for the activism that the environmental justice movement would begin to use. The concept of environmental racism emerged; it describes a reality in which natural burdens and benefits are disproportionately available to certain groups based on their race. In 1982 Warren County, Alabama, brought this issue to the forefront when a commercial toxic waste dump located itself in this predominantly African American community (see Box 1.3). In the early 1990s scholars developed an understanding of *ecofeminism*, the idea that environmental destruction threatens the spheres of life in which women are primarily responsible and that patriarchy and natural degradation are related elements of power and oppression (Mies & Shiva, 1993). Environmental racism and ecofeminism are the forebears of the modern-day environmental justice movement—even so, mainstream environmental preservation organizations remained predominantly white (Taylor, 2014). Ecofeminism and environmental racism were the first two fields to identify that human social identity categories, such as race, gender, and socioeconomic status, mediate a person's experience with nature. In doing so, these groups began to redefine the term *environment* to reach far beyond the wilderness to include our homes, our neighborhoods, where we work, and areas often considered urban (Agyeman, 2005). During this time the initial combined conceptualizations of social work and the natural environment emerge, with writings provided by Germain (1973), Pincus and Minnahan (1973), and Grinnell (1973). These social work forebears extended lightly into environmental issues, while holding a strong focus on social and economic issues. Social work's extension into this area continued into the 1980s and 1990s, while independently, recognition of environmental justice as a serious area of inquiry and academic discourse grew.

THE FOURTH WAVE OF ENVIRONMENTALISM

The fourth wave of environmentalism is our current experience. This wave of environmentalism is deeply exploring the intersection of human social identity categories, lived experiences, and access to the benefits and burdens of nature. It has environmental justice as its nexus. This fourth wave of environmentalism critically addresses human and environmental inequities within the same intellectual system because the efforts to eradicate these injustices share a simultaneous effort,

---

Box 1.3 People, Places, and Issues—Warren County, North Carolina

The spark of the modern environmental justice movement in the United States is considered to be a landfill fight in Warren County, North Carolina.

> In 1982, a small, predominately African-American community was designated to host a hazardous waste landfill. This landfill would accept PCB-contaminated soil that resulted from illegal dumping of toxic waste along roadways. After removing the contaminated soil, the state of North Carolina considered a number of potential sites to host the landfill, but ultimately settled on this small African-American community. (Office of Legacy Management, 2017)

More than 500 people showed up to protest the Warren County landfill site, leading to a growing recognition that financially poor communities of color were being used as sites to dispose of and store toxic waste, threatening human health. This recognition brought about a new wave of data collection. *Toxic Waste and Race*, a 1987 study conducted by the United Church of Christ, found that race was a determining factor in the siting of toxic and hazardous waste (Commission for Racial Justice, 1987) and that communities of color were disproportionately exposed to human health threats due to their geographic location. In fact, race proved to be the most significant variable in determining hazardous waste sites, and this pattern was consistent across the United States (Commission for Racial Justice, 1987).

This racially divisive land use continues today in other ways. Houston has been noted to have other unwanted facilities located predominantly in black neighborhoods, including salvage yards, garbage incinerators, and recycling operations (Bullard, 2005). Bullard states that in many places across the United States, "the racial character of the neighborhoods had been established long before the industrial facilities invaded the neighborhoods" (p. 56).

---

locally and globally. Environmental injustice is described as "inequitable exposure of communities of color, and communities in poverty, to environmental risks due primarily to their lack of recognition and political power" (Agyeman, Schlossberg, Craven, & Matthews, 2016, p. 322). Jones (2008, p. 105) states that progressives "are passionate about the environment, fair trade, economic justice and global peace. Unfortunately, many do not yet work in concert with people of color in their own country to pursue this agenda; they champion 'alternative economic development strategies' across the globe, but not across town." Attention to local disparities is as important as attention to those beyond our borders. The base of the sustainability movement has been broad, albeit white, and so too is the environmental justice movement, though largely people of color (Agyeman, 2005). Current efforts to coalesce sustainability activism with social and environmental justice are at the heart of this fourth wave of environmentalism. In our own profession social workers have already begun the development of ecological social work (Besthorn, 2000), green social work (Dominelli, 2012), and theories and practice methods responding to and fitting for the fourth wave of environmentalism. Social work is likely just beginning its broadening of the contributions and methodologies for continued environmental social work ideas to emerge.

Defining Environmental Justice

There is no easy way to define *justice*. When it comes to applying justice to the day-to-day lives we live and work in, it becomes even harder. We grapple with issues of justice as social workers, even though it is a signature element of our work. In a recent podcast (Episode 189, 2016) several social work leaders define environmental justice through the eyes of our profession, considering it a subset of social justice. Environmental justice occurs when all people equally experience high levels of environmental protection and no group is excluded from environmental decision-making or affected disproportionately by environmental hazards (Episode 189, 2016). Environmental justice also affirms ecological unity and the interdependence of all species—and the right to be free from ecological destruction (Episode 189, 2016). In social work we don't just try to define and understand the concept of justice—we work on creating and sustaining systems and relationships of justice. "The pursuit of environmental justice engages citizens in local to international struggles for economic resources, health, and well-being, and in struggles for political voice and the realization of civil and human rights" (Rogge, 2008, p. 1). In this book, we focus on the struggles of justice-making and the practical potential inherent in environmental justice social work. Distributive justice, a concept explained by Rawls (1971), describes justice as a fairness or equality in resources or burdens within a society. Recognition is also a form of justice that suggests that until the past is faced objectively and we reconcile our history, a viable future just isn't possible (Hawken, 2007). "By receiving sorrow, hearing admissions, allowing reparation and reconciliation, people and tribes whose ancestors were abused give new life to all of us in the world we share" (Hawken, 2007, p. 188).

The U.S. Environmental Protection Agency (EPA) offers a definition of environmental justice that highlights the intersection of social identity categories and laws, regulations, and policies. This definition focuses exclusively on the actions of the government of the United States but can apply to nearly any setting. The first sentence in the definition states that environmental justice is "The fair treatment and meaningful involvement of all people regardless of race, color, national origin, or income with respect to the development, implementation, and enforcement of environmental laws, regulations, and policies." As you'll see in Chapter 9 on policy practice, nearly any law or policy has environmental components to it. See Box 1.4 for the full definition of environmental justice used by the U.S. EPA.

In February 1994, President Clinton signed Executive Order 12898, Federal Actions to Address Environmental Justice in Minority Populations and Low-Income Populations. This set a standard for assessing and ameliorating environmental injustices experienced by communities impacted by the federal government. An executive order is not a law, but it is a way that the president can intervene in the actions of the agencies that do the work of the federal government. Executive orders are requirements that become institutionalized into the process of federal governmental agencies. The executive order states that "each Federal agency shall make achieving environmental justice part of its mission by identifying and addressing, as appropriate, disproportionately high and adverse human health or environmental effects of its programs, policies, and activities on minority populations and low-income populations." To do this work, the executive order required the creation of an Interagency Working Group on Environmental Justice, comprised of heads of departments across the federal government system. In addition to data collection on human health issues, the group was required to collaborate with Native American programs, provide information and allow access to citizen participation, and review food consumption guidelines regarding fish and wildlife. A precursor to the federal act, the Principles of Environmental Justice, provides a delineated set of ideas expressing areas of problem and solution. These principles were developed at the first summit of the National People of Color Environmental Leadership group in 1991—3 years before the executive order by President Clinton. Review Box 1.5 for the Principles of Environmental Justice.

Box 1.4 **Definition of Environmental Justice**

The fair treatment and meaningful involvement of all people regardless of race, color, national origin, or income with respect to the development, implementation, and enforcement of environmental laws, regulations, and policies. Fair treatment means that no group of people, including racial, ethnic, or socioeconomic groups, should bear a disproportionate share of the negative environmental consequences resulting from industrial, municipal, and commercial operations or the execution of federal, state, local, and tribal programs and policies.

U.S. Environmental Protection Agency (2017).

Box 1.5 **More to Explore—Principles of Environmental Justice**

In 1991 a defining moment in the environmental justice movement occurred. The first National People of Color Environmental Leadership Summit was held in Washington DC. Bringing together leaders, it sparked a document that has guided the environmental justice movement ever since. Delegates drafted and adopted 17 principles of environmental justice. Since then, the principles have served as a defining document for the growing grassroots movement for environmental justice. Succinct in its wording yet holistic in its view of the interconnections between people and environmental problems, the principles of environmental justice serve as a marker for continued decision-making today. The principles are relevant to social work as they touch on the values so prevalent in and consistent with the social work profession. The principles can be another reference point when considering ethical actions and the impact on humans and Earth, and they speak directly to environmental racism and the foundational concepts of justice we have as a profession.

PREAMBLE

WE, THE PEOPLE OF COLOR, gathered together at this multinational People of Color Environmental Leadership Summit, to begin to build a national and international movement of all peoples of color to fight the destruction and taking of our lands and communities, do hereby re-establish our spiritual interdependence to the sacredness of our Mother Earth; to respect and celebrate each of our cultures, languages and beliefs about the natural world and our roles in healing ourselves; to ensure environmental justice; to promote economic alternatives which would contribute to the development of environmentally safe livelihoods; and, to secure our political, economic and cultural liberation that has been denied for over 500 years of colonization and oppression, resulting in the poisoning of our communities and land and the genocide of our peoples, do affirm and adopt these Principles of Environmental Justice:

1. **Environmental Justice** affirms the sacredness of Mother Earth, ecological unity and the interdependence of all species, and the right to be free from ecological destruction.
2. **Environmental Justice** demands that public policy is based on mutual respect and justice for all peoples, free from any form of discrimination or bias.
3. **Environmental Justice** mandates the right to ethical, balanced and responsible uses of land and renewable resources in the interest of a sustainable planet for humans and other living things.

4. **Environmental Justice** calls for universal protection from nuclear testing, extraction, production and disposal of toxic/hazardous wastes and poisons and nuclear testing that threaten the fundamental right to clean air, land, water, and food.

5. **Environmental Justice** affirms the fundamental right to political, economic, cultural and environmental self-determination of all peoples.

6. **Environmental Justice** demands the cessation of the production of all toxins, hazardous wastes, and radioactive materials, and that all past and current producers be held strictly accountable to the people for detoxification and the containment at the point of production.

7. **Environmental Justice** demands the right to participate as equal partners at every level of decision-making, including needs assessment, planning, implementation, enforcement and evaluation.

8. **Environmental Justice** affirms the right of all workers to a safe and healthy work environment without being forced to choose between an unsafe livelihood and unemployment. It also affirms the right of those who work at home to be free from environmental hazards.

9. **Environmental Justice** protects the right of victims of environmental injustice to receive full compensation and reparations for damages as well as quality health care.

10. **Environmental Justice** considers governmental acts of environmental injustice a violation of international law, the Universal Declaration On Human Rights, and the United Nations Convention on Genocide.

11. **Environmental Justice** must recognize a special legal and natural relationship of Native Peoples to the U.S. government through treaties, agreements, compacts, and covenants affirming sovereignty and self-determination.

12. **Environmental Justice** affirms the need for urban and rural ecological policies to clean up and rebuild our cities and rural areas in balance with nature, honoring the cultural integrity of all our communities, and provided fair access for all to the full range of resources.

13. **Environmental Justice** calls for the strict enforcement of principles of informed consent, and a halt to the testing of experimental reproductive and medical procedures and vaccinations on people of color.

14. **Environmental Justice** opposes the destructive operations of multinational corporations.

15. **Environmental Justice** opposes the military occupation, repression and exploitation of lands, peoples and cultures, and other life forms.

16. **Environmental Justice** calls for the education of present and future generations which emphasizes social and environmental issues, based on our experience and an appreciation of our diverse cultural perspectives.

17. **Environmental Justice** requires that we, as individuals, make personal and consumer choices to consume as little of Mother Earth's resources and to produce as little waste as possible; and make the conscious decision to challenge and reprioritize our lifestyles to ensure the health of the natural world for present and future generations.

_____

Principles of Environmental Justice (1991)

Environmental Justice and Human Health

Threats to human health were the main impetus for the environmental justice movement (Bullard, 2005). Several major events were flashpoints causing closer analysis of human-made environmental threats to health: toxic chemicals in the Love Canal neighborhood found in the 1970s; war in the 1960s and 1970s; a chemical leak in Bhopal, India, in 1984; and the Chernobyl nuclear disaster in 1986. Cancer, disability, death, and other health conditions were some of the frightening outcomes of each of these major events. They also created recognition that industries and businesses cannot be trusted to take caution for the human health of people in areas in which they operate; creating heightened awareness and igniting a flame of fear and consciousness-raising—stepping stones for the environmental justice movement. When Warren County is identified, we in the United States begin to recognize that we don't need major disasters to jeopardize our health—common, daily experiences can post threats to our health as well.

The intersection of health risks and environmental problems was the initial impetus for environmental justice (Bullard, 2005). Disproportionate health burdens are problems carried with us into contemporary environmental justice issues. Endemic to environmental injustice is the inequality of natural environmental benefits and burdens that intersect with race, socioeconomic status, and gender. "Every person has an equal right to obtain social benefits and an equal obligation to carry social burdens" (Dolgoff, Loewenberg, & Harrington, 2009, p. 123). Pioneering research clearly identified the unethical placement of toxic waste stations near African American neighborhoods (Commission for Racial Justice, 1987). Contemporary concerns regarding health and toxic exposures continue today with concerns ranging from asthma, neurological disorders, cancers, developmental concerns, and others. Our understanding of the interplay of toxicity and human health is an area of growing evidence. Moreover, our understanding of mental health in relation to access to the benefits of nature is evolving. "Understanding the esteem and identity of a locality helps us better understand the locality's meaning for both residents and non-residents" (Locke, Garrison, & Winship, 1998, p. 77). It seems reasonable that living near a garbage dump or toxic waste site has the potential to impact our self-esteem and understanding of who we are. It also seems reasonable that living on beautiful land you love has the potential to build a sense of place and identity essential to human happiness and even a responsive citizenry.

Environmental Justice and the Economy

Another impetus for environmental justice action is economics. A significant amount of our economy is built upon natural resources. Accessing and using these resources leads to jobs. Contemporary issues of the economy, environment, and employment include coal mining, fishing, logging, fracking, mining for metals, and industrial farming. There is a tension that must be grappled with: living on Earth and operating an economic system with a safe and comfortable quality of life requires the use of Earth's resources. People must eat, use water, and modify the temperature of their homes, so we sacrifice natural resources to create a standard of living that provides safety and comforts. Environmental justice asks us to question how far our use of natural resources needs to extend to truly find safety, comfort, and happiness—and to consider the exploitation and needs of workers and nonhuman beings as we strive to improve our standard of living.

Ownership of land is a sign of economic stability for families in many parts of the world. Ownership of beautiful natural land is a privilege for a very small number of people around the world. In a recent review of real estate listings, land in Sanibel Island, Florida, USA, with an ocean view and not near power plants, manufacturing sites, or landfills, was over 2 million dollars for a lot for one home. Being close to natural beauty greatly increases land values. There are other variables that impact the cost of land—access to employment, the utility of the land and water availability. But what does hold true is that land that has great natural beauty is far more expensive than land that does not. The more financially poor a person is, the more likely he or she will have to breathe motor exhaust from having excessive traffic in front of his or her home; live near a dump site; have less green space in his or her immediate area; live near a polluting industry or a distribution center with excessive truck traffic; have less visually appealing views; be overexposed to public lighting and public noise; have less ability to find relief from heat waves, cold spells, or superstorms; be more likely to live in a food desert; and the list goes on and on. Middle- and upper-class families excuse themselves from these degradations by being able to live in more expensive areas and purchase amenities that shield them from the most uncomfortable of these issues. Even more grinding are those families forced from their land due to international conflict, instability, or climate change so serious their land has become unlivable. Millions of people are estimated to be refugees each year (United Nations High Commissioner for Refugees, 2016). They are often forced to live in marginal ecological areas that decrease their social and economic capacities—linking environmental degradation with their own poverty (Jager & Kok, 2007). These inequalities, felt at the micro level, are deeply disproportionate.

The economy and the environment are linked across social structures and within individual lives. Studies have shown that greater inequity in the micro lived experiences of people is reflected in inequities in social and economic justice on a macro scale. Countries with greater income distribution, more political rights, and higher literacy rates have better environmental quality—specifically better air and water quality and sanitation (Torras & Boyce, 1998). "This emphasis upon greater equity as a desirable and just social goal is intimately linked to a recognition that, unless society strives for a greater level of social and economic equity, both within and between nations, the long-term objective of a more sustainable world is unlikely to be secured" (Agyeman & Evans, 2002, p. 6). Economic tensions cause us to simultaneously deplete and revere Earth's beautiful natural resources. This suggests that the triplet goals of securing social equity, economic justice, and environmental justice must be simultaneously pursued.

Human Rights and Earth's Rights

Human rights are inherent rights for simply being human. They are considered to be essential in the development of individuals and collective societies. Without these, survival is in jeopardy, but so too is the development of our full capacity. A human rights perspective, or framework, is useful in social work practice because it provides grounding to consider the experiences of the clients we serve and a universal framework to think about changes that impact larger social systems and, hence, many, many people. Essential to human rights is the understanding that necessities provided for some must be provided for all. In this way, it aligns too with our commitment to justice. Common human rights include the right to access clean air and water, healthy food, education, a responsive and capable medical system, safety from harm, and freedom to build and maintain family units of one's choosing.

Human rights refer to concepts about human dignity, respect for people, and responsibility to each other. The term *human rights* often refers to the rights and freedoms that we need simply because we are human. These rights and freedoms are for all people, regardless of geographic location, race, country of origin, gender, or educational status. What we have come to learn over time is that human rights are deeply connected to the rights of Earth, for without Earth, we have no capacity to grant and secure human rights. Safeguarding human rights requires the protection of place and space. Cultural competence and cultural safeguarding require the protection of the land that creates that culture, the rhythms of the natural world there, the food that grows there, the cycles of life that naturally emerge from the world in that area. Today, human rights are threatened not only by war, dictatorship, or corruption but also by long-standing environmental degradations to land, water, and food sources as well as rapidly rising temperatures.

For at least 150 years Earth has been considered only as a resource for what it can offer humans. "Non-human nature is regarded as a conglomerate of resources without intrinsic value and prized only in terms of what it can produce or absorb" (Coates, 2003, p. 23). We have come to recognize the rights of Earth as the degradation of the natural ecosystems health has compromised our own health. Recognition of our vulnerability on a decimated planet is the instigator of our readiness to consider environmental justice. "The rights of people to use and enjoy the air, water and sunlight are essential to life, liberty, and the pursuit of happiness. These basic human rights are impaired by those who discharge toxic substances into the air, water, and land. Contaminating the commons must be recognized as a fundamental wrong in our system of laws, just as defacing private property is wrong" (LaDuke, 1999, p. 199). Earth's rights are integral to our own rights. If we do not stop the pressures that exploit Earth, we are unlikely to be able to stop the pressures that exploit people. Box 1.6 provides a declaration on the rights of Earth.

Environmental Social Work, Ecological Social Work, Green Social Work

Incorporating a natural environment perspective only adds to the existing knowledge, values, and skills of the professional social worker. Social work has thoughtful contributors to our understanding of environmental social work, and while the terminology varies, there are strong threads of commonality among the language and practice efforts of social workers involved in the environmental justice movement. Ecological social work or deep-ecological social work (Besthorn, 2000, 2012) has been developing for several years and has three dimensions of influence that forge its conceptual framework: first, this orientation is environmentally aware of the dependence of humankind on our environmental system; second, it suggests that spirituality cannot be removed from our work with the environment; and third, deep-ecological social work is political and recognizes the social construction of disparities (Besthorn, 2000). Dominelli, another leader in our thinking on social work and the environment, defines green social work as "practice that intervenes to protect the environment and enhance people's well-being by integrating the interdependencies between people in their socio-cultural, economic and physical environments, and among peoples within an egalitarian framework that addresses previously structural inequalities and on equal distribution of power and resources" (2012, p. 8).

Box 1.6 **More to Explore—Universal Declaration of the Rights of Mother Earth**

World People's Conference on Climate Change
and the Rights of Mother Earth
Cochabamba, Bolivia
April 22, 2010

Preamble

We, the peoples and nations of Earth:

considering that we are all part of Mother Earth, an indivisible, living community of interrelated and interdependent beings with a common destiny;

gratefully acknowledging that Mother Earth is the source of life, nourishment and learning and provides everything we need to live well;

recognizing that the capitalist system and all forms of depredation, exploitation, abuse and contamination have caused great destruction, degradation and disruption of Mother Earth, putting life as we know it today at risk through phenomena such as climate change;

convinced that in an interdependent living community it is not possible to recognize the rights of only human beings without causing an imbalance within Mother Earth;

affirming that to guarantee human rights it is necessary to recognize and defend the rights of Mother Earth and all beings in her and that there are existing cultures, practices and laws that do so;

conscious of the urgency of taking decisive, collective action to transform structures and systems that cause climate change and other threats to Mother Earth;

proclaim this Universal Declaration of the Rights of Mother Earth, and call on the General Assembly of the United Nation to adopt it, as a common standard of achievement for all peoples and all nations of the world, and to the end that every individual and institution takes responsibility for promoting through teaching, education, and consciousness raising, respect for the rights recognized in this Declaration and ensure through prompt and progressive measures and mechanisms, national and international, their universal and effective recognition and observance among all peoples and States in the world.

Article 1. Mother Earth

(1) Mother Earth is a living being.

(2) Mother Earth is a unique, indivisible, self-regulating community of interrelated beings that sustains, contains and reproduces all beings.

(3) Each being is defined by its relationships as an integral part of Mother Earth.

(4) The inherent rights of Mother Earth are inalienable in that they arise from the same source as existence.

(5) Mother Earth and all beings are entitled to all the inherent rights recognized in this Declaration without distinction of any kind, such as may be made between organic and inorganic beings, species, origin, use to human beings, or any other status.

(6) Just as human beings have human rights, all other beings also have rights which are specific to their species or kind and appropriate for their role and function within the communities within which they exist.

(7) The rights of each being are limited by the rights of other beings and any conflict between their rights must be resolved in a way that maintains the integrity, balance and health of Mother Earth.

Article 2. Inherent Rights of Mother Earth

(1) Mother Earth and all beings of which she is composed have the following inherent rights:

    (a) the right to life and to exist;

    (b) the right to be respected;

    (c) the right to continue their vital cycles and processes free from human disruptions;

    (d) the right to maintain its identity and integrity as a distinct, self-regulating and interrelated being;

    (e) the right to water as a source of life;

    (f) the right to clean air;

    (g) the right to integral health;

    (h) the right to be free from contamination, pollution and toxic or radio-active waste;

    (i) the right to not have its genetic structure modified or disrupted in a manner that threatens its integrity or vital and healthy functioning;

    (j) the right to full and prompt restoration for violations of the rights recognized in this Declaration caused by human activities;

(2) Each being has the right to a place and to play its role in Mother Earth for her harmonious functioning.

(3) Every being has the right to wellbeing and to live free from torture or cruel treatment by human beings.

Article 3. Obligations of human beings to Mother Earth

(1) Every human being is responsible for respecting and living in harmony with Mother Earth.

(2) Human beings, all States, and all public and private institutions must:

(a) act in accordance with the rights and obligations recognized in this Declaration;

(b) recognize and promote the full implementation and enforcement of the rights and obligations recognized in this Declaration;

(c) promote and participate in learning, analysis, interpretation and communication about how to live in harmony with Mother Earth in accordance with this Declaration;

(d) ensure that the pursuit of human wellbeing contributes to the wellbeing of Mother Earth, now and in the future;

(e) establish and apply effective norms and laws for the defence, protection and conservation of the rights of Mother Earth;

(f) respect, protect, conserve and where necessary, restore the integrity, of the vital ecological cycles, processes and balances of Mother Earth;

(g) guarantee that the damages caused by human violations of the inherent rights recognized in this Declaration are rectified and that those responsible are held accountable for restoring the integrity and health of Mother Earth;

(h) empower human beings and institutions to defend the rights of Mother Earth and of all beings;

(i) establish precautionary and restrictive measures to prevent human activities from causing species extinction, the destruction of ecosystems or the disruption of ecological cycles;

(j) guarantee peace and eliminate nuclear, chemical and biological weapons;

(k) promote and support practices of respect for Mother Earth and all beings, in accordance with their own cultures, traditions and customs;

(l) promote economic systems that are in harmony with Mother Earth and in accordance with the rights recognized in this Declaration.

Retrieved from Global Alliance for the Rights of Nature (2010).

This green social work perspective (Dominelli, 2012) includes a few key perspectives:

- Current economic structures devalue the relationship and interdependency among people and their ecosystem.
- Current modern infrastructure and communities were not developed with a sense of understanding of limited and finite natural resources.

- Geographic localities support community relationships, the first line of defense in social welfare.
- There is currently a neglect of cultural diversity especially from those of First Nations or indigenous cultures.
- Economic structures continue to perpetuate inequalities between people and between people and their environments.

Environmental justice work merges neatly with our existing social work practices on social and economic injustices. With our understanding of the past, we move forward with preventive actions, built on principles of equality. Social work can be an architect of this kind of change. As we move through this book we will continue to think about the linking of environmental justice, social work practice, and our theories and conceptual foundations.

Critical Thinking Questions

1. When you were growing up, what were key environmental justice issues of the time? Have they changed since then? How?
2. What are current environmental justice events that will one day be part of the historical record of environmental justice?
3. Robert Bullard claims that human health has been the first entry point for environmental justice work. Do you agree or disagree? Identify a modern-day human health problem with environmental tenets
4. Describe environmental justice in your own words. Imagine you have a 30-second "elevator" speech. What is most salient?

Key Terms

Civil Rights Act
Earth's rights
Ecofeminism
Environmental justice
Environmental preservation
Environmental racism
Human rights
Justice of recognition
Social burdens
Social resources
Toxic waste
Wilderness Act

Additional Learning Activities

1. View the 70-second clip on sustainable development by the United Nations. Describe in your own words three things you learned through this visual synopsis. https://www.youtube.com/watch?v=kyliZP3xI1g&feature=youtu.be
2. View this short video of Robert Bullard, identified by some as the father of the environmental justice movement. Explain his perspective of why environmental justice came to be. https://www.youtube.com/watch?v=EL1FTRNPU08
3. Begin a conversation with a trusted person 20 to 40 years older than you. Ask questions about environmental issues in the years in which this person grew up. What does he or she remember? How does this impact your understanding of problems today?

References

Agyeman, J. (2005). *Sustainable communities and the challenge of environmental justice.* New York: New York University Press.

Agyeman, J., & Evans, B. (2002). Environmental quality and human equality. *Local Environment, 7*(1), 5–6.

Agyeman, J., Schlossberg, D., Craven, L., & Matthews, C. (2016). Trends and directions in environmental justice: From inequity to everyday life, community, and just sustainabilities. *Annual Review of Environmental Resources, 41*, 321–340.

Bell, J., Mora, G., Hagan, E., Rubin, V., & Karpyn, A. (2013). *Access to healthy food and why it matters: A review of the research.* Oakland, CA: PolicyLink. Retrieved from http://thefoodtrust.org/uploads/media_items/access-to-healthy-food.original.pdf

Berger, R., & Kelly, J. (1993). Social work in the ecological crisis. *Social Work 38*(5), 521–526.

Berman, M. G., Jonides, J., & Kaplan, S. (2006). The cognitive benefits of interacting with nature. *Psychological Science, 19*(12), 1207–1212.

Besthorn, F. H. (2000). Toward a deep-ecological social work: Its environmental, spiritual and political dimensions. *The Spirituality and Social Work Forum, 7*(2), 2–7.

Besthorn, F. H. (2012). Deep ecology's contribution to social work: A ten-year retrospective. *International Journal of Social Welfare, 21*(3), 248–259.

Brune, M. (2016). A hard and heartbreaking week. Retrieved from http://www.sierraclub.org/michael-brune/2016/07/hard-and-heartbreaking-week

Bryan, M. L. M., & Davis, A. F. (Eds.). (1990). *100 years at Hull House.* Bloomington: Indiana University Press.

Bullard, R. (2005). *The quest for environmental justice.* San Francisco, CA: Sierra Club Books.

Carson, R. (1962). *Silent spring.* Boston: Houghton Mifflin.

Coates, J. (2003). *Ecology and social work: Toward a new paradigm.* Halifax, NS, Canada: Fernwood.

Commission for Racial Justice. (1987). *Toxic waste and race in the United States: A national report on the racial and socioeconomic characteristics of communities with hazardous waste sites.* New York, NY: United Church of Christ. Retrieved from https://www.nrc.gov/docs/ML1310/ML13109A339.pdf

Dolgoff, R., Loewenberg, F. M., & Harrington, D. (2009). *Ethical decisions for social work practice* (8th ed.). Belmont, CA: Brooks/Cole.

Dominelli, L. (2012). Green Social Work: From Environmental Crisis to Environmental Justice. Malden, MA: Polity Press. *International Journal of Social Welfare, 22*, 431–439.

Episode 189—Rachel Forbes, Dr. Andrea Nesmith, Meredith Powers, and Cathryne Schmitz: Environmental Justice. (2016, April 11). *inSocialWork* Podcast Series. [Audio Podcast] Retrieved from http://www.insocialwork.org/episode.asp?ep=189

Finney, C. (2014). *Black faces, white spaces: Reimagining the relationship of African Americans to the great outdoors*. Chapel Hill: University of North Carolina Press.

Friends of the Earth (2007). *A citizen's guide to climate refugees*. Collingwood, VIC, Australia: Friends of the Earth. Retrieved from http://archive.foe.org.au/sites/default/files/CitizensGuide2007.pdf

Germain, C. B. (1973). An ecological perspective in case work practice. *Social Casework, 54*(6), 323–330.

Global Alliance for the Rights of Nature. (2010). Universal Declaration of Rights of Mother Earth. Retrieved from http://therightsofnature.org/wp-content/uploads/FINAL-UNIVERSAL-DECLARATION-OF-THE-RIGHTS-OF-MOTHER-EARTH-APRIL-22-2010.pdf

Grinnell, R. M. (1973). Environmental modification: Casework's concern or casework's neglect. *Social Service Review, 47*(2), 208–220.

Hawken, P. (2007). *Blessed unrest: How the largest social movement in history is restoring grace, justice, and beauty to the world*. New York, NY: Penguin.

Jager, J., & Kok, M. T. J. (2007). Vulnerability of people and the environment: Challenges and opportunities. In *Global environment outlook: Environment for development (Geo-4)* (pp. 301–360). New York, NY: United Nations Environmental Programme. Retrieved from http://web.unep.org/geo/assessments/global-assessments/global-environment-outlook-4

Jones, V. (2008). *The green collar economy: How one solution can fix our two biggest problems*. New York, NY: Harper One.

Kemp, S. P., & Palinkas, L. A. (with Wong, M., Wagner, K., Reyes Mason, L., Chi, I., Rechkemmer, A.). (2015). Strengthening the social response to the human impacts of environmental change. (Grand Challenges for Social Work Initiative Working paper No. 5). Cleveland, OH: American Academy of Social Work and Social Welfare.

Kuo, F. E., & Sullivan, W. C. (2001). Environment and crime in the inner city: Does vegetation reduce crime? *Environment and Behavior, 33*(3), 343–367.

LaDuke, W. (1999). *All our relations: Native struggles for land and life*. Cambridge, MA: South End Press.

Locke, B., Garrison, R., & Winship, J. (1998). *Generalist social work: Context, story and partnerships*. New York, NY: Brooks/Cole.

Marsh, J. C. (2005). Social justice: Social work's organizing value. *Social Work, 50*(4), 293–294.

Marx, J. D. (2004). *Social welfare: The American partnership*. New York, NY: Pearson.

McKinnon, J. G. (2008). Exploring the nexus between social work and the environment. *Australian Social Work, 61*(3), 256–268.

Mies, M., & Shiva, V. (1993). *Ecofeminism*. London: Zed Books.

Nesmith, A., & Smyth, N. (2015). Environmental justice and social work education: Social workers' professional perspectives. *Social Work Education 34*(5), 484–501.

Neumann, P., & Carreck, N. L. (2010). Honey bee colony losses. *Journal of Apicultural Research 49*(1), 1–6.

Office of Legacy Management. (2017). Environmental justice history. Retrieved from https://energy.gov/lm/services/environmental-justice/environmental-justice-history

Pincus, A., & Minnahan, A. (1973). *Social work practice model and method*. Itasca, IL: F. E. Peacock.

Principles of Environmental Justice. (1991). Retrieved from http://www.ejnet.org/ej/principles.html

Raanan, R., Balmes, J. R., Harley, K. G., Gunier, R. B., Magzamen, S., Bradman, A., & Eskanazi, B. (2016). Decreased lung function in 7-year-old children with early life organophosphate exposure. *Thorax, 71*(2), 148–153.

Rasmussen, L. (2013). *Earth honoring faith: Religious ethics in a new key.* New York, NY: Oxford University Press.

Rawls, J. (1971). *A theory of justice.* Cambridge, MA: Harvard University Press.

Richardson, E. A., Pearce, J., Mitchell, R., & Kingham, S. (2013). Role of physical activity in the relationships between urban green space and health. *Public Health, 127,* 318–324.

Rogge, M. (2008). Environmental justice. In T. Mizrahi & L. E. Davis (Eds.). *Encyclopedia of social work* (e-reference ed.). New York, NY: Oxford University Press.

Taiaiake, A. (2015, January 28). The Indigenous Exhibit at the Canadian Museum for Human Rights. Retrieved from http://www.taiaiake.net.

Taylor, D. E. (2002). *Race, class, gender and American environmentalism.* Gen. Tech. Rep. PNW-GTR-534. Portland, OR: U.S. Department of Agriculture, Forest Service. Retrieved from https://www.fs.fed.us/pnw/pubs/gtr534.pdf

Taylor, D. E. (2014). The state of diversity in environmental organizations. Green 2.0. Retrieved from http://vaipl.org/wp-content/uploads/2014/10/ExecutiveSummary-Diverse-Green.pdf

Teixeira, S., & Krings, A. (2015). Sustainable social work: An environmental justice framework for social work education. *Social Work Education, 34*(5), 513–527.

Torras, M., & Boyce, J. K. (1998). Income, inequality, and pollution: A reassessment of the environmental Kuznets curve. *Ecological Economics, 25,* 147–160.

United Nations High Commissioner for Refugees. (2016). Figures at a glance. Retrieved from http://www.unhcr.org/figures-at-a-glance.html

U.S. Environmental Protection Agency. (2017, September 26). Learn about environmental justice. Retrieved from https://www.epa.gov/environmental justice/learn-about-environmental-justice

CHAPTER 2

Social Work's Foundational Concepts

VALUES AND SKILLS FOR ENVIRONMENTAL JUSTICE

Assuming that we could define love satisfactorily, would it set limits on knowledge or on the way in which knowledge is acquired? —David Orr, Earth in Mind, p. 43–44

In this chapter, we discuss the foundational concepts of social work and how they are applied to environmental justice. The social work profession is built on a long tradition of core values and a growing body of evidence-informed practice methods. Working alongside professionals from a variety of disciplines, in a myriad of professional arenas in which social workers find themselves, we address issues with individuals, families, groups, organizations, and communities in our work. In this same way, we can extend our practice knowledge and skills to environmental justice.

As social work has developed we have held strongly to the disciplines of sociology and psychology, and our inclusion of biology never expanded beyond the human body. In the past few decades, social work thinkers have expanded our understanding of the environment and explored and defended the expansion of the environment to that of the natural environment (Coates, 2003; Mary, 2008; Dominelli, 2012; Gray, Coates, & Hetherington, 2013; Besthorn, 2012). As we'll see, the foundational concepts of social work are integral to environmental justice practice too. In this chapter, we address, arguably, six of the most salient concepts of social work (justice, strengths perspective, person in environment, power, lifespan perspective, and micro, mezzo, macro) and identify their relationship with environmental justice. While we address them distinctly for clarity, we know these are interrelated and overlapping concepts. We will then review our social work values and extend these initial six concepts to incorporate three more as foundational to our profession: sustainable development, deep ecology, and the environmental justice framework (Bullard, 2005). We'll finalize this chapter with the addition of another important concept, love.

Justice

Social workers have been tugging at the economic, social, cultural, and political threads of society for years to cultivate justice. Adding the natural environment is, well, only natural! As justice is a main tenet of social work, inclusion of environmental justice, so intrinsic to our physical, mental, and economic health, integrates well with the concepts and methods we have already developed in our discipline. Justice is understood as a balance of numerous interlinked elements of distribution, recognition, participation, and capability (Schlossberg, 2007). Social work has long singled out distributive justice as paramount. As social workers, we understand justice to be the sharing and allocating of social goods for the betterment of people but also of society as a whole, an equitable distribution. Modern-day environmental justice movements also define justice in other ways, including ways individuals and communities are recognized for the environmental degradations they face or the opportunity to participate and lead in change-making (Schlossberg, 2007). Justice is useful in practice more than definition. A helpful concept is to consider transactions.

> A contemporary view of social justice can be defined by transactions that genuinely value all people, all peoples, and all life; foster inclusion while deeply respecting diversity of values and cultures; support the human rights of individuals and the collective rights of groups; and reduce reliance on adversarial power operating through coercion, oppression, and violence. Most of the injustice found in the contemporary world is at its roots structural, grounded in interlocking social, economic, and political institutions and established practices that marginalize and exploit some while benefiting others. (Mattaini & Holtschneider, 2016, p. 4)

Social workers believe there is an injustice in the distribution of resources if they are based on social, political, or economic power rather than human need or the value of equality. Social workers also believe there is an injustice if the distribution of hazards (Kemp, Whittaker, & Tracy, 1997) is disproportionate so that some people's physical, mental, or social health is compromised. Social workers are concerned about economic inequality, as well as about air inequality. If compromised air quality is related to income or race, then we know an injustice is occurring. Social workers address injustices. Environmental justice is within our purview.

Strengths Perspective

The strengths perspective (Saleeby, 2002) is a foundational concept in social work and a practice skill that becomes fully integrated into the practice of social workers.

It is integral to practice and has been explicated in work with individuals, families, organizations, and communities in various helpful ways; and it can be useful with environmental justice. The natural environment has been ignored or even demonized by some throughout history, and recognizing the beauty and strengths of nature in the ecosystems of all of our lives is the first step to true appreciation and caretaking of Earth and its resources, which in the end is caring for ourselves.

The strengths perspective provides us a place to begin in social work practice. In addition to focusing on diminishing negative environmental experiences, it is as important to enhance the environmental strengths of the clients we are working with. This perspective is foundational as we consider an individual's relationship to, and impact on, Earth. Families, groups, communities, and organizations can all begin by identifying the benefits they receive from the natural environment around them. Recognizing nature as an asset to communities', families', and individuals' physical, mental, and social health is essential to contemporary social work practice as we now understand the impact of our natural environmental spaces, including what we eat and the air we breathe, on our human health and vitality. Saleeby (2002) states that even in the toughest and most demanding environments there is a bounty of natural resources within that place and community. He suggests that our resilient species and the planet's longevity are surely signs of our capacity for health and healing. Imagine using these principles of the strengths perspective, modified to include nature, with people and their environment (Saleeby, 2009):

> Every client system and every ecosystem has strengths
> Struggles can be a source of challenge and opportunity
> Assume that none of us know the upper limits of human or nature's capacity
> All aspirations should be taken seriously
> The best way to serve is collaboration
> Every environment is resource rich

Person in Environment

Person in environment is the perspective that makes social work unique from its foundational academic disciplines of sociology, psychology, and biology. This important perspective recognizes the influence of factors on human function beyond the scope of the individual. This perspective takes into account variables in an individual's or family's life that grow out of social, political, environmental, and economic structures of the time period. History, traditions, culture, geography, weather, and land use are also part of the environment. Despite the advancement of the person in environment perspective in social work practice, the dominance of problem assessment continues to focus on individuals and how they should respond to the environment in which they live. However, person in environment is part of what makes social work unique—that the environment is equally a target of change as the individual in that environment. Person in environment has a basic understanding that humans constantly engage in transactions with their environment. These transactions, long described as solely with other humans and human social constructs, are expanding to include nonhumans, land, weather, and places in which we live, work, and learn together. These transactions shape lives. A stripping of the natural context encourages individualistic reasoning for problem occurrence and removes the opportunity for environmentally focused interventions.

Expanding our understanding of person in environment will also help us see the people with whom we are in relation, though it is not readily apparent. We are, for example, in relationship with the people who create our clothes, harvest our coffee beans, pick and pack our fruit, butcher our meats, sweep our streets, collect our recycling, deliver our mail, and educate our children. Globalization assures that these relationships are far beyond our local borders, with international supply chains that most people are unaware of (Powers & Slominski, 2017). This perspective is often displayed with the individual at the center and nested circles of ecological influence that an individual experiences. These include family, community, society (which includes political, social, and economic structures). The nested circles also contain nature, nation, economy, and geography. Think of the nested circles as dynamic and evolving in a three-dimensional perspective that changes over the course of time and over the course of one's life.

Lifespan Perspective

As social workers, we take the long view. We recognize that human joys and sorrows will rise and fade over the developmental lifespan of a person from birth to death. It also reminds us that no two points in time are the same; people and the environment are always changing. Time runs through the nested circle diagram and the person in environment perspective. Time reflects the developmental life course of humans and recognizes that both human and Earth systems change over time. As we continue in this text we will explore how systems theory and time continue to interact and interplay with humans and the environment in which we live. Earth too is different from years previous or years ahead. Understanding this concept of time helps us imagine the influences of history, the power of the now, and the possibilities of the future. Person in environment and lifespan are connected through the context in which they operate. The connections are simultaneously intangible yet influential.

Some of the ways to think about the context of how we change over the course of our lifespan are found in the study of human development. Built on research from many academic disciplines, human development is viewed as changing over the lifespan in different ways (Berger, 2008). We cannot expect the same trajectory of development for every group of people—the diversity within a specific group can be vast. And we know that lived experiences impact that trajectory in ways that are unique to every individual. The sum of life's experiences and the person him- or herself create a unique identity. At the same time, universal needs, such as clean air and water, are understood to be influential for the entirety of people. Human development occurs in multiple ways (Berger, 2008). It is multidirectional as change can occur in any direction and not necessarily in a straight line. There may be growth, but there can be setbacks too. Human development is also multicontextual. Human beings are embedded in multiple contexts that reflect their gender, culture, nation, geography, educational and economic status, that impact life development.

Power

Power is an important concept to social workers. It depicts who in society has access to resources, freedoms, and decision-making. While power has tangible influences, it is not always easily identified. Structural forces such as power and privilege require an abstract view of society and culture. Charlton (1998) describes how *hegemony*, a process in which dominant norms are impressed on others as natural or even ideal, is a source of power. "Hegemony is projected multidimensionally and multidirectionally. It is not projected like a motion picture projects images. The impulses and impressions, beliefs and values, standards and manners are projected more like sunlight. Hegemony is diffuse and appears everywhere as natural" (p. 31). While we cannot see sunlight, we know it is there. Power and privilege are much like sunlight: we know they are there, but we cannot always describe them in a tangible way. We can, however, often see the impacts of power and privilege. Power intercedes across all levels of human society, and in our current anthropocentric era, humans have used power widely over Earth, animals, and their resources.

Often social work clients are experiencing diminished power in their lives. Their access to resources and freedom for self-determination may be very limited.

> Decisions that have significant environmental and social consequences are often made without the involvement of those whose interests are directly at stake. For people whose lives and livelihoods often depend on natural resources and are therefore most vulnerable to environmental risks, the consequences of exclusion can be especially severe. Weak access to decision-making may expose poor communities to high levels of pollution, remove them from productive land, and deprive them of

the everyday benefits provided by natural resources. (Foti & de Silva, 2010, p. v)

One of the roles of the social worker is to identify the slivers of power clients have in their world and find ways to leverage and expand that power to the benefit of the client's life. This process, called *empowerment*, is an effort to create shared power. Power is not finite. Empowerment expands the opportunity for power to additional people, especially over the capacity to conduct and to self-determine one's life. If we consider Earth as a client of the social worker, we can begin to imagine ourselves advocating and standing up for our client to assure that it has the resources it needs to live a full and healthy life. Power can be shared in multiple, infinite ways.

Power that is shared between client and social worker is a growing concept in professional culture, such as within social work (Birkenmaier, Berg-Weger, & Dewees, 2011). While social workers bring power through their expertise, education, and professional status, the contemporary practice of shared power calls for social work to assure the client has power to direct his or her life. Each relationship must be explored at the boundaries of shared power. Some clients may need you to provide your expertise and direction at times but to reassess and pull back your direction as they become more able to lead the process. More likely, the social worker will need to shift his or her own practice skills to assure that he or she is not patronizing or blurring the capability for power the client already holds. Thinking creatively, with intention, clients and social workers can build a nuance of shared power that works for both of them. The most effective social workers allocate power and responsibility according to the strengths of those within the working relationship. Built on American Indian views (Lowery & Mattaini, 2001), shared power can capture the strengths of the participants and build toward ever-greater equality in the change-making process (see Box 2.1).

In the process of social work, sources of power can be found in multiple places. There is power in agency resources, power in knowledge of history and culture, expert knowledge by those who have credentials and experience, interpersonal power based on relationships and reputation, and power that comes from legal processes and actions (Birkenmaier et al., 2011). All of these power sources can be made transparent and shared with clients to build intentional and thoughtful action and communication.

Micro and Macro

Social work divides its work into three levels. *Micro* social work, sometimes called direct practice, refers to the practice of social work with individuals and families. Our profession has strong roots in micro practice, stemming from our work in charity organization societies at the beginning of our profession (Marx, 2004). Micro social

---

Box 2.1 **People, Places, and Issues—Indigenous
Environmental Network**

Indigenous Environmental Network (IEN) is an "alliance of indigenous peoples whose shared mission is to protect the sacredness of Earth Mother from contamination and exploitation by respecting and adhering to indigenous knowledge and natural law." As an international organization, they use empowerment as a foundation for the work they do. IEN defends water rights for indigenous people around the world. Their most visible efforts have been to stop oil-bearing pipelines from crossing land and water in sovereign states or those that have potential to harm anyone's land or water sources. Their organizing led to strong opposition to the Keystone XL pipeline, with an influential social media presence and international news coverage. Their work is broader than pipeline opposition, covering food sovereignty, clean energy options, and climate change. One of their main goals is to empower and educate indigenous people in strategies to protect their environment and their health—for all life forms. To do this they advocate for and develop strategies to impact policy, build alliances among indigenous communities, and advocate for and create awareness about environmental justice issues. They work to broaden the power base to be inclusive of women, other people of color and all faiths, and other environmental justice organizations. They respect the entire lifespan in their work by including elders and youth. IEN is an example of creating and sharing power in infinite ways (see www.ienearth.org).

---

work is crucial in helping individuals and families deal with the struggles of living in contemporary society. With a strong focus on connecting people to resources and assuring that local environments and services meet the developing needs of individuals and families across a lifespan, micro social workers are experts at helping individuals and families at any stage of the life course. Micro social work embraces a broad range of social problems and is prepared to work across issues, people, and the environments in which they are found. Adept at engaging and assessing humans where they are, micro social work is able to respond to environmental justice implications as they affect the daily lives of people and those they care for.

Mezzo social work is considered to be practice with middle-size groups and communities. This includes task groups—groups set aside to accomplish specific tasks or lead specific efforts—and therapeutic groups—groups that address a specific therapeutic or supportive need (Toseland and Rivas, 2017). Few social workers would consider themselves solely a mezzo-level social worker; often we are micro or macro social workers utilizing mezzo practice skills to effectively influence the problems we are addressing.

Macro social work is practice with communities, organizations, and policies. This practice is called macro because it works toward social work solutions that impact larger groups of people and has a reach that is broader than an individual, family, or small group. The interventions are focused on entire communities or organizations with methods that affect organizations, communities, government entities, and policy. The demarcations among these three levels of practice are used to assist us in our critical thinking and planning for change. In real life, expert social workers recognize the connections between these levels of practice and can holistically connect the practice levels with outcomes for their clients, no matter at which level they enter into practice.

These six concepts are, arguably, the most important concepts in social work practice and they are foundational—cutting across all social work education and professional arenas. However, they are not enough for current and future social work, which must address a natural environment that is in crisis. To begin to address the expansions needed in social work, let's first turn to our values.

Values

Social work is a profession and an educational endeavor based on a set of core values that are accepted as essential to our practice. Our social work values have focused exclusively on the human condition. But the expansion of these values to natural systems and other living beings is easy to imagine. In 1973 Levy developed a system for classifying our professional social work values, called "preferential conceptions." These values, embraced by the profession, have provided the foundation to create frameworks, methods for our practice, and guidance in decision-making. In analyzing Levy's classification system and expanding it to include the natural environment and other living beings, we identify the value system for environmental justice social work practice (see Box 2.2, the added words are in italics).

Box 2.2 **Preferential Conceptions of People *and Earth***

Belief in:
- Inherent dignity and worth of all *living things and Earth*
- Capacity for change *and adaptation of all living things and Earth*
- Mutual responsibility *for all living things and Earth*
- Need to belong *and recognize our interdependence on each other and nature*
- Uniqueness and respect *for biodiversity*
- Common human and *nonhuman* needs *that include a healthy environment*

These additions to Levy's values do not reduce the intention of his work. Instead, they expand on what can be included and what can be considered in the practice of social work. These values and the six conceptual foundations of social work practice provide us a rich understanding of where to begin our environmental justice work as social workers. But as knowledge and problems change, incorporating additional concepts to our perspectives and models of social work is necessary. Toward that end, I suggest that two additional concepts and a framework become part of the foundational concepts of social work.

Sustainable Development

Because social workers care about improving the quality of living for people, especially in regard to access to education, healthcare, and meaningful work, sustainable development is an important addition to the foundational concepts of social work practice. Generally, *sustainable development* refers to the idea that we can adequately meet the needs of the current population on Earth, without compromising the needs of future generations. In general, we want to maintain some of the benefits of modernity—in improved health, improved education, and expansion of choice and experience. However, we must counter material overabundance for some with the continued deep grinding poverty for others. In an excellent review of sustainable development, Dylan (2013) identifies the connections of sustainable development to social work's understanding of practice, suggesting that power analyses must be integrated into sustainable development practices to address the inequities that prevail and encourage criticism as part of communities in which overconsumption has become a norm. In other words, social workers can work to address the injustice of those who use too many resources as much as fighting for those who have too little. The Brundtland Report, titled *Our Common Future*, underscored three important components of sustainable development: economic stability, environmental protection, and social equity (United Nations, 1987). In recent years, activists have also called this the "triple bottom line" (Jones, 2008). Essentially, the triple bottom line suggests that all three of these elements are attainable, worthy of measuring, and necessary for a sustainable future. Mary (2008) culled key principles of sustainable development relevant to social work. She states that these principles of sustainability can be applied to all institutions (p. 33):

> An increase in the value of human life as well as other species
> Fairness, equality, economic and social justice
> Decision-making that involves partnership and an enhanced participation
> Respect for the ecological constraints of our natural environment

These principles guide our work as we consider the need to improve the living conditions of people in poverty and diminish the overuse of resources by a select few. Sustainable development is also about culture, place, and biodiversity. It is a perspective and a practice that can ground how we operate in the world, like the strengths perspective. Sustainable development is about large open spaces for wildlife and highly populated urban spaces. Sustainable development includes maintaining our human languages and our animal species. Sustainable development demands participation rather than just inclusion. Sustainable development is against environmental degradation and human exploitation. Sustainable development is about human wellness and Earth wellness. Sustainable development is for fair wages and restoring natural resources. Sustainable development wants a comfortable and safe quality of life for humans and enough natural space for animals. Sustainable development recognizes the need for human opportunity and the limits of finite resources. Sustainable development is worthy of becoming a normalized concept of social work practice. Like the strengths perspective, it can be applied across settings, levels of practice, and intervention strategies.

Deep Ecology

Deep ecology requires us to question the long-held and privileged perspective that humans are the central organizing framework for life on Earth. Deep ecology requires us to seriously consider the premise that separation between humans and other living species on Earth is simply a social construction. With a deep ecology perspective, humans begin to see themselves not as independent but as interdependent with other humans, species, and diverse life forms on Earth. This perspective requires social workers to think beyond the diversity among human beings and recognize the diversity among living beings.

A related perspective, the Gaia hypothesis, suggests that the Earth is a living organism in itself. The interdependence of human and other life forms is only possible if Earth itself is a healthy organism. The Gaia hypothesis suggests that Earth is able to self-maintain, adapt, and heal wounds. Like the deep ecology perspective, it suggests that our understanding of our relationship to Earth and all its inhabitants has been limited by modern social structures. Deep ecology provides a deep and abiding respect for Earth and an intentional positioning of Earth's needs in concert with human needs. Indigenous communities around the world have struggled to maintain their perspectives, which are fundamentally in line with deep ecology and Gaia hypothesis. Social work authors have criticized modernity and capitalism for divorcing humans' lived experiences from the natural world (Coates, 2003) and privileging Western norms of relationships rather than indigenous ways of understanding human and natural connections (Gray, Coates, Yellow Bird, &

Box 2.3 **More to Explore—Are You an Environmental Social Worker?**

Do you believe Earth has rights? Do you believe nonhuman animals have rights?

Do you believe nature and species should be protected by law?

Do you think more people should be educated about environmental issues?

Would you be willing to advocate on behalf of people and the environment?

If you answered "yes" to all or most of these questions, you just might be an environmental social worker!

_____

(Adapted from Kirst-Ashman & Hull, 2015)

Hetherington, 2013). One of the founding values of the social work profession is to respect the dignity and worth of every human being, and "when we do not respect the worth of the natural environment, we do not respect the worth and dignity of the people who reside in and depend on it" (Besthorn and Saleeby, 2003, p. 10). Deep ecology also warrants a place as a foundational concept of social work (Box 2.3).

Environmental Justice Framework

The environmental justice framework, developed by Robert Bullard (2005), provides a framework to help us understand and address the environmental injustices we face. The five-point framework provides guidance on solving problems that humans face in response to natural environmental crises and human-made environmental concerns (Box 2.4). The framework aligns with the social work values of our profession as presented through Levy's (1973) work. Because the framework includes the human impact alongside the environmental impact, it is a natural fit for social work.

ALL INDIVIDUALS HAVE A RIGHT TO BE PROTECTED FROM ENVIRONMENTAL DEGRADATION

Because we believe in the dignity and worth of all people, as a profession, we must put into practice the right of all individuals to be protected from environmental degradation. Evidence gathered over the past few decades has identified the differential environmental degradations for certain groups of people; as a profession with roots in equality and justice, we can easily stand behind equal protection.

Box 2.4 **Mitigating Environmental Injustices—A 5-Point Framework**

1. All individuals have the right to be protected from environmental degradation.
2. Prevention is the preferred strategy; eliminate a threat before harm occurs.
3. Use the precautionary principle when introducing a new product or process for which the effects are unknown or disputed.
4. Shift the burden of proof to polluters and dischargers and away from those potentially harmed.
5. Change disproportionate human experiences by targeting actions and resources.

———————

(Bullard, 2005)

PREVENTION IS THE PREFERRED STRATEGY; ELIMINATE A THREAT BEFORE HARM OCCURS

Prevention is always the preferred strategy in social work; difficult to implement but definitely a preference. Reacting to environmental degradation and human health problems is the course we have been on for some time. With our lifespan perspective, we are acutely aware of the need for prevention as early exposure to negative environmental variables can have long-lasting results.

USE OF THE PRECAUTIONARY PRINCIPLE FOR PROTECTING WORKERS, COMMUNITIES, AND ECOSYSTEMS

The precautionary principle states that protection of workers, communities, and ecosystems must be prioritized. Before decisions are made that have potentially harmful impacts on Earth or the community, proof of safety and nontoxicity is required. Evidence informs decision-making, and until quality research with evidence of safety is determined, implementation should not proceed. Acting without evidence of safety or effectiveness could be considered an ethical breach.

SHIFT THE BURDEN OF PROOF TO POLLUTERS AND DISCHARGERS WHO DO NOT GIVE EQUAL PROTECTION

Currently, when there is a concern of pollution or toxic exposure within a community, it is the responsibility of the community members themselves to prove that pollution has or will occur and that this pollution has a direct impact on their health. This is a burden of responsibility that many individuals and communities cannot afford. This burden must be shifted to the polluters themselves. The onus of responsibility to prove that no harm is being caused to the community and the environment should not be on the backs of community members, taxpayers, and activists. It must be borne by the industry creating the pollution itself.

CHANGE DISPROPORTIONATE HUMAN EXPERIENCES BY TARGETING ACTIONS AND RESOURCES

Documentation has revealed that there are deeply disproportionate experiences of the benefits and the burdens of nature. People of color, the economically poor, women, and children experience more environmental burdens. This disparity needs to be corrected in the near term. To do so we must increase environmental resources while simultaneously reducing the burdens for these groups with targeted actions that redress the burdens in the near term.

Implementing the environmental justice framework is the prerogative of multiple stakeholders in a community. The framework can be used by individuals, organizations, community groups, and government. In fact, partnership in use of the framework is likely necessary to make it effective at addressing widespread environmental justice problems. A shared commitment to investing in solutions for the environment, equity, and economy, rather than solving problems, can yield new outcomes. "The time has come for a public–private community partnership to fix this country and put it back to work" (Jones, 2008, p. 88). Interfaces among nonprofits, community organizations, business, and government can be some of the most important areas in which the framework, and social work practice, can be applied. These three additions to our foundational knowledge of social work, sustainable development, deep ecology, and the environmental justice framework, will help propel social work into a modern and influential profession—while still holding true to our roots.

On Loving

Social work is a practice, like practicing law or medicine; and we continue to refine and evolve our methods over time. Social work for me is also my spiritual practice. My willingness to be with, suffer with, and rise with other people in our shared journey toward a fulfilling life is a practice to cultivate in a most humane and tender way. Vulnerability. Love. Togetherness. We need doses of this in our work as well. Social worker and researcher Brenee Brown reminds us that, "The absence of love, belonging, and connection always leads to suffering" (2012, p. 11). Much of what we learn in social work practice asks us to consider research, efficiency, and effectiveness. And so I have learned to love evidence and outcomes. In turn, I work to love the vulnerabilities of these ways of practicing. Our efficiencies are never enough; our scientific evidence does not tell the whole story, nor does it always offer insight into the solution. But if we enter social work practice understanding the strengths and weaknesses of these efficiencies, accept them with love of what is, and open up the storytelling and decision-making to be inclusive, the answer often emerges.

In their book on upcycling, McDonough and Braungart (2013) ask, "How can one design or manufacture in a way that loves all of the children, all of the species, for all time?" Can we ask social workers to imagine a work that calls us to love not only all of the children but all of nature and species that children encounter, now and in the future? Might this not be the most sustainable design in social work practice we could ever imagine? In accepting our own need and even desire, to have relationships with other life forms, known as *biophilia* (Wilson, 1984), we recognize love as a legitimate motivation for the work we do on behalf of people and the environment. And if we acknowledge love as a legitimate motivation, it is a legitimate component of our social work practice, worthy of our conversation, our study, and our application to our core values and foundational concepts. In including love "it requires a greater consciousness about how language, models, theories, and curricula can sometimes alienate us from our subject matter. . . . We need better tools, models and, theories, calibrated to our innate loyalties—ones that create less dissonance between what we do for a living, how we think, and what we feel as creatures who are the product of several million years of evolution" (Orr, 2004, p. 46).

Now, using these foundational concepts, remembering our expanded values, and focusing on the love and joy we experience in our relationships, in our community, and with nature is the approach that social workers can and should employ. When we approach our work with questions such as *How has love helped you overcome strife?* and *Where is joy found for you?* we will find our responses to the environmental justice issues of our time, and they will be linked to social and economic justice. When we plan our social work interventions around joy, love, and meaningful relationships, we find interventions and solutions that could not have been discovered any other way. This moves us beyond solving conflicts or garnering resources and pulls us into lived solutions that respect the fullness of individual lives (see Box 2.5).

Barriers to Environmental Justice as Social Work Practice

Despite our growing interest in environmental issues and social work practice, we must be aware of barriers to creating real transformational social work practice in the environmental realm. Some of these barriers grow out of long-standing marginalization of macro practice. For example, funding through insurance agencies and a focus on individual practice and case management has dominated the landscape of the social work workforce for a number of years (Plitt-Donaldson, Hill, Ferguson, Fogel, & Erickson, 2014; Hill, Ferguson, & Erickson, 2010). There has been a tendency to view as less professional the assessment and intervention methods in the

---

Box 2.5 **Organizations in Action—Sustainable South Bronx**

The South Bronx was a hazardous area to live. A predominantly African American community, the South Bronx bore a disproportionate burden of commercial waste, fumes from diesel trucks, and power plants. Recognizing that changing these environmental conditions could not be separated from the economic disparities the community was facing, Sustainable South Bronx was created in 2001. Sustainable South Bronx works to combat two human problems in one fell swoop, environmental degradation and unemployment. Through a combination of job training, greening of community spaces, and social enterprise, Sustainable South Bronx works to provide local jobs to people in their community while simultaneously improving the environment of the city in which they live. These jobs are technical and require training and education, and they also include skill-building that helps with communication, leadership, community-building, and creativity. They are also extending their reach beyond the employable age sector and connecting with high school students to reach them even earlier, a good example of the lifespan perspective. This organization helps individuals with job training on the micro level, helps the community identify concerns and address them on the mezzo level, and organizes and campaigns to create a united front for change for the entire city on the macro level. Programs that span the micro to macro divide are often the most successful. For more information go to www.ssbx.org.

---

mezzo and macro realms (Kemp et al., 1997). The effective intervention of environmental injustices will need to occur on all three levels of social work practice. Our clinging to micro methods will not work to address the seriousness of environmental degradation. Moreover, single social workers won't make enough of a dent; we need our group, organizational, and policy practices to align with environmental justice. This requires that methods be developed, implemented, measured, and shared on all three levels of practice.

Another barrier is our lack of understanding of the differences in ways humans perceive and experience the environment around them. In 1997 Kemp and coworkers suggested that they were making a beginning contribution to the development of social workers' awareness of the "potent relationships between diversity and environmental contexts." (Kemp et al., 1997, p. 175). Twenty years later, our understanding of the full recognition of human and environmental diversity intersections is yet incomplete. This limits our ability to synthesize and catalyze transformational intervention efforts. Nonetheless, we are headed in the right direction, and our commitment is strong. Like all barriers, these too will eventually deteriorate.

We have covered some of the most fundamental concepts of social work practice and suggested new ones. These eight concepts and the environmental justice framework are fundamental to social work practice. History tells us that the context and the environment surrounding human beings are always underexplored as a cause for human problems in modern society. It is easy to explain a human problem by looking through the behavioral or biological lens of the human being. But if we hold to our foundational concepts, we know that the context and the environment in which the person is operating have a deep explanatory power in describing the person's lived reality. We will continue to explore the environmental explanations and causation for the human experience. Doing so allows us to consider more broadly what is identified and defined as a problem. Understanding and expanding our own view of oppression and the privileges that we experience are part of this process. When we view problems as part of the external environment rather than only internal to the individual, we see the solutions in much different ways; and through this process, social change occurs.

Critical Thinking Questions

1. Explain how social work can be a leader in environmental justice work.
2. Describe the environmental justice framework in your own words. Give an example of how it can be applied.
3. Make a list of what you love about nature. Make a list of what you love about people. Can you find connections? Write a paragraph analyzing the similarities and differences.

Key Terms

Biophilia
Deep ecology
Empowerment
Gaia hypothesis
Hegemony
Lifespan
Macro
Mezzo
Micro
Person in environment
Power
Privilege
Strengths perspective

Sustainable development

Values

Additional Learning Activities

1. Identify an environmental justice issue in your community or use one from history. In small groups, apply the five points of the environmental justice framework. Analyze ways the points in the framework have been addressed and ignored. Write a paragraph detailing each segment.
2. Draw the nested circles, person in environment perspective, for your life right now. Where do nature and nonhuman beings fit? At which level(s) in the circle? Share with a classmate and compare and contrast what you identified. Do you see areas you would like to change?
3. If you were to organize a value tour of your natural environmental community, where would you go? What elements of nature would show how you value or do not value the environment surrounding your community? (Adapted from Finn and Jacobson, 2008). Draw a map of your community and indicate what is valued and what is not. What have you discovered?

References

Berger, K. S. (2008). *The developing person through the life span* (7th ed.). New York, NY: Worth.

Besthorn, F. (2012). Deep ecology's contributions to social work: A ten-year retrospective. *International Journal of Social Welfare, 21*(3), 248–259.

Besthorn, F., & Saleeby, D. (2003). Nature, genetics and the biophilia connection: Exploring linkages with social work values and practice. *Advances in Social Work, 4*(1), 1–18.

Birkenmaier, J., Berg-Weger, M., & Dewees, M. (2011). *The practice of generalist social work* (2nd ed.). London, UK: Routledge.

Brown, B. (2012). *Daring greatly: How the courage to be vulnerable transforms the way we live, love, parent and, lead.* New York, NY: Gotham.

Bullard, R. (2005). *The quest for environmental justice: Human rights and the politics of pollution.* San Francisco, CA: Sierra Club Books.

Charlton, J. I. (1998). *Nothing about us without us: Disability oppression and empowerment.* Berkeley: University of California Press.

Coates, J. (2003). *Ecology and social work: Toward a new paradigm.* Halifax, NS, Canada: Fernwood.

Dominelli, L. (2012). *Green social work: From environmental crisis to environmental justice.* Malden, MA: Polity Press.

Dylan, A. (2013). Environmental sustainability, sustainable development, and social work. In M. Gray, J. Coates, & T. Hetherington (Eds.). *Environmental social work* (pp. 62–87). New York, NY: Routledge.

Finn, J. L., & Jacobson, M. (2008). *Just practice: A social justice approach to social work* (2nd ed.). Peosta, IA: Eddie Bowers.

Foti, J., & de Silva, L. (2010). *A seat at the table: Including the poor in decisions for development and environment.* Washington DC: World Resources Institute.

Gray, M., Coates, J., & Hetherington, T. (2013). Introduction: Overview of the last ten years and typology of ESW. In M. Gray, J. Coates, & T. Hetherington (Eds.). *Environmental social work* (pp. 1–28). New York, NY: Routledge.

Gray, M., Coates, J., Yellow Bird, M., & Hetherington, T. (2013). Introduction: Scoping the terrain of decolonization. In M. Gray, J. Coates, M. Yellow Bird, & T. Hetherington (Eds.). *Decolonizing social work* (pp. 1–24). Farnham, UK: Ashgate.

Hill, K. M., Ferguson, S. M., & Erickson, C. L. (2010). Sustaining and strengthening a macro identity: The association of macro practice social work. *Journal of Community Practice, 18,* 513–527.

Jones, V. (2008). *The green collar economy: How one solution can fix our two biggest problems.* New York, NY: Harper One.

Kemp, S. P., Whittaker, J. K., & Tracy, E. M. (1997). *Person–environment practice: The social ecology of interpersonal helping.* Hawthorne, NY: Aldine de Gruyter.

Kirst-Ashman, K. K., & Hull, G. H., Jr. (2015). *Generalist practice with organizations and communities* (4th ed.). Belmont, CA: Brooks/Cole.

Levy, C. S. (1973). The value base of social work. *Journal of Education for Social Work, 9*(1), 34–42.

Lowery, C. T., & Mattaini, M. (2001). Shared power in social work: A Native American perspective of change. In H. E. Briggs & K. Corcoran (Eds.). *Social work practice: Treating common client problems* (pp. 109–124). Chicago, IL: Lyceum.

Marx, J.D. (2004). *Social Welfare: The American Partnership.* New York: Pearson.

Mary, N. L. (2008). *Social work in a sustainable world.* Chicago, IL: Lyceum.

Mattaini, M. A., & Holtschneider, C. (with Lowery, C. T.). (2016). *Foundations of social work practice: A graduate text* (5th ed.). Washington DC: NASW Press.

McDonough, W., & Braungart, M. (2013). *The upcycle: Beyond sustainability—Designing for abundance.* New York, NY: North Point Press.

Orr, D. W. (2004). *Earth in mind: On education, environment, and the human prospect.* Washington DC: Island Press.

Plitt-Donaldson, L., Hill, K., Ferguson, S., Fogel, S., & Erickson, C. (2014). Contemporary social work licensure: Implications for macro social work practice and education. *Social Work, 59*(1) 52–61.

Powers, M., & Slominski, E. (2017). Threadbare: The role of social work in addressing ecological injustices of the fashion industry. In M. Rinkel & M. Powers (Eds.). *Social work: Promoting community and environmental sustainability. A workbook for global social workers and educators* (pp. 258–274). Berne, Switzerland: International Federation of Social Workers. Retrieved from http://ifsw.org/product/books/social-work-promoting-community-and-environmental-sustainability-free-pdf/

Saleeby, D. (2002). *The strengths perspective in social work practice* (3rd ed.). Boston, MA: Pearson.

Saleeby, D. (2009). *The strengths perspective in social work practice* (5th ed.). Boston, MA: Allyn & Bacon.

Schlossberg, D. (2007). *Defining environmental justice: Theories, movements and nature.* New York, NY: Oxford University Press.

Toseland, R. W., & Rivas, R. F. (2012). *An introduction to group work practice* (7th ed.). Boston, MA: Allyn and Bacon.

United Nations. (1987). Report of the World Commission on Environment and Development: Our Common Future. Retrieved from http://www.un-documents.net/our-common-future.pdf

Wilson, E. O. (1984). *Biophilia.* Cambridge, MA: Harvard University Press.

CHAPTER 3

Theoretical Foundations

SYSTEMS, NARRATIVE, AND STRUCTURAL THEORIES

It is the theory that decides what can be observed. —Albert Einstein, Goodreads

There is a dynamic relationship between theory and practice, in that, through the application of the theory, the theory itself is transformed,. —Collen Lundy (2004, p. 49)

Because social work is an applied profession—meaning what we study we apply to life—theories are deeply important to understanding the meaning behind our methods of social work practice. Without understanding theories integral to our work, social work fails to live up to its full potential. Theories are applied in what we call models or frameworks of practice. Some theories have well-developed frameworks for practice backed up by research. Others do not. Not because they are not good or important but because the models or frameworks are difficult to implement or hard to complete research on. Perspectives are important too; they reflect our outlook and help us see beyond what is readily apparent, but they do not have explanatory power or provide guidance in the steps of our work. Most importantly, we want to consciously choose our theories, models, frameworks, and perspectives to assure that they reflect our values, our foundational concepts, and the needs of our clients. Theories come alive in our practice, in the moment-to-moment interactions and decisions we make while working with our clients. We want our theories, models, frameworks, and perspectives to complement each other, provide us knowledge and guidance when challenges occur, and remind us of our priorities during ethical conundrums. While theories and perspectives may appear abstract and hard to apply to the individual client systems we face, that is the challenge of social work; and recognition of the difficulty is warranted. As we reflect on our practice, we can see where we stayed true to our theories, models, frameworks, and perspectives and where we can apply them with more intention. In social work education, we call these our "practice behaviors," and we link them to our social work competencies (Council on Social Work Education, 2015).

Theories describe the relationship between components that are connected and can sometimes make predictions about outcomes. Models describe what happens during practice in a general way to give us an idea of how theory may be expressed in the work we do with people in their environments. Frameworks provide us a step-by-step process for our practice. Perspectives express a view or a lens through which we observe or interpret the world based on social work values. It is common in social work practice to interchange the words *theory, model, framework*, and *perspective*. While they are different, there is often overlap and interplay in the application of our work; and conflating the terminology has become quite common.

Adding to the complexity is that theories do not emerge fully formed. Theories are a dynamic force; they evolve over a number of years and even decades. As society changes, the ability to change and adapt with society is one hallmark of a well-constructed theory (Boss, Doherty, LaRossa, Schumm, & Steinmetz, 2004). Good theories have clarity of their concepts, are simple, and have openly stated assumptions. A good theory acknowledges that it has a value position, recognizes it has limits, acknowledges that it was birthed out of other theories, and, most importantly, is open to change over time (Boss et al., 2004).

In addition to theories that inform our practice, social work is a values-based profession; and values, too, are abstract concepts that we apply to real life. These values are applied through what we call "perspectives," or ways of looking at the world. Values and perspectives are as important as theories. These can be even harder to make tangible because they cannot be made into frameworks or models. Nonetheless, if we look, observe, and reflect, we will begin to identify when our values and perspectives are applied and begin to shift our social work practice to match our values. This is called *praxis*.

We know that practice without bias is impossible. And so adopting theories, frameworks, values, and perspectives is a way to assure that we shape our biases in the best possible way for the clients we work with. Be open about the theories you espouse, the practice frameworks you employ, and what your values are. This transparency is the antidote to a biased practice that continues the oppression and marginalization clients often face on a day-to-day basis in society. "Practice frameworks provide a view of social work practice related to the process of the work" (Birkenmaier, Berg-Weger, & Dewees, 2011, p. 7). Practice frameworks often provide a standard utilization of the steps of the process. Introduced in Chapter 6 of this text, you will see that we use the phases of practice as the guiding framework for environmental justice as social work practice. But there are many frameworks for practice, some that are general and others that are specific to theories, methods, or populations.

In this chapter, we cover three (only three!) important theories that impact environmental justice and social work. While you may know that there are many theories that can be applied, these three constitute important aspects of our understanding of environmental justice and reflect the important interface of humans and Earth. Moreover, they can be utilized with all system sizes. As you grow in your understanding and use of social work theories for environmental justice work, apply them and share your findings.

Social Work's Theoretical Contribution to Environmental Justice

Social work theories are used to explain a set of phenomena, and sometimes multiple theories are necessary to understand experiences. We have an important road ahead; the natural environment, including its benefits, must be integrated more fully into social work theoretical development and practice (Rogge, 2000). It is important because theories help us explain the action that occurs within a given context. Theories also help us make decisions on the actions we should take to help solve a problem. When we become adept at applying theories, we often apply more than one in any given situation. Because we recognize that problems are complex and multisystemic, the sophisticated social work practitioner utilizes multiple theories to help address environmental injustices in the community.

Environmental interventions are key to the practice of environmental justice social work. While not discounting intervention efforts that focus on the biology or psychology of the individual, we lift up the efforts to intervene in a wide array of environmental variables that impact the quality of life of the people we serve. In their book *Person—Environment Practice*, Kemp, Whittaker, and Tracy (1997, pp. 86–87) identify six core themes that are still pertinent to contemporary environmental intervention. These six themes inform and guide each of our theoretical orientations at all levels of practice.

1. Recognition that an environmental or contextual focus is central to efforts to facilitate the empowerment of individuals, families, groups, and communities.
2. A focus on the actual and potential resources available in the environment to bolster a client's strengths and resiliency.
3. Understanding that environmental practice is inherently developmental, that is, that the progressive development of individual, family, group, and community competence and empowerment are supported by a spectrum of environmental interventions that themselves represent different levels of complexity and goals.
4. Recognition that the environment must be addressed both as objective reality and in terms of its meaning for individuals, groups, and communities and that the meaning of the environment is strongly influenced by variables such as race, gender, sexual orientation, culture, and class.
5. The related understanding that environmental intervention encompasses both intervention in the environment and the process of transforming individual and

collective perspectives through critical analysis of the impact of environmental conditions.

6. A commitment to incorporate into social work practice the understanding that the environment represents both opportunities and constraints and that environmental intervention necessarily includes both critical reflection and action with regard to the impact of environmental conditions in individual and collective well-being.

Most of our practice methods grow out of a theoretical perspective. Often, these links between theory and practice go unrecognized or unnamed. As I teach future social workers, I like them to think about the kernels of theory that reside in the practice methods they are using. Sometimes there is more than one. In this chapter I describe the theories that can be tagged to the methods given in future chapters. I hope this helps you see how the theoretical constructs are manifested in the behaviors of a social worker. These are not the only theories manifested in environmental justice social work practice, so feel free to flex your critical thinking muscles and try applying other theories you have learned.

When evaluating theories to choose for this chapter, I considered the ethical implications of the theory, the theory's sensitivity to humans and Earth, and the potential of the theory to inform all phases and levels of social work practice, from individuals to organizations, communities, and policy. The theories covered in this chapter connect to our foundational concepts, building from a base of systems theory and then proceeding to narrative theory, which informs our applications of our phases of practice. We end with structural theory, which requires action in ameliorating the disparities that have become known to us.

Systems Theory

Systems theory is a central theory for social work practice. A *system* is a set of interrelated elements that organize to make a whole. The theory can be applied to a wide range of phenomena. A family can be a system, an organization can be a system, and so can an economy. In every system, multiple components work together to create the whole. These systems can be small, medium, or large. Mirroring our understanding of micro, mezzo, and macro practice, systems theory applies to all levels of social work. Systems theory provides a conceptual framework for social workers to understand the interrelated parts that exist in every ecosystem. The parts of the system interact with each other and change as other parts of the system change. As a result, systems theory shows that change in the dynamics of a system is normal and can influence many other parts of the system. This theory informs the person in environment perspective and the macro to micro levels of social change introduced in Chapter 2, explaining the interdependence between levels in the system and people in their environments.

Social workers identify how a presenting problem is connected to other parts of the system and determine which parts of the system (often multiple) should be pursued in finding a solution. One of the benefits of using systems theory in social work is that it requires the social worker to see problems beyond, or in addition to, the simplistic problem first encountered (see Box 3.1). For example, we may meet a family with a child who has behavioral difficulties. A simplistic solution would be to respond to the behaviors in a specific way, directing behavior change at the child. Social workers also know to consider what else in the environment may be influencing the child's behaviors. Conflict in the home, a poor diet, and lack of access to fresh air and exercise are additional areas in which interventions can occur on behalf of the child. Using systems theory, the social worker views the child with behavioral struggles as a complex system with many parts that need to be nurtured and cared for to reach success. Methods of practice in systemic social work include the following:

1. Identifying connections to other areas in the person's life
2. Assessing context and the environment
3. Implementing interventions that include the person and the systems around the person

Narrative Theory

Narrative theory is an examination of the stories people carry about themselves and their experiences and how they are expressed in their life. Narrative theory believes that words have power and that descriptors and storylines shape the lived experiences and the future opportunities for people. Like systems theory, narrative theory has expansive use across many disciplines (Herman, Jahn, & Ryan, 2005) and can be used in a variety of settings and with any size of practice. Social work has used narrative theory to develop practice approaches to encourage people to share their perception of an experience, tell their story, and then, through expanding and reframing the meanings of clients' words, help people to a broader understanding of the problems they are experiencing. It includes the history of their life and images of the future, encompassing a lifespan perspective, one of the foundational concepts of social work practice.

One way narrative theory is useful in social work is the connection of multiple injustices and oppressions that one can experience. Psychological recognition is a crucial element of environmental justice. When people are not recognized or cared for because of the environmental degradations they bear, it shapes their understanding of themselves and their community. A lack of recognition inflicts damage, and this lack of recognition is the foundation of disparities in distribution in resources (Schlossberg, 2007), furthering the cleavage between those with privileges and those without. Rarely is one a victim of environmental injustice without finding oneself at an intersection with another injustice. These layers of injustice, especially

---

Box 3.1 **More to Explore—A Day in the Life of Environmental Justice Advocates**

It can be tough to explain exactly what environmental justice (EJ) advocates do. To understand a day in the life of organizing with the community around environmental justice issues, I spent a day with two EJ colleagues, Janiece and Mahyar, two powerhouse female community organizers of color fighting everything from urban air pollution to oil pipelines.

Janiece is a 28-year-old organizer of African American and Cherokee descent. We started our day at her office at Neighborhoods Organizing for Change (NOC), a nonprofit where she leads their EJ campaign focused on food justice, air pollution, clean energy, and empowering women. She spoke about the constant battle against patriarchy as a female organizer of color in a male-dominated space, as well as the intersection of how climate change globally impacts women and children the hardest, rippling into food insecurity, representation, and governance.

"I've organized mostly around air pollution and recently with metals plants, which became a spitfire campaign as an organic community-driven issue when community members came to NOC saying they needed the organizational support to bring the issue to the pollution control agency," Janiece shared. With the backing of NOC and working with the community, they achieved a victory when the state pollution control agency moved to shut down the metals plant for repeated violations of air quality, including emitting high levels of lead. This kind of frontline, community-driven EJ work has become more common in recent years, and organizations are taking an intentional approach to building leaders from communities directly affected.

As a climate justice program manager, Mahyar has worked with communities on how climate change affects health. "In college I started working against the expansion of a waste incinerator, and now Janiece and I both work on shutting down the incinerator to create a zero waste model. I've done a lot of work on the Alberta Clipper, Sandpiper, Keystone, and Dakota Access Pipelines and serve on the board of 350, the local branch of the national organization 350.org, working toward a just transition from fossil fuels. I spend a lot of time in rural parts of the state, and as a woman of color it can be difficult to work in rural spaces," Mahyar shared.

Both fierce female organizers navigating white male-dominated spaces have had to overcome a lot to have their voices heard and to lift up the voices of the communities they work with. Their advocacy can fall on deaf ears. With their collaborative work with the pollution control agency, they both shared frustration over the processes of community engagement, often feeling that institutions listen to those directly affected by environmental injustice merely as an afterthought.

"How is engagement validated if we provide ideas but we don't know how the decisions are being made?" Janiece noted that deliberations impacting the community are often made behind closed doors, and the pending outcome may end up with polluting agencies simply moving to another community while operating in the same manner. "Janiece and I work in coalition spaces a lot together." Building an intersectional EJ movement crosses many different individuals, communities, and organizations. Across the spectrum are broad coalitions such as with clean energy, food access, and social justice. Each organization builds their respective bases to move issues forward and fight everywhere from the streets to the capitol. "Getting through to communities of color and financially poor communities the message has to be centered around health, energy bills, well-being, and done in a way that speaks to the communities' immediate needs," Mahyar added.

Together Janiece and Mahyar have done incredible work in their careers fighting for the environment. With each other's support, they have shifted the power dynamics back to women, youth, communities of color, and indigenous people most directly affected by climate change. We ended our day with their message to others fighting for change. "To the youth, don't stop fighting and resisting. To youth of color, stick together and to white allies, step up. We need young people. Keep the conversation open with people close to you on a local level and keep going," said Mahyar.

───────────────

Contribution by Ryan Stopera, MSW, MBA

---

when underrecognized, wreak havoc on a person's understanding of self. Narrative social work provides the opportunity for recognition—and hence the beginning of justice-making: "justice requires attention to both distribution and recognition" (Schlossberg, 2007, p. 15).

Social workers are the receivers of stories of suffering; in our reception of them, we can begin to name and acknowledge the sufferings that people have experienced (Denborough et al., 2013), as a means to begin healing injustices. Especially if we use the words of the people themselves, we can then "find ways that these can be richly witnessed and acknowledged in resonant ways" (Denborough et al., p. 15). As we listen to the stories of suffering, we will find an opportunity to identify ways of survival, values that transcend the suffering, for ideals that are larger than the present problem. As we help people identify and name these, we find ways to contribute to furthering the positive ideals—this is the process of doing justice (Denborough et al., 2013). This making of justice with narrative theory can be used at all levels of practice, from micro to macro. On a macro level, a narrative theory can be applied to help us understand the story-making about, and hence the marginalization of, certain groups of people. Bullard describes one of these overarching stories.

for the most part, the dominant media have stereotyped native peoples as fighting a losing battle against the onslaught of industrial civilization. . . . This process has frequently been described as modernization but is more accurately characterized as developmental genocide for those who stand in the way of the economic exploitation of valuable resources. The basic element of this process is the devaluation of the victims, which makes them seem inferior or worthless. Native communities occupy lands that contain untapped resources are frequently described as primitives and savages or obstacles. (Bullard, 2005, p. 169)

This quote suggests that using narrative theory on the macro level can help us explore the stereotyping and social construction of certain groups of people and their relationship to Earth (see Box 3.2). Methods of practice in narrative social work include, but are not limited to, the following:

Box 3.2 **Organizations in Action—White Earth Land Recovery Project**

White Earth is an American Indian reservation in northern Minnesota. The White Earth Land Recovery Project (WELRP) works to facilitate land recovery of the White Earth Reservation through a variety of human- and nature-focused programs. Headed by Executive Director Winona LaDuke, an organizer, activist, and previous vice-presidential candidate, the organization has grown to encompass a wide array of projects that address local, cultural, and geographic needs. "The mission of the White Earth Land Recovery Project is to facilitate recovery of the original land base of the White Earth Indian Reservation while preserving and restoring traditional practices of sound land stewardship, language fluency, community development and the strengthening of our spiritual and cultural heritage." Programs include seed saving, indigenous farming conferences, renewable energy sourcing, radio programming to preserve native languages, and food sovereignty efforts linking farms to schools and communities. "We work to continue, revive, and protect our native seeds, heritage crops, naturally-grown fruits, animals, wild plants, traditions, and knowledge of our indigenous and land-based communities. We strive to maintain our culture and resist the global industrialized food system that corrupts our health and freedom through inappropriate food production and genetic engineering" (www.welrp.org). The WELRP works to change the predominant cultural narrative of the region and empower and promote indigenous ways of people's connections to and strengths in their natural and cultural environment.

1. Externalizing the problem
2. Identifying exceptions to the stories or times when the problem did not exist or was triumphed over
3. Reauthoring the story in ways that show strengths and resiliency and offer pathways of hope

Structural Theory

Structural social work theory was developed by Canadian social work educator Maurice Moreaux. "It is an analysis which places alongside each other the divisions of class, gender, race, age, ability/disability and sexuality as the most significant social relations" (Moreau & Leonard, 1989, p. 1). Arguably, environmental injustices would be welcome to Moreau in the contemporary development of this theory. Attending to deep disparities and injustices and highly attuned to power differentials, Moreau developed a theory of social work practice that views the powers of society as endemic in the social worker/client relationship, and he worked to unchain these oppressive practices from the profession he cared so much about. Moreau's view of oppression included all forms equally and did not determine that any form of oppression was more important than any other (Mulally, 2007). This is why it is such an important theory for environmental justice in social work practice. It elevates environmental justice to the importance of social or economic justice and extracts the problematizing away from the individual. Land use is one good example: "people who are well-resourced have much more choices about where and how they live, and have the ability to live distant from, or to move away from, environmental risks such as air, and land pollution. On the other hand, people with less economic resources or social capital may be forced to live with risks that would not be acceptable to others" (McKinnon & Alston, 2016, p. 2). There are several dynamic forces of inequality with multitudes of intersectionality: inequality is an inherent part of capitalism; is visible in the categories of class, age, geographic location, race, etc.; excludes groups from opportunities and quality of life; and is self-perpetuating (Mulally, 2007, p. 244). Daily experiences with inequalities provide each and every person a portion of oppression or a portion of privilege. Those daily rations add up, provide new doorways to more oppression or privilege, and ensure that it is passed on and shared with those the person loves most. Oppression and privilege spread through families like the germs of a common cold. When one member of the family has some of it, the rest of the family has some too, and so the perpetuation continues. The oppression is often based on a multiplicity of social identity categories. A person may be poor, female, and of color, creating a combination of oppressions that must be borne on a daily basis. This is an inequitable distribution of social stigma. "A structural approach to social work can be viewed as a practice that acknowledges the role of social structures in producing and maintaining inequality and personal hardship and the importance of offering concrete help to those in need or difficulty" (Lundy, 2004, p. 56).

Structural social work has focused on making collective what appeared to be the personal troubles of people and facilitating critical thinking and empowerment for people to recognize those structures. We know that not all of the problems individuals face are completely structural. However, structural social work requires an analysis that focuses on the immediate concerns and needs of the client being served but also attends to the power arrangements in society that create and maintain economic, social, and environmental systems that generate stress, illness, degradation, and deprivation (Lundy, 2004). Moreau and Leonard (1989) highlighted the simultaneous contradiction that social work is able to reproduce and rise up against the injustices and inequities clients face. Structural social work requires praxis, the ability to reflect and act. Often this includes the steps of (1) critical thinking about the situation, (2) a connection of that which is a personal problem to a similar and wider social problem, and (3) a building of resources, personal and social and tangible, to address and facilitate change. This means that every step of the phases of practice should include this powerful dialectic questioning—what is personal? what is communal?

Some structural social work theorists use the language of colonialism as they describe the relationships among humans and Earth. *Colonialism* refers to a sense of domination, even ownership, especially politically and economically, of a place or a people. Behaviors of colonists reinforce this sense of ownership and decision-making by some, while simultaneously keeping some humans and other living things in a position of limited power. Human behaviors of colonizing Earth (exploiting it for economic gain without care for the people and others who reside here) are in many ways the roots of the environmental justice problem (see Box 3.3). Structural social work methods are tactics that can correct the distorted ideas of what can be exploited and by whom. Using structural social work theory helps illuminate the subjugation of people of color, financially poor people, and Earth itself.

Limitations and Strengths of Theories

Various theories and perspectives are useful to the social worker addressing environmental justice issues. I find systems, narrative, and structural theories to be useful in understanding, learning, and intervening in environmental justice problems. Systems theory helps us understand the multiplicity of connections and ties us to the outcomes of our clients and Earth in recognition of the connections between all. It grounds us in an overall understanding and perspective-making. But it doesn't suggest interventions that can target and ameliorate injustices. We need a deeper understanding and sometimes radical techniques to do that. Narrative theory is key to equity within practice relationships. It provides the social worker a methodology

---

Box 3.3 **Organizations in Action—Climate Reality Project**

One good example of structural theory in action is the Climate Reality Project. It works to end the structural foundations that contribute to continued fossil fuel dependence, the source of climate change. Founder and chair Al Gore leads this organization in its efforts to reach and educate people about the negative impacts of climate change and the potential for change and opportunity in clean power energies. The Climate Reality Project hosts initiatives such as 24 Hours of Climate Reality, Climate Reality Campus Corps, and I am Pro Snow. It works to reach a broad spectrum of people to engage them to work toward addressing and building inclusive resiliencies to climate change: "we're uniting millions from all corners of the globe and all walks of life—factory workers and farmers, teachers and taxi drivers, students and shop clerks, and more—to make our leaders honor and strengthen their commitment to climate action" (www.climaterealityproject.org/our-mission). Because climate change is a problem for everyone, the Climate Reality Project aims to build the solutions in everyone.

---

for engaging interpersonal work and assures power for the client. It also helps social workers, often saturated in the larger social structures of the time, a method to assure that they practice without bias and discrimination. Structural theory creates the space for action and advocacy and the commitment to changing macro forces so pertinent to justice-making work.

When faced with understanding the landscape of environmental injustices, it can be overwhelming and daunting to imagine using social work theories, knowledge, and skills to make a tangible impact on problems that we face. While the magnitude of what we face is large, the wellspring of care, concern, and professionals who want to make changes is heartening. People are motivated by the wellspring of love and compassion that can be seen within and among species of all kinds. It does seem that one of the most popular types of video threads on Facebook reflects the friendships and relationships built between species of all kinds. We are fascinated by the potentiality of love that can be bestowed from one living being to another. The orangutan raising a tiger cub, the dog and deer who play unabashedly, the baby elephant cuddling with a human. When we link arms with other groups, professionals, and organizations working on mending the fabric of environmental, social, and economic justice we begin to see the ripening of our shared work and commitment. When we integrate all social institutions into understanding the connections between environmental, social and economic justice, we begin to transform all of society.

Theories are so important because they provide the foundation, the undergirding, of the work we do. Whether we realize it or not, they provide our building blocks.

As theories help us to describe or even predict the behavior of people in their environments, they help us determine what we need to research and where we need to focus our problem-solving efforts, and they help us build our knowledge as a profession. They are part of our daily lives as social workers. As we integrate environmental justice into our theories, environmental social work becomes part of our typical practice methods. Becoming proficient at identifying theory and how it is applied in social work practice is a developmental process. As you begin to identify the theories that inform who you are and the kind of social work practice that you will embark on, you will become more confident in the work you do and able to express the complexity of the problems and the solutions. Talk with your colleagues about how you intend to inform your current social work practice, talk with your peers about how environmental justice problems might be explored, documented, and resolved. As you do so you too will be contributing to the dynamic evolution of theories over time.

Critical Thinking Questions

1. Which of the theories presented resonated the most with you? Explain what you found fascinating or meaningful about the theory.
2. What theory do you find complex? Write down three sentences that explore how it is complex from your perspective. Share with a partner and discuss this complexity. As you begin to find words to explain this, does it become clearer?
3. It was stated in this chapter that theories can be combined to help solve problems. Consider theories you have learned in other classes. Are there times you have combined more than one theory to understand something?
4. Albert Einstein said, "It is the theory that decides what is observed." What do you think he meant? If true, how does this help us in our social work practice? Hinder our social work practice?

Key Terms

Colonization
Framework
Integration
Model
Narrative theory
Systems theory
Perspective
Practice
Structural theory

Additional Learning Activities

1. Choose one of the theories from this chapter. How does this theory become tangible in your life or community? Describe one way you can apply the theory to your life. Write a paragraph describing this.
2. Read the newspaper over the next week. Clip out an article to which you can apply one of the theories described in this chapter. Identify at least two connections that demonstrate how the theory relates to the story. Share your findings with classmates.
3. Each member of the class brings a contemporary newspaper or magazine article that reflects an environmental justice issue. Review and discuss each class member's contribution. Build a collective archive over the course of the semester. Consider how elements of justice are revealed. Identify any connections to injustices to your community. How might these be challenged? Consider sharing your environmental justice scrapbook beyond the borders of your classroom (Finn and Jacobson, 2003).

References

Birkenmaier, J., Berg-Weger, M., & Dewees, M. (2011). *The practice of generalist social work* (2nd ed.). New York, NY: Routledge.

Boss, P., Doherty, W. J., LaRossa, R., Schumm, W. R., & Steinmetz, S. K. (2004). *Sourcebook of family theories and methods: A contextual approach.* New York, NY: Springer.

Bullard, R. (2005). *The quest for environmental justice.* San Francisco, CA: Sierra Club Books.

Council on Social Work Education. (2015). *2015 Educational policy and accreditation standards.* Retrieved from https://www.cswe.org/getattachment/Accreditation/Accreditation-Process/2015-EPAS/2015EPAS_Web_FINAL.pdf.aspx

Denborough, D. (2013). Healing and justice together: Searching for narrative justice. *International Journal of Narrative Therapy and Community Work, 3,* 13–17.

Finn, J. L., & Jacobson, M. (2008). *Just practice: A social justice approach to practice.* Peosta, IA: Eddie Bowers.

Herman, D., Jahn, M., & Ryan, M. L. (2005). Introduction. In D. Herman, M. Jahn, & M. L. Ryan (Eds.). *Routledge encyclopedia of narrative theory.* New York, NY: Routledge.

Kemp, S. P., Whittaker, J. K., & Tracy, E. M. (1997). *Person–environment practice: The social ecology of interpersonal helping.* Hawthorne, NY: Aldine de Gruyter.

Lundy, C. (2004). *Social work and social justice: A structural approach to practice.* Peterborough, ON, Canada: Broadview Press.

Moreau, M., & Leonard, L. (1989). *Empowerment through a structural approach to social work.* Montreal: Ecole de Service Sociale, Université de Montréal and Carleton University School of Social Work.

Mulally, B. (2007). *The new structural social work.* New York, NY: Oxford University Press.

Rogge, M. E. (2000). Children, poverty and environmental degradation: Protecting current and future generations. *Social Development Issues, 22*(2/3), 36–53.

Schlossberg, D. (2007). *Defining environmental justice: Theories, movements, and nature.* New York, NY: Oxford University Press.

CHAPTER 4

Ethics for Environmental Justice

*The situationist enters into every decision-making situation fully armed with the
ethical maxims of his community and its heritage, and he treats them with respect
as illuminators of his problems. Just the same he is prepared in any situation to
compromise them or set them aside in the situation if love seems better served by
doing so. —Joseph Fletcher*

*North American indigenous tribes and many non-western cultures have held for
centuries that ethical decision-making must be grounded in and subordinate to the
interests of the natural world. —Fred Besthorn*

Ethical social work practice is essential to the spirit of our work. We have a mandate to address human well-being, especially as it relates to the basic needs of life. It
comes as no surprise then that the basic needs of clean air, water, access to natural
spaces, have now become part of our mandate for human health and well-being.
" . . . it is becoming increasingly clear that realities such as climate change, soil ero-
sion, pollution, and deforestation are affecting human health and well-being and,
as the consequences of environmental devastation, social injustices fall disproportionately upon the most disadvantaged." (Gray & Coates, 2012, p. 239). In the past,
ethical principles and guides for social workers have not included the natural environment. But in our quest to respond to people's needs, we find ourselves addressing
the environmental injustices our clients face—spearheading a need to include the
natural environment as part of our ethical practices. To do so we must stand stead-
fast on our eight foundational concepts, our environmental justice framework and
our values and theories.

As we practice social work, our actions and the means in which we work to
attain them are just as important as the final outcome. Like other professional
groups that serve people, including nurses, physicians, and lawyers, social
workers follow ethical guidelines put forth by our professional organizations
that guide and give language to the ethical conundrums we face. Our professional ethical standards are a must to review and consider in our day-to-day practice. We have to remember, though, that our ethical statements are principles and

guidelines—they are not recipes to be followed. We have to use the gui apply it to the story we are confronted with, and then imagine how the be sible scenario can be created. Often, there is no perfect ethical endpoint. _____ with the ambiguity of these outcomes is part of the maturity we develop as we grow as professionals. After more than 25 years of social work practice, my best advice is to encourage you to be honest and transparent in your decision-making and action, tell others, write it down, and be prepared for some disappointment. There are often losses in making an ethical decision. Lean on your colleagues in your social work practice as you address the losses and the gains in the ethical problems you face.

Previous focus on ethics within social work has centered on human rights and human needs with complete exclusion of Earth and the natural world. Rights of Earth and nonhumans have been blatantly ignored within social work practice. This suppression of the natural world is harmful to us but was not made visible until our understanding of environmental problems grew. An eco-centric informed understanding of ethics includes natural systems and other living things as having an equal moral standing in the process of decision-making. "Ordinary behavior guided by a shared ethic is considered 'natural', simply the way things are" (Rasmussen, 2013, p. 128). This is the new goal for social work; to make environmental ethics the way things are, much like ethics around mandatory reporting or confidentiality have grown to become normalized practices within our profession. In considering our ethical mandate, we must consider our extension of ethics beyond the human realm to include other species, plants and all of nature—with similar tools, concepts, and language (Schlossberg, 2007).

Moral Norms of Ecological Justice

Within an ethical framework, norms help us to clarify our thinking. As we build natural systems into our ethical framework for social work, I suggest the inclusion of the moral norms of ecological justice, (Martin-Schramm and Stivers, 2003 & Martin-Schramm, 2010). Ecological refers to species and their habitats. Justice has traditionally referred more distinctly to the human realm, though we will question that assumption here. These moral norms provide a broad ethic of eco-justice, with terms and concepts to consider in our personal lives, in how we act with our clients, and how we build and lead our organizations. While moral norms are not an applied step-by-step analysis, that is provided later in this chapter, the norms provide guideposts to consider in practice from a broad view. The following four moral norms of ecological justice reflect the foundational concepts and values of our profession: sustainability, sufficiency, participation and solidarity (Martin-Schramm, 2010).

Sustainability—Good stewardship is one in which ancestors and future generations share in present decision making. Sustainability calls us to think about the outcomes we need in the near future, but also about the outcomes generations in the future will need. It is considered unethical to not consider the sustainability of the activities of our lives. It is also unethical to assume that the use of these resources only impacts the current people involved. How might a child born today, or in 5 more years, need those very same resources?

Sufficiency—All forms of life on Earth are entitled to share in the goods of creation. Unlimited consumption is not part of sufficiency nor is refusing consumption. Instead, sufficiency encourages a sense of frugality of precious resources and a simultaneous generosity of abundance. "To care is to practice restraint" (Martin-Schramm, 2010, p. 32). It also asks us to consider what we truly need to be sufficient. What else can be provided, in abundance, to heal the aches of inefficiency? Love and belonging are two possibilities.

Participation—This is an affirmation of all forms of life, and the inclusion of multiple forms of life should be part of decision-making that affects well-being. As advocates, diverse forms of life can be part of what we advocate for. Building on the sense of deep ecology, Earth may not be human-centric as we have imagined, but relational in all forms, beyond those described and identified by humans.

Solidarity—Joining in common cause, with those who are suffering as well as those who are privileged, is part of an ecological ethic. The separation between individual welfare and the common good is very thin for environmental problems. Our interdependence requires a common, shared, healthy, home. We are fundamentally interdependent.

These moral norms of ecological justice are closely aligned with our own professional values. They also give us four clear conceptual pillars to consider as we aim to act ethically in our daily lives. Box 4.1 will give you an understanding of permaculture, a method for sustainability that can be used in a myriad of ways and applied to efforts of environmental justice.

Choosing Issues Is a Privilege

Many people reading this text can choose which types of environmental issues they would like to work on. Choosing which issues one would like to be involved in, and when, is a part of having privilege (Reitman & Ewall, 2007). Most community groups affected by environmental injustices do not have this privilege. The toxic soil their home rests on, or the nearby manufacturing plant is a part of life they cannot choose to get away from. Because of these disparities, society has a responsibility to align resources in the near term to contribute to these often overlooked groups who are addressing environmental problems they did not choose to deal with.

Box 4.1 **People, Places, and Issues—Permaculture:**
Designing for Sustainability

At this critical time when systems around the world are reaching the point of collapse and chaos, permaculture is a positive and life-affirming practice that can contribute to regenerative and sustainable change.

Permaculture is a system of design that is rooted in the laws of nature. Developed by Australians Bill Mollison and David Holmgren, permaculture design draws on the knowledge and practices of indigenous peoples, and on natural ecological systems. Permaculture is now part of a global grassroots revolution that is taking place in communities all over the world where people are working for social and ecological change. It relies on an understanding that humans exist as part of an interdependent, interconnected whole, and that to exist sustainably we must exist respectfully in that web of relationship. By observing patterns that exist in nature, we can begin to see how to design in ways that respect and promote healthy relationships. A forest, for example, knows how to keep itself healthy and balanced through cycles of decay, death, rebirth, and growth, and through a riotous diversity of life, from the underground mycelia to the tallest fir. All forest plants, animals, and systems exist in complex relationships and patterns with one another and serve various and sometimes redundant functions. Because natural earth systems tend to sustain and regenerate themselves, they are good models for how to design all kinds of sustainable systems.

We are all designers of our own lives and most of us are designers of other systems too, at work and at play. So, how we design is important. Are we designing in ways that harm the Earth and each other, or that regenerate and sustain healthy relationships? Permaculture offers ethics and principles that are simple but help to guide all design decisions. Permaculture ethics include 1) Earth care; 2) people care; and 3) fair share, which means being aware of our limited resources and only using what we need while fairly distributing the rest (not just to people, but to animals, plants, soil, water systems, etc.). In each design decision, we can ask: Does this care for the earth? Does this care for people? Does it allow for equity, justice, and distributing the surplus?

Permaculture also consists of 12 principles that offer simple but profound guidance for how to live and design in ways that are regenerative. Some of these principles are: observe and interact, produce no waste, design from patterns to details, integrate rather than segregate, use and value diversity, and apply self-regulation and accept feedback. Permaculture principles can be applied to land-based projects, social systems, or the art of living. For example, observe and interact is the first permaculture principle and probably the most important aspect of any permaculture design. One must deeply observe a system, ask questions, do research, and interact with any stakeholders as the first step in any design. As Charlie Mgee (2012) of the permaculture-themed band *Formidable Vegetable Sound System* croons, "Before you intervene, don't do anything, anything." In order to know how and what to design, one must know what already exists, what's working and what's not, what relationships are in place, what patterns exist, and what is needed. For an excellent overview of permaculture principles, I recommend David Holmgren's (2004) book Permaculture: Principles and pathways beyond sustainability. Another great resource is Sustainable [r]evolution: Permaculture in ecovillages, urban farms and communities worldwide (Birnbaum & Fox, 2014) which provides numerous examples of permaculture design and principles in action. Additionally, many educational centers all over the world now offer training which results in a permaculture design certificate.

What can you design with permaculture? Almost anything. In the Leadership for Sustainability Education (LSE) graduate program at Portland State University, students who take our Permaculture and Whole Systems Design courses create designs for all kinds of projects. Recently several students created a design for a water catchment system at an urban community orchard. Their design used roof catchments, water storage tanks, a wetland, and a hand washing station in which the soapy grey water can be used to apply to fruit trees to ward off aphids.

Each design project took into account Earth care, people care, and fair share and used permaculture principles to design based on natural patterns. Using a permaculture design process often results in a design that feels good and flows well. People who interact with permaculture design often report feeling in right relationship with the world around them. As an added benefit, using permaculture design contributes positive local solutions for a more regenerative and sustainable world.

Contributed by Dr. Heather Burns, assistant professor, Portland State University

Professional Social Work Ethics and Environmental Ethics

Ethical principles are written in a certain time, so they are built on a language and context that is dynamic and shifting. Culture changes and so too does the need to update principles that help inform us on decision-making. However, ethical principles that are well constructed and broad enough to include diversity often have good staying power. Multiple good frameworks of sequential steps for the process of ethical decision-making exist in the social work literature (Dolgoff,

Box 4.2 **People, Places, and Issues—The Green Belt Movement**

The Green Belt Movement began in Kenya in 1977, by Professor Wangari Maathai. She became concerned about human and environmental health when she learned women were traveling farther to find water, and that their food supplies were becoming less stable. In an effort to build community, as well as benefit the natural environment, Wangari began aiming to increase the quality of life for women, improve their resources and help the planet— with an entry point of planting tree's together. The Green Belt Movement has lived beyond their fearless leader, who died in 2011. People who are part of the Green Belt Movement have planted millions of trees—even beyond the borders of Kenya—and the connection to people and planet has been the backbone of the movement from the beginning. Combining gender livelihood advocacy, tree planting, and water harvesting, and connecting these micro issues to the macro issue of climate change, makes this organization a clear leader in connecting environmental, economic and social justice.

_____

www.greenbeltmovement.org

Loewenberg, & Harrington, 2009; Reamer 1995; Congress, 1999). These ethical frameworks reflect well-reasoned strategies for making ethical decisions. When multiple variables, constituencies, and legal issues apply, decision-making can become very complex especially in the field of environmental justice. Flexible facilitation of these ethical steps, in consultation with social workers and other professionals, when necessary, will assure you are practicing with the highest regard to ethics.

Because the context of the situation is so important in our perspective of person and environment practice, it is sometimes necessary to use a framework that has more fluidity and a broader scope for looking at ethical environmental dilemmas. One way to include these contextual factors and situational aspects of ethical decision-making is to include the concepts of motives, means, ends, and the likely effects (Fletcher, 1966, Cournoyer, 2014). Using these broad concepts allows us to include contextual variables, and integrate existential questions that impact a wider audience in addition to the individual client you may be considering. Such reflection and consideration are appropriate in the environmental justice social work context in which the connection between the individual and community is paramount (see Box 4.2).

There is a place where professional social work ethics and environmental ethics overlap. They can even be considered helpful playmates in the difficult world of environmental decision-making. There are many social work texts and writers on ethics, and their work is important and ever-evolving, as the context in which social work practice occurs is dynamic and shifting.

> *"One of the hallmarks of professional social work status is continuous and ongoing consideration of moral and ethical issues in service to others [include Earth here]. Because you have the potential to harm as well as help, to exploit as well as empower, and to restrict as well as liberate, you must consciously, deliberately and reflectively examine your thoughts, feelings, and actions in both moral and ethical terms."* (Cournoyer, 2017)

Cournoyer, building off the work of Fletcher (1966), lays out a useful framework for environmental justice. If we consider the motives, means, ends and effects of our decisions, if we walk through these steps, we may come to an answer that is best for our clients and the environment. This situational ethics (Fletcher, 1966) is realistic in the world of social work practice. There are no universal answers that transcend situations. However, a framework for us to consider the ethics of the situation helps us move forward in ways beneficial to multiple stakeholders, and give us a sense of the best possible answer, often in a situation of no perfect answers.

Situational Ethics in Environmental Justice

A situational ethical framework does not provide step by step instructions on solving problems, but does give us points to ponder to lead to a final decision that is the best available at the time—one we can act upon knowing we have the best available evidence and critical dimensions to guide us in the actions we are taking. You'll see in this framework that the final posed question for any ethical scenario asks what would happen if social workers everywhere acted in the way you are considering. This is especially important in environmental justice where all actions have unacknowledged environmental outcomes (see Box 4.3). The following descriptions of the situational ethicist are based on work by Cournoyer (2017):

MOTIVES

Explore your motives as a person and as a professional. Social workers have responsibilities to individuals and society as whole, to act in ethical ways. Is your purpose consistent with our profession's values? In addition, acknowledge what your personal motives are. ". . . acknowledge your personal aims as you shift focus and emphasize your professional motives. Once we consciously recognize our personal motivations, we can then gently put them aside in order to do our best professional work." (Cournoyer, 2017, p. 178). Ask yourself, "If I was the client(s), what would I experience if my social worker acted on these motives?" "If social workers

Box 4.3 **Ethical Case Studies**

Consider these two ethical case studies; one micro and one macro. Apply the four ecological norms and the situationist ethical framework (see Box 4.4). What are the motives, means, ends and effects in each of these stories?

SIGHTSEEING

Liz is a new staff member at a small eldercare facility. In her unit she has four clients. They all range in age from 64 to 79 and need some assistance with daily life. Her title is personal care attendant and she spends time providing dinner, assisting with recreational activities, and helping with activities of daily living. One of her colleagues who has been working at the agency for three years is taking the week off for a vacation. This staff member worked two evenings per week, on opposite days of Liz. When Liz starts her shift, one of the clients asked where her colleague was. Liz explained that she is on vacation and she is covering her shift this week. One of the clients responds with relief saying "Good, I don't want to go on a sightseeing drive again." Liz inquires further, and the client tells her that for the last year their evening activities have been to drive around town for two hours. Liz inquired a little bit further and learned from other clients that this was their weekly activity. She looked back in the activity logs and discovered that sightseeing trips seemed to be recreational activities that this staff person planned every week. She also looked in the vehicle logbook and learned that the company had paid for gas on those nights or the next morning. This was an expense as the old agency van only got 8 miles to the gallon. Liz felt this was a recreational activity not in the best interest of the clients, the agency budget, or the environment.

Liz approached her boss, a social worker, and mentioned her findings. When the staff member came back from vacation the social worker supervisor spent some time in private supervision with the staff. The staff member confessed to feeling overwhelmed and burnt out. She felt driving around town for two hours was easier then meeting demands for her workload at the agency.

MACRO—LOVE CANAL

History provides us a rich repertoire of ethical issues to dig through. Learning from history is one of our greatest assets. Love Canal, an area that was once used as an industrial dump for chemicals, became the site of a community of about 100 new homes in the late 1950's. What was sold as a beautiful community to the mostly white working and middle class families who bought homes there, became a tragic source of toxins by 1978. Rainfall caused leakage in underground storage tanks, and corroding waste-disposal drums were emerging from underground in back yards. Puddles of toxic chemicals emerged, with leakage into homes and gardens. Birth defects were identified. Cancers were noted. Families were evacuated, federal and state funds were used to provide emergency assistance, purchase homes from the families and address the enormous cleanup. The story doesn't end there, as the Environmental Protection Agency of the United States believes there are hundreds of similar dumpsites for chemical waste across the US with homes on them. Love Canal is the most famous, but more contemporary examples are likely to exist.

From https://archive.epa.gov/epa/aboutepa/love-canal-tragedy.html

---

Box 4.4 Key Questions in Environmental and Human Ethics

Motives—

Is your purpose and motives consistent with our profession's values?

If I was the client(s), what would I experience if my social worker acted on these motives?

If social workers everywhere manifested these motives, how would society respond? Is it sustainable for current and future generations?

Means—

Are the means consistent with my professions' ethics?

Will my means generate the desired end state?

Have I genuinely considered all other means that would help me stay true to my profession's ethics?

If I was the client(s) and my social worker implemented these means, what would be my reaction?

If these means were applied routinely and universally by all social workers, what would be society's reaction?

Is it sufficiently frugal and generous?

Ends—

Who participated in the identification of these ends?

Toward whom are the ends targeted?

Are the persons affected by these goals aware of their existence?

Would I be proud to accomplish this goal?

If these goals were pursued and achieved by all social workers and environmentalists, what would be society's response?

Is their participation and solidarity between individual welfare and the common good?

everywhere manifested these motives, how would society respond?" Using the moral norms of ecological justice ask, are my motives sustainable for current and future generations?

MEANS

Means include both the process of decision making as well as the nature of the plan for action. You are considering the ways in which you may proceed. Ask, *Are* the means consistent with my professions' ethics? and *Will* my means generate the desired end state?. If not, ask yourself, Have I genuinely considered all other means that would help me stay true to my profession's ethics? Also, if I was the client(s) and my social worker implemented these means, what would be my reaction? If these means were applied routinely and universally by all social workers, what would be society's reaction? Using the moral norms of ecological justice, ask, Is it sufficiently frugal and generous?

ENDS

Envision the nature of the end goals. Ask yourself, Who participated in the identification of these ends? Toward whom are the ends targeted? Is the person(s) affected by these goals aware of their existence? Would I be proud to accomplish this goal? Ask yourself, if these goals were pursued and achieved by all social workers, and their clients, what would be society's response? Using the moral norms of ecological justice, ask yourself, Is their participation that affirms multiple life forms?

EFFECTS

As you explore the effects of the decision-making, consider what impacts should be for others, now and in the future, in relation to this decision-making. There are always unexplored areas, sometimes called unintended consequences, to our decision-making. How might the side effects be positive or negative or might they create new opportunities? Ask yourself, If I were subject to these side effects how would I react? Would I be personally willing to accept the side effects? If the side effects were experienced widely throughout society how would society react? Using the moral norms of ecological justice, ask yourself, Does it build solidarity?

Ethical Environmental Economics for Everybody

The poorest people on the planet are expected to suffer the most with the environmental degradation we are currently experiencing and is yet to come. While people in poor parts of the world do degrade the environment around them, it is hard to blame them when their meager subsistence is so deeply dependent on the natural world. For those of us who live in countries that are called developed, we have grown accustomed to divorcing our recognition of our own deep reliance on nature for our survival. Over time, many people in developed areas have lost an ethical understanding, a moral norm of sufficiency, of what it is enough to live a happy and fulfilling life. The measure of a successful economy has relied exclusively on indicators of economic growth. Yet, for the sake of Earth, we are in deep need of applying restraint from our reliance on consumer supported happiness. Happiness that is measured on a community level with indicators such as freedom, health, relationships, and joy could free us from the concept of constant economic growth. A new economic paradigm would focus on that which is common to us all: soil, air, water, food, energy, and how these essential components for quality-of-life can be cared for and shared. In this paradigm, economic activity operates within the ecological limits of the planet. Eco-nomics, joining ecology and economics (Rasmussen, 2013, p. 149) is one way to think about shifting our current measurement of what a successful economy is.

Ethical Principles Screen

When faced with an ethical problem, it is helpful to have tools to use to help make decisions and walk us through the application of our values, perspectives, and theories. These tools act as a type of assessment, one we can use to consider the decisions being made. Dolgoff, Loewenberg and Harrington (2009) offer an ethical principle screen, developed for generalist social work practice that fits well with environmental social work practice. They provide seven principles to guide the process of making decisions. The ethical principles developed are provocative when you consider their application to environmental justice issues people face. Let's look more closely and apply an environmental justice lens to the principles developed by Dolgoff et al. (2009).

> Principle 1: Protection of life—Reducing chances of death, for humans, plants, animals, and Earth are all forms of protection of life.
> Principle 2: Equality and inequality—Equality of environmental blessings and burdens.
> Principle 3: Freedom and autonomy—Self-determination is important in social work and we guard the practice through our shared power.
> Principle 4: Least harm—People and other beings have the right to be protected from environmental or manufacturing harms. Prevention is always our preference rather than amelioration after an environmental harm has occurred.

Principle 5: Quality of life—Having access to nature that is not degraded is an enhancement to our quality of life.

Principle 6: Privacy and confidentiality—People and other beings have a right to privacy of their story. Simultaneously, part of environmental justice work is about sharing stories so people find others sharing similar difficulties. Empowering clients to share their own story can build bridges and create momentum for large-scale change.

Principle 7: Truthfulness and disclosure—Sharing with clients all of the information known about the environmental justice issue they are facing is important in their own ability to make informed decisions.

As you can see, the tried and true ethical principles screen for social work can be extended beyond social, economic, and biological principles to include the environment, and still maintain the integrity of our social work practice.

Ethical Audit

An intrinsic ecological ethic views the natural world as primary to the health of human economies and development. Natural world interests are held in prevailing or at least equal consideration when addressing ethical issues. Ecological justice proponents hold that there is a justice of " . . . humanity in service to the environment" (Besthorn 2013, p. 35). If social work believes this to be true, and mounting evidence suggests it is so, then attending to our decision-making and the impacts on the natural environment are indeed part of an ethical practice. Reamer (2001) suggests ways that social workers at an agency can conduct an ethical audit, we can extend this to an environmental ethical audit, to assess what agency practices may need to be shifted to address the needs of the environment the agency operates in. Reamer suggests the following steps in such a process (p. 3):

- Identify pertinent issues related to the practice setting: consider what about the agency, the way it operates, who it serves and the work it does to identify specific environmental ethical implications.
- Assess the adequacy of what is currently done: what has been done so far and what else could be done to improve the environmental ethical response?
- Develop a practical strategy to modify what is needed: what can be done, and who can do the work in the agency?
- Monitor the practical strategies: determine if they really work or what modifications are needed.

If you consider an ethical environmental audit to be about "practices, procedures and policies" (Reamer, 2001, p. 5) you see that it falls squarely in the realm of macro practice skills with organizations. However, the advocacy and energy for such an endeavor may develop out of direct line staff who request such a review and may even provide leadership and membership to such an effort. A cross-section of participation from membership within the agency would be crucial to "seeing" the many varieties of ways in which environmental ethical issues may emerge in the way an organization conducts itself.

Ethical Limits of Anthropocentrism

In the field of philosophy, many philosophers believed that existing ethical frameworks were limited in addressing the natural environment (McShane, 2009). One of the reasons for this limitation is anthropocentrism, a belief founded on the assumption that human beings, and things that impact human beings, are what matters in moral considerations. It was not yet fully considered, at least not in Western cultures, that the natural world has a profound impact on humans; a knowledge known by indigenous cultures worldwide for thousands of years. Hence, humans would not have a direct ethical need or responsibility for the natural world. To move beyond anthropocentrism, one must view nature and other beings as having value in their own right, and simply not only in relation to how they are useful to the human experience. If something has value in it's own right, it is said to have intrinsic value (McShane, 2009) and moral considerations should be applied.

Social workers hold an explicit value in the dignity and worth of every human being. It is not a stretch for social workers to value things that are non-human, it fits within the social work worldview because we know from systems theory that all of the components of our world are interconnected. Extension of this belief system calls us to also consider intergenerational justice; the concept that future peoples, who do not exist right now, have interests that we are morally responsible for responding to in an ethical way.

Ethics Embedded with Love

We have already learned of the deep and abiding place that justice holds in the social work profession. We already understand that justice requires sharing burdens and blessings of the natural environment, without disproportionate suffering placed on some humans and other beings. Within an ethical framework, we can include the nature of love. "Justice divorced from love easily deteriorates into a mere calculation of interests and finally into a cynical balancing of interest against interest. . . . Love forces the recognition of the needs of others. Love judges abuses of justice." (Martin-Schramm, 2010, p. 27). In the second chapter of this text, I made a call to consider love as integral in our social work practice. I suggest here that love is also a foundational concept in social work's ethical practice. It is what takes social work beyond calculations of disproportionality and provides the will to seek change. It motivates us to create means and effects that honor place, people, and other living beings in our social work practice, in our lives, and in our world.

Critical Thinking Questions

1. Choose one principle from the ethical principle screen that speaks to you the most. How does it impact you emotionally? Why do you think you chose it?
2. Consider the moral norms of ecological justice: sustainability, sufficiency, participation and solidarity. Define them using your own terms, and give an example of how you think they are, or can be, lived out.
3. In this chapter, we suggest that choosing ethical issues is a privilege. Do you agree or disagree? Explain.
4. Should the federal, state or local government establish policies to provide resources for cleanup of environmental pollutants or health care for people who become sick due to pollutants? Is this an ethical mandate?

Key Terms

Applied
Anthropocentric
Common good
Eco-centric
Ends
Ethical principles
Ethical framework
Inherent
Motives
Means
Norms
Universal

Additional Learning Activities

1. On the National Association of Social Workers (NASW) website, find the Code of Ethics for social workers. Do they mention environmental justice? Where would you explicitly add environmental justice? If so, identify what that language could be.

2. Identify an ethical dilemma a class member has experienced working with humans and the environment. Or, you may identify an ethical dilemma you feel likely to experience or have heard of. Then choose one response to the dilemma and examine the dilemma using the motives, means and ends framework. Write down your answers and be prepared to share them with the class.

3. Look up the United Nations Environmental Programme website. Why do you think the United Nations is involved in environmental programs? Can you find examples of the kind of work the United Nations is currently doing in regards to the environment? Find one example and describe it in two paragraphs. Share in class.

References

Besthorn, F. (2013). Radical equalitarian ecological justice: A social work call to action. In Gray, M., Coates, J., & Hetherington, T. (Eds.). *Environmental social work*. New York, NY: Routledge.

Birnbaum, J., & Fox, L. (2014). *Sustainable [r]evolution: Permaculture in ecovillages, urban farms, and communities worldwide*. Berkeley, CA: North Atlantic Books.

Congress, E.P. (1999). *Social work values and ethics*. Chicago: Nelson Hall.

Cournoyer, B.R. (2017). *The social work skills workbook*. Belmont, CA: Brooks/Cole.

Dolgoff, R., Loewenberg, F.M., & Harrington, D. (2009). *Ethical decisions for social work practice*. (8th ed.). Itasca, IL: F.E. Peacock.

Fletcher, J. (1966). *Situation ethics: The new morality*. Philadelphia. PA: The Westminster Press.

Gray, M., & Coates, J. (2012). Environmental ethics for social work: Social work's responsibility to the non-human world. *International Journal of Social Welfare, 21*, 239–247.

Holmgren, D. (2004). *Permaculture: Principles and pathways beyond sustainability*. Hepburn, Australia: Holmgren Design Services.

Martin-Schramm, J. (2010). *Climate justice: Ethics, energy, and public policy*. Minneapolis, MN: Fortress.

Martin-Schramm, J. B. & Stivers, R.L. (2003). *Christian environmental ethics: A case methods approach*. Maryknoll, NY: Orbis.

McShane, K. (2009). Environmental ethics: An overview. *Philosophy Compass 4/3*, 407–420.

Mgee, C. (2012, Aug 10). *Look around (Permaculture principle 1: Observe & interact)*. Retrieved from https://www.youtube.com.

Rasmussen, L. (2013). *Earth-honoring faith: Religious ethics in a new key*. New York, NY: Oxford University Press.

Reamer, F.G. (1995). *Social work values and ethics*. New York: Columbia University Press.

Reamer, F. G. (2001). *The social work ethics audit: A risk management tool*. Washington D.C.: NASW Press.

Reitman M. & Ewall, M. (2007). *Campus-community organizing guide: Building power for lasting change in the youth movement for clean energy*. Energy Justice Network. Retrieved from http://www.energyjustice.net/files/campus/ccog.pdf

Schlossberg, D. (2007). *Defining environmental justice: Theories, movements, and nature*. New York, NY: Oxford University Press.

CHAPTER 5

Understanding Yourself and the Natural Environment

Our need is not to find something to believe, but rather to discover that our lives indicate what we believe right now. —Edith Hunter, Welcome: A Unitarian Universalist Primer, p. 62

If you know wilderness in the way you know love, you would be unwilling to let it go. —Terry Tempest Williams, Red: Passion and Patience in the Desert, p. 76

In this chapter, we ask you to consider your own experiences with the natural environment. How did you experience childhood in the outdoors? In what ways does nature have meaning for you now? When do you think of nature? Do you ever crave the outdoors? What kind of language do you use as you discuss nature, weather, or animals?

Our experiences with nature, our culture, the way we grew up, and our spiritual life have a profound impact on our view of the natural world. The natural world might be a space to welcome and bring into our lives, or nature might be a place to avoid, to mitigate its impact on our life. Nature has a social construction that is not neutral (Evans, 2002). The social construction of nature has elements that empower some members of society while simultaneously disempowering others. Like much of social learning, these messages are often unexamined, along with their consequences. "We (as otherwise educated people) lack language to describe the value of commonplace experiences in the outdoors or our affiliation with other species" (Gray, Coates, & Hetherington, 2013, p. xix). Our relationship with nature is reflective of more than just the surface; we need to consider "how our unhealthy relationships with the natural environment are intimately linked to our unhealthy relationships with each other" (Finney, 2014, p. 34).

For some, the natural world is something to be avoided and tamed. Weather is awful unless warm and sunny, all bugs are to be avoided, and the walk back and forth to our car is our outdoor adventure. In his groundbreaking book on nature deficit disorder, Louv (2008) describes the lack of outdoor activities, including general free play, that young people have been able to experience in recent generations (see Box 5.1). For many middle-class young people in contemporary U.S. society, this is the way they have grown up. Rather than playing in the open green

---

Box 5.1 **People, Places, and Issues—Nature Deficit Disorder**

Richard Louv's groundbreaking book *Last child in the woods* (2008) looks at both the multiple causes and the effects of the increasing separation between children and nature. This largely anecdotal work is organized by the obstacles that come between children and free play in nature. Studies show that 65% of parents are concerned about the lack of time kids spend outdoors in nature (Nature Conservancy, 2014). Early on, Louv elucidates the loose-parts theory, which is the conception of nature as an open-ended toy that is only limited by a child's imagination. Louv sees the standardized education system—and focus on organized sports as the primary physical play of children—as the functional opposite of loose-parts play, "when children played in an environment dominated by play structures rather than natural elements, they established social hierarchy through physical competence; after a grassy area was planted with shrubs their social standing became based less on physical ability and more on language skills, creativity, and inventiveness" (p. 88). Many of the children he interviewed thought of team sports more as work than play and discussed it in the same way as homework.

There are many barriers between the twenty-first-century child and natural learning: electronics are everywhere, parents are more fearful of strangers than ever before, and litigation has become too extreme to allow open use of empty lots. Louv is able to even-handedly discuss the pros and cons of each of these hurdles and proposes solutions to all of them. For instance, litigation can be avoided by creating protected play spaces near construction sites or by liability insurance mandates for property owners of areas that arouse the natural curiosity of a child.

One of the broader issues tackled in the book is what Louv terms *ecophobia*, which is the fear of environmental degradation. Louv posits that an educational focus on abstract, far-away environmental problems, like rainforest deforestation, in lieu of local natural history has a polarizing effect on children:—"Children are so disconnected with nature that they either idealize it or associate it with fear—two sides of the same coin, since we tend to romanticize what we don't know" (p. 134)—polarizing the environmental movement and our relationship to nature, further and further.

Contribution by Charles Exner

spaces in their community, young people are scheduled with structured activities, are plugged into screens that keep them inside, or live in communities that may not provide beautiful, safe, and nontoxic opportunities to be outdoors. Financially poor people may have limited green space in urban settings and extensive space in rural settings. And, like other social concepts, the expressions, beliefs, and attitudes of our larger culture and society are impressed upon and shape our view of the world. Without reflection, we cannot see, know, or modify the beliefs handed down to us. Social work has built into its educational programs the practice of deep reflection to improve our skills for practice. Methods of self-reflection and behavior adjustment can be applied to our experiences with the natural environment. We call this *praxis*. In this chapter, we will provide you the opportunity to reflect on your unexamined assumptions, your attitudes, and the resulting practice behaviors of your early learning on the natural environment. We'll also explore our own complex relationship with humans and nature and consider our role as oppressor and oppressed, gaining a deeper understanding of our relationship in the perpetuating systems that mark environmental injustices.

Perspectives on Nature

There are many views and perspectives of nature, as diverse as any other phenomenon. We'll touch on three of them here, to give you some idea of the range of ways in which individuals and cultures view the natural environment they are placed in. Many good resources on nature can be found, and I encourage you to access them over the course of your life.

NATURE AS ECONOMIC RESOURCE

Many human communities have viewed nature and its bounty as a natural resource for economic development. Striving for modernization and industrialization in a growing economy, humans separated themselves from all but the economic potential in natural spaces. With this view of nature as economy, humans took on a perspective of superiority that allowed us to extract, pollute, and harvest at will. Woods and forests are potential timber sales, mountains contain minerals and elements for extraction, waterways are opportunities to build dams for energy or corporatize for bottling and sale. "No one owned the forest but everyone sold it out" (Sanjayan, 2010, p. 8). Some animals are bred on a massive scale and slaughtered for meat production, and waters are harvested for the sale of fish and other edibles. The economic basis for this perspective is relevant. We humans are absolutely reliant on these natural resources for our dietary intake, for our work, and to build homes and institutions that provide a healthy way of life and satiate our desire for human progress. However, the history of colonization, colonization of people over Earth and often of white communities over First Nations peoples, began to skew our reliance on nature, or change the perspective from one of interdependence to one of domination. In current society, deep controversy exists over the use of nature as an economic resource, especially in relation to coal and oil extraction, overharvesting of waterways, and mountaintop mining, to name just a few. On the one hand, we need affordable sources of energy, food to eat, and minerals to power our electronic devices. On the other hand, the cleanup of what is left after extraction is often unclaimed, the dirty vestiges of burning oil and coal are warming our planet, and the potential depletion of Earth's natural resources can take hundreds to thousands of years to regenerate, if at all.

NATURE AS DIRTY OR DANGEROUS

Nature is also viewed as a place where people participate in work that is dirty, sometimes keeping them in marginalized groups, such as agricultural laborers and miners. Work that is dirty may be perceived as having less pay, keeping people in poverty-class or working-class status. Physical enjoyment of the outdoors may have reduced over the past few decades as people become less comfortable with sweat, dirt, and other effects of outdoor play. Evans (2002) persuasively argues that nature—I add outdoor nature that is beautiful—is overly identified as a white and male experience, and that has led to unexplored assumptions about who gets access to environments of natural beauty and who must tolerate environments that are contaminated or considered dirty.

Nature can also appear dangerous due to threatening species that may attack or bugs that may infect or weather events that can kill. Truly, there is power in nature in all of these forms, and this view of nature grew out of the need to protect oneself and family members from potential dangers. It is not without merit. However, the unexamined assumptions about this perspective have led to skewed perceptions of danger. Communities in places in which natural dangers are very real have often developed responses to these dangers to remain safe, for example, traveling in groups in wild spaces. In contemporary cultures with high material development, often called "Western" or "developed," the actual access to danger in nature is extremely minimal. In cultures with low access to natural danger, people have taken on attitudes that increase the levels of perception of danger or dirtiness in natural spaces—for example, children not playing outdoors for fear of kidnapping, limiting outdoor play for fear of illnesses transmitted by insects, adults exercising indoors so they can have access to showers, driving individual cars to transport ourselves so as to assure our travel no matter the weather. Slowly, over time, these activities shape our actual time outdoors and in nature and limit our relationship with the natural world in our very own communities (see Box 5.2).

Box 5.2 **Organizations in Action—The Trust for Public Land**

The Trust for Public Land is a nonprofit organization working to conserve natural spaces that people care about. Founded in 1972, the organization created parks to protect lands for people to access, to ensure healthy livable communities now and for generations into the future. They also aim to ensure that everyone has parks, gardens, playgrounds, and trails close to their home. Believing that natural spaces provide inspiration, education, recreation, and more to human communities, the trust purchases lands for public use in an effort to permanently protect outdoor spaces. "Creating Parks and Protecting Land for People" is their motto. Their work is urban and rural and focuses on the connections of humans to the natural spaces they are part of. In addition to conserving large swaths of public lands and assuring they are safe from private interests, the Trust for Public Land helps create parks that express cultures and strengthen human communities (for more information, see www.tpl.org).

NATURE AS SPIRIT

One of the ways cultures around the world have viewed nature is as a spiritual resource. Natural places provide respite from the stressors and hassles of modern and contemporary life. Natural spaces provide opportunities for people to get in touch with themselves or their faith. There are often culture-bound expectations that someone heading off into a natural encounter will experience a transformation of their identity in a meaningful way (Evans, 2002), especially if the natural encounter is in a place of beauty. It reminds people to slow down, be present, and discover the many things humans can be grateful for. Nature can literally be awe-inspiring—awe is an emotion that can have "profoundly positive effects on people" (Abrahamson, 2014, p. 38). For many cultures around the world, God is found and realized through natural spaces. Animist faith traditions view nature as representative of God. Nearly every faith tradition around the world, Muslim, Buddhist, Jewish, or Christian, provides guidance on caring for the Earth. This view of nature as spirit has anchored many communities to live harmoniously with natural places. Their collective understanding of the natural world as a source of faith can be a touchstone for many individuals and communities.

These are just some of the ways nature is viewed by individuals and communities; there are others. Disagreements over human perceptions of nature can be found around the world and have caused enormous conflict, in global and local ways. If we return to our foundational concepts and values, we begin again to identify new ways of thinking. If nature is only an economic resource, then we are quickly decimating our account and simply not saving enough for the future. If nature is dirty and dangerous, we lose the opportunity for adventure, new discoveries, and a relationship with nature. If nature is only spirit, we may not be able to provide the economic development necessary to lift people out of chronic poverty. Like all perspectives, we can examine and critically analyze them, decide if they are right for us, and choose a new or shifted perspective. We can hone our perspectives; they are not unchangeable views of the world, nor are they mandated. We can freely choose our perspectives on nature; it simply requires us to identify the perspective we have and begin to decipher a new one.

Environmental Privilege

Most people today, including college students, would not condone environmental injustices. No reasonable person would suggest that some groups should suffer with poor air quality, live on land without access to water or ability to grow food, or be burdened with all of a city's landfills. However, these very visible injustices are only part of the story. As racism did not end when slavery was abolished and women's rights did not become equal with the right to vote, we have learned that confronting and addressing racism and sexism requires an understanding of white privilege and male privilege. Confronting one's environmental privilege is akin to confronting these social privileges. When we dismantle the privilege that we experience, we often see that there are benefits, material and nontangible, that come out of our privilege and have been passed down in ways that are often unacknowledged by us or our society. These privileges are persistent, and they raise ethical questions that we must struggle with. Understanding and dismantling privilege, in all its forms, is part of a larger effort toward social equity. Some privileges are based on the color of our skin or gender, others on the socioeconomic class we belong to. Here we explore environmental privilege. *Environmental privilege* is defined as access to nature's bounty and resources to elevate one's standard of living (such as green spaces, beautiful views, clean air, and water) while simultaneously being sheltered from environmental hazards (such as industrial sites, roadways, and dangerous weather events) (see Box 5.3).

As we recognize, identify, and begin to dismantle environmental privilege, we will move toward protection of, and resistance to, environmental injustices in their explicit and subtle forms. A kind of hierarchy within land conservation has emerged as groups have identified lands more important to save than others. While this has merit, especially as you consider the big and bold places of the world such as the Grand Canyon or the Maasai Mara, it may have caused us to lose sight of the smaller and closer-to-home locales and need for green spaces. This consciousness-raising can help us move beyond the concepts of only protecting the big and beautiful animals or the large and grand natural spaces. It will help us see that natural spaces exist all around us and that some humans and nonhumans are oppressed within this social structure. Like race, our relationship with the natural environment is socially

---

Box 5.3 **Definition of Environmental Privilege**

Environmental privilege results from the exercise of economic, political, and cultural power that some groups enjoy, which enables them exclusive access to coveted environmental amenities such as forests, parks, mountains, rivers, coastal property, open lands, and elite neighborhoods. Environmental privilege is embodied in the fact that some groups can access spaces and resources, which are protected from the kinds of ecological harm that other groups are forced to contend with every day. These advantages include organic and pesticide-free foods, neighborhoods with healthier air quality, and energy and other products siphoned from the living environments of other peoples.

———————

(Park & Pellow, 2011, p. 4)

---

constructed, and that social construction has preferred the big and beautiful among animals and landscapes. In actuality, these privileged environments and animals are not the only ones worth saving. These decisions are reflections of power and colonization.

Privilege, based on the history of colonization, is a powerful and time-tested process that inculcates every fabric of our existence. It is one way power is manifested. It is pervasive, yet nearly impossible to see. The vigilance necessary to identify the effects of privilege is an impossible mission to carry out on one's own. It calls for joint efforts, collaboration. While the efforts are significant and the effects of colonization and privilege will take generations to unravel, the rewards of a just society are great.

Breaking patterns of privilege may feel unnatural, unbalanced, and difficult, enlisting the constant forces and barriers that push the context back into the privilege/marginalization balance we have come to know. For this reason, constant contestation is needed. The daily transactions within the hegemonic system are constantly pushing for the privilege to continue. Without rational thought and acceptance of this feeling of the unnatural, of being off balance, the easiest response is to go back to the system in which one feels most comfortable.

Because privilege lies in multilayered contexts within the lives of individuals and groups, understanding colonization of Earth and its resources is a lifelong process of discovery. Some of this journey of discovery comes from participation within groups where individuals learn about the oppression that they have been subjected to or have participated in. These movements then provide a basis for discussing these multilayered contexts that must be examined on the macro level of social systems and on the micro level of individual interactions. This leads us to examine environmental privilege and environmental injustices as flip sides of the same coin.

Before social workers practice helping others to identify problems of environmental justice, it is essential that they first examine the privileges and oppressions inherent in their own life. Social workers must engage in a critical questioning of their own assumptions and how those assumptions affect their practice. One of the ways to check one's environmental assumptions is to consider one's environmental privileges.

Coates (2013) suggests steps to work through in addressing systemic privileges. First, one must be willing to celebrate and recognize diversity in its human and natural forms, this requires validation of alternative worldviews, especially those that are non-Western or even nonhuman. This can help weaken paradigms of exploitation. Second, one must recognize the level of one's own privilege and oppression and identify the privileges and the losses—and the distortion this serves to purport. Third, understanding the history of who and what has been made poor, marginalized, and degraded can help social workers see the existing relationships of power and subordination. It is important to see the consequences of exploitation and privilege on people and Earth to really understand the impacts on daily life (see Box 5.4).

Nature Is Public Welfare

There is no more important shared, common, public welfare benefit than a healthy natural environment. Clean air to breathe, clean water to drink, predictable weather, land capable of growing food—these are the foundations of any human society. In many rural or financially poor communities around the world it is the ecosystem that provides their needs—not a government-sponsored entitlement program (Sanjayan, 2006). Indeed, it has been said that the original social welfare was a natural environment that could sustain you and your family from youth to old age. "Indeed, although industrialized countries may feel more removed from their natural environment, people in these countries are also dependent on natural systems" (Erickson, 2011, p. 185). Contemporary *social welfare* is defined as any service, good or money granted to people by its government (Segal & Brzuzy, 1997). In looking at social welfare through this lens, we see that there are many social welfare benefits provided by local, state, and national governments. These include things like fire departments, public libraries, road signs, schools, museums, long-term care facilities, roadside rests, national forests and wildlife refuges, and our national park system. The year 2016 was the 100th anniversary of the national park system in the United States. It was in 1916 that the Organic Act established the National Park Service to promote and care for national parks. In 2009 American Public Television shared a series called *The National Parks: America's Best Idea*. The film series is the story of a very important idea—that the most special places in the nation, those of great beauty and grandeur, should be preserved for everyone. It was 1906 when

Box 5.4 **More to Explore—Unpacking the Invisible Backpack**

In 1989 Peggy McIntosh wrote a classical piece on white privilege. Titled, "Unpacking the invisible knapsack," she brilliantly helped shape individuals' understanding of how privilege operates, specifically white privilege in the United States. In her article, McIntosh simply addresses 26 ways white privilege is experienced, unknowingly, through social structures that are invisible to the eye. In this modification of her work, we explore environmental privilege. McIntosh's concepts are blatantly borrowed and applied to environmental privilege as we unpack the proverbial naturalist's backpack.

1. I have access to beautiful views of nature where I live, work, or play.
2. I can breathe clean air at home, school, and work.
3. I take vacations to places with lots of natural beauty but do not give up human comforts such as hot water, Internet access, and gourmet food.
4. I drink clean water.
5. I use as much water as I choose for my daily activities, such as bathing and cooking, without thinking about it.
6. Year round, I eat fruits and vegetables that are not grown in the region in which I live.
7. My trash is hauled far away from my home.
8. I heat and cool my home, work, or school space as I wish, depending on the season.
9. I choose to eat only certain animals.
10. I can avoid toxic chemicals by being selective about my purchases.
11. I own land.
12. I eat fruits and vegetables that I have never grown.
13. I have shelter options from weather's most violent storms.
14. Where I live has green spaces with trees, plants, and flowers.
15. When I go to parks or nature preserves, I see people who look like me.
16. I feel safe in the outdoors near my home.
17. I have the appropriate gear to wear when I go out in nature.

How many of these are true for you? As you unpack your environmental privilege, consider how these experiences can be different for people based on their social identity categories. How do race, gender, economics, and age impact one's environmental privilege?

President Theodore Roosevelt signed the Antiquities Act, allowing the creation of national monuments to protect areas of natural, cultural, or scientific significance; he pushed forward the notion that natural spaces hold unique information culturally and scientifically. The Public Television series was filmed at some of the most spectacular locations in the United States including Acadia, Yosemite, Yellowstone, and the Grand Canyon. While a story of natural places, it is also the story of people from many different backgrounds, who devoted themselves to saving some portions of these precious lands that they loved. In saving land to be shared by all of us, even owned by all of us, we are reminded of the true meaning of citizenry and democracy. These places are part of what we are most proud of in the United States. These national parks and monuments are shared property, owned by all U.S. citizens, as a public good, provided by our government to every citizen; they are a public welfare. The public parks in cities and villages around the world are a shared natural resource too, provided by governments for people's enjoyment, cultural opportunities, and experiences of wonder. Indeed, even our urban forested canopies maintained by our municipal systems provide benefits. People who live on streets with more and larger trees report better perceptions of their own health (Kardan et al., 2015). The economic value of nature's public welfare benefit is literally priceless.

Leave No Trace (www.lnt.org) offers a set of outdoor ethics that provide guidance for people visiting national parks and other wild outdoor spaces. The principles provide guidance for visiting the great outdoors and ensuring minimal impact on the natural spaces humans come in contact with. Leave No Trace is an effort to assimilate specific language and ideas into the culture of backpackers, hikers, and others using the outdoors. These same principles are extended here and applied to any natural space, including those in urban settings. I suggest we treat all of nature the way we would treat our national parks.

Leave No Trace Principles

Wild Areas	Urban Areas
1. Plan ahead and prepare	1. Plan ahead and prepare
2. Travel and camp on durable surfaces	2. Travel on durable surfaces
3. Dispose of waste properly	3. Refuse, reduce, reuse, and recycle
4. Minimize use and impact of fires	4. Minimize use and impact of energy
5. Respect wildlife	5. Respect wildlife and city life
6. Leave what you find	6. Leave nature, pick up trash
7. Be considerate of other visitors	7. Be considerate of others, human and nonhuman

Speciesism

One value of the social work profession is believing in the inherent worth and dignity of every human being. In an interesting piece titled "Social work and speciesism" (2000) Wolf describes the -ism social workers have yet to face, that of relegating nonhuman species to a lesser position than ourselves. Speciesism requires us to consider the dignity and worth of the nonhuman counterparts in our world. Speciesism asks us to reflect on the nature of all of our relationships, beyond those of other humans, and critically question the assumptions inherent in our actions. If the inherent dignity and worth of all beings were part of your life, how would that change your relationship with animals? How might it change your actions in the world? Ted Strong states in LaDuke's book, *All our relations* (1999, pp. 5–6),

> If this nation has a long way to go before all of our people are truly created equally without regard to race, religion, or national origin, it has even farther to go before achieving anything that remotely resembles equal treatment for other creatures who called this land home before humans ever set foot upon it. . . . While the species themselves—fish, fowl, game and the habitat they live in—have given us unparalleled wealth, they live crippled in their ability to persist and in conditions of captive squalor. . . . This enslavement and impoverishment of nature is no more tolerable or sensible than enslavement and impoverishment of other human beings.

This is antithetical to what we learn in our social work education, in fact all education, where the focus is completely human. "The academy as we know it was founded by humanists, promoters of all things human-centric, and speciesism runs rampant in it. Think of how many courses, programs, centers, colleges, and entire institutions devote themselves exclusively to the study and benefit of human animals" (Hood, 2017, para. 15). Social work has focused its profession on justice-making. Expanding who deserves to be inside this realm of justice and who is kept out is a conversation our profession should explore. The attention paid to other species, while minimal, has often continued to extend colonization. It is common to hear of pets referred to as a "rescue" and as wild animals being "saved" from a deleterious fate. A recent bumper sticker asks the question, "Who rescued who?" It is doubtful that animals want to be pitied and controlled any more than humans do.

We can again consider Coates's (2013) process of dismantling human privilege and extend it to nature. First, celebrate and recognize diversity in its human and non-human forms. We might consider factory farming as one example. Massive animal farming of a single species for the meat industry could be viewed differently with this lens. Doing so can help weaken paradigms of mass exploitation. Second, recognize the level of our own participation in environmental privilege and oppression—the privileges and the losses, as well as the distortion these serve to purport—and recognize human exploitation of land and animal, especially when completely built on economics. Third, understanding the history of who and what has been made poor, marginalized, and degraded can help social workers see the existing relationships of power and subordination. Loss of animal diversity and poaching of animals for unique properties related to luxury or the economy are some areas in which the speciesism perspective can be applied. Speciesism is an important element in the work of some specialists in our profession. Veterinary social workers are on the front lines addressing this divide. See Box 5.5 for one veterinary social worker's story.

Sufficiency and Self-Care

Much of social work's justice-making has focused on sharing the wealth, or redistribution of resources to financially poor people, to at least provide a basis of dignity for their lives—housing, access to food and healthcare. While even wealthy countries are still struggling to implement justice in regard to these commodities, it is time to consider what is true "wealth" in regard to the human experience. Is it access to greater consumerism and material wealth? This appears to be the unstudied answer many contemporary societies have provided. But beyond a respectable access to resources for human existence, happiness and wholeness may not increase relative to income. What is the poverty we need to shield people from? What is the wealth we hope to provide?

Reflect back to our four moral norms, sufficiency, participation, sustainability, and solidarity (Martin-Schramm & Stivers, 2003; Martin-Schramm, 2010). Orr (2004) calls for a sufficiency revolution, recognition of what it actually takes to live a decent life—how little it can be. How can we shape community so that exploitation of resources is condemned and despised and care and efficiency in the resources of Earth are condoned and sanctified?

> There is a nobility and duty to care for creation through little daily actions, and it is wonderful how education can bring about real changes in lifestyle. Education in environmental responsibility can encourage ways of acting which directly and significantly affect the world around us. . . . Reusing something instead of immediately discarding it, when done for the right reasons, can be an act of love which expresses our own dignity. We must not think these efforts are not going to change the world. They benefit society, often unbeknown to us, for they call for a goodness, albeit unseen, inevitably tends to spread. Furthermore, such actions can restore our sense of self-esteem; they can enable us to live more fully and to feel that life on earth is worthwhile. (Pope Francis, 2015, p. 154–155)

Box 5.5 More to Explore—Veterinary Social Work

The pager at my waist begins to vibrate as I hear the page overhead: "Family Services to the ER, STAT." I arrive at the emergency room door within minutes, and I am met by a panicked doctor and two nurses who explain that the patient, who arrived in septic shock, was brought to the hospital by her only living family member. This family member is reportedly in the family consult room, crying for help and resources because the patient is not insured and the family cannot afford to provide the patient with the surgery that might save her life.

Supporting people during medical crises is part and parcel of a medical social worker's job—and in that regard, this is a normal event. But what would it mean if the patient presenting to the emergency room that day had four legs and fur? How might you proceed if you found out that the patient—a 14-year-old dog—was the primary source of social and emotional support for an elderly and disabled veteran who brought her to the hospital, using the last of his monthly check to put gas in his car for the 2-hour drive?

Working with these issues, and any issues arising at the intersection of human and animal needs, is the task of veterinary social workers. Veterinary social workers are social workers who specialize in addressing the many ways in which human and animal lives are interwoven. While veterinary social work emerged out of interventions in veterinary hospitals (the University of Pennsylvania's veterinary hospital was likely the very first "host" for a social worker), veterinary social workers now work with a wide range of issues related to how nonhuman animals influence individual, family, and community well-being. Focal areas of practice may include the creation of animal-informed social policies and community programs (e.g., how to make sure a housing program is compliant with Americans with Disabilities Act regulations related to service animal access); the creation, administration, and evaluation of animal-assisted interventions; the provision of education and support to animal welfare and veterinary professionals, particularly around professional risk and well-being; and, of course, the provision of crisis intervention, medical case management, and grief support in veterinary and/or animal welfare practice settings. It goes without saying, then, that choosing a career in veterinary social work requires not just an expertise in social work theories and methods but also advanced training and professional experience working with the diversity of human–animal relationships (whether based on companionship, service, work, or chattel) and the impact of those relationships on human health, social programs, and social policy.

T. R. AND BELLA: A VETERINARY SOCIAL WORK CASE

I introduced myself to T. R. after receiving a case brief from the emergency room team triaging Bella. Bella was in rough shape, and she would likely die that day without emergency surgery to address the source of her infection. In talking with T. R., an army veteran, and former county sheriff, I learned that Bella had been with him since puppyhood, arriving shortly after a life-threatening injury on the job that ended his career and his marriage. I learned that Bella provided T. R. with critical companionship, as well as the motivation to persevere through chronic pain and social isolation. I learned that in a lifetime peppered with multiple traumatic events, animals had become a profound source of meaning and safety for T. R. I also learned that he had no money to pay for his own most basic needs, let alone for Bella's surgery—although he was willing to do anything and everything, even selling his sole source of transportation, to save her life.

So our partnership began. Social workers, regardless of their work setting or primary population, provide not only direct service but also education, resource brokering, mediation, and advocacy. In the case of T. R. and Bella, I spent multiple days working to help him problem-solve around his and Bella's needs, recognizing that T. R.'s health and well-being were intimately tied with hers. Of primary importance that first day was problem-solving around the financial restrictions to emergency surgery. With information and support, T. R. was able to apply for emergency grant funding from multiple sources, including his faith community and other nonprofit organizations, securing just enough money to send Bella to surgery. That small measure of success opened the door to more detailed conversations about T. R.'s psychosocial and health needs, particularly in light of the risk that Bella might not survive her infection. As Bella's health crisis stretched into multiple days of watching and waiting in intensive care, T. R. was provided with support for day-to-day decision-making on her behalf, as well as behind-the-scenes brokering of resources and services that would eventually reconnect him with critical resources (including energy assistance for his home, food shelf referrals, and person-to-person links to trauma support programming at the local Veteran's Administration hospital). And when Bella acutely took a turn for the worse, T. R. was provided with grief support and a referral to a local pet loss group. T. R.'s relationship with the veterinary team, beyond providing him with veterinary services, became the link to many other life-sustaining services—in large part due to the presence of an animal-informed social worker.

ANIMAL-INFORMED SOCIAL WORK

The social work profession's focus on the person in environment perspective has long been anthropocentric, missing the richly reciprocal relationship between humans and the natural world. This oversight leads to countless missed opportunities to engage the individuals, families, and communities we serve. In the United States alone, almost two-thirds of the population keeps animals for some form of companionship, making animals a wonderful conduit for rapport-building, client assessment, and client treatment. But social workers do not have to specialize in veterinary social work to be "animal-informed" practitioners. Instead, knowing how to assess and leverage human–animal relationships may be the key to fully understanding what our clients need, removing unnecessary barriers to service, and creating sound social and organizational policies that more accurately reflect the wide range of needs emerging from human–animal relationships in both personal and public environments. Social workers may start by educating themselves on the forms and functions of human–animal relationships and the many ways animals are employed to serve human needs and enhance personal and public health. From there, it is necessary to educate ourselves on the presence (and, more likely, absence) of animals in policy—particularly as policy dictates who can receive services and from whom. For instance, knowing how animals are reflected in the Americans with Disabilities Act, Fair Housing Administration regulations, and disaster relief policies (such as the PETS Act of 2006) prepares social workers to advocate for, and broker resources on behalf of, clients. Finally, foundational knowledge about how animals are utilized in therapeutic, social, and educational programs prepares social workers to more effectively evaluate, deliver, and refer clients to necessary services.

As described by MacNamara and Moga (2014, p. 162), "The social work profession, at its best, has a large toolbox of potential strategies to assist clients in navigating their world. In fact, the field of social work is ideally situated to explore this more expanded perspective of humans and their environment." Regardless of specialization and target population, each of us has the capacity—if not responsibility—to embrace and apply the many ways in which nonhuman animals influence our lives and the lives of those we serve.

Contribution by Jeannine Moga, MA, MSW, LCSW

In consideration of the world's resources, one can wonder how high of a standard of living we need to aim for. Might we consider that material wealth can be restrained and replaced with luxuries of relationships? Can the word *poverty* be changed so as not to describe people without economic means but to describe those void of a relationship with nature and others? A poverty of nature or a poverty of human relationships? To effectively understand ourselves, we must examine our own thoughts and beliefs with intention. Box 5.6 provides an assessment to help us begin.

Taking care of yourself and living your values are important parts of a fulfilling life and a fulfilling career as a social worker. You may have chosen a career in social work because you care about young people, you have an interest in homelessness,

Box 5.6 **Natural Environment Self-Exploration and Assessment**

To understand someone in social work we often conduct what is called an assessment. Assessments include questions that help us understand the experiences and perspectives of a person. We can also assess ourselves. Use the following set of questions to explore and assess your own relationship with nature.

1. How would you characterize the natural environment of the neighborhood you grew up in? Of the larger community you grew up in?
2. Take out a sheet of paper and create two columns. In the first column write down five behaviors from the list that seem to be most valued in the family you grew up in. Then, in the opposite column write down the five behaviors that seem to be the least valued in the family you grew up in. How did these influence you?
   a. Recycling
   b. Showing off wealth or materialism
   c. Giving to others, especially those in need
   d. Turning off lights when leaving a room
   e. Spending time outdoors for pleasure
   f. Spending time outdoors for work or labor
   g. Complaints about the weather
   h. Reusing items
   i. Using one-time-use items and then throwing them away
   j. Gardening without pesticides or herbicides
   k. Gardening with pesticides and herbicides
   l. Caring for pets
   m. Family vacations to the natural spaces
   n. Family vacations to human-made spaces
   o. Gratitude for nature
   p. Worry about pollution
   q. Lack of care for environmental issues
   r. Fear or disgust of nature
   s. Ignoring the outdoors
3. Think of one or two people who you perceive to have a different environmental view from you. What tells you they might be different? How would you characterize their values?
4. What do you appreciate having learned from your environmental background?
5. What has been hard for you to accept from your environmental background?
6. What impact does your environmental background have on your current attitudes, behaviors, and feelings toward nature?

(Adapted from a questionnaire developed by Prof. Susan Smulyan at Brown University.)

you care about social work in healthcare settings, you want to write policy, or you want to help families in times of crisis. Whatever your interest in social work is, environmental justice can be part of your practice. You don't have to become a full-time environmental social worker. You don't need to change what drew you to social work, and you don't need to find a different location or area of interest. Incorporating environmental justice is for all social workers in all kinds of organizations, with all kinds of people.

Critical Thinking Questions

1. Are experiences in nature a component of human diversity? Explain.
2. Identify your own environmental privilege. What experiences have you been given access to because of the color of your skin, your economic class, your gender, or another component of your social identity?
3. Identify your own environmental oppression. What experiences have you been kept out of because of the color of your skin, your economic class, your gender, or another component of your social identity?

Key Terms

Anthropocentric
Nature deficit disorder
Praxis
Privilege
Public welfare
Speciesism
Use of self

Additional Learning Activities

1. Leave your classroom and explore the area outside. Where is nature in your community? How is it expressed? Is it respected? revered? distrusted? ignored?
2. Identify the social, economic, political, cultural and spiritual traditions that influence how nature is treated in your locale.
3. Write an environmental history of yourself. Consider your relationship with nature. Who taught you to have this kind of relationship? Do you notice nature's impact on your life? How do you remove yourself from a relationship with nature? How do you engage yourself in a relationship with nature? What do you want for your future relationship with nature?

4. Nature analysis. Record your experiences in the natural world for 1 week. Collect data on the amount of time you spent in nature. Include the kind of nature you were in and the weather during that time. Comment on your emotional and intellectual response to each of the natural experiences. Explore with partners in class. What surprised you?

References

Abrahamson, J. (Nov/Dec 2014). The Science of Awe. Sierra Magazine. 99(6), 36-39 & 54.

Coates, J. (2013). Ecospiritual approaches: A path to decolonizing social work. In Gray, M., Coates, J., Yellow Bird, M. & Hetherington, T. (Eds) Decolonizing Social Work. New York: Ashgate.

Erickson, C. L. (2011). Environmental degradation and preservation. In L. M. Healy and R. J. Link (Eds.). Handbook of International Social Work (pp. 184–189). New York, NY: Oxford University Press.

Evans, M. M. (2002). "Nature" and environmental justice. In J. Adamson, M. M. Evans, & R. Stein (Eds.). The environmental justice reader: Politics, poetics, and pedagogy (pp. 181–193). Tucson: University of Arizona Press.

Finney, C. (2014). Black Faces: White Spaces: Re-imagining the relationship of African Americans to the great outdoors. Chapel Hill: University of North Carolina Press.

Gray, M., Coates, J., & Hetherington, T. (2013). Preface. In M. Gray, J. Coates, & T. Hetherington (Eds.). Environmental social work (pp. xvii—xx). New York, NY: Routledge.

Hood, J. W. (2017). How to teach about nature while we destroy it. Chronicle of Higher Education, 63(21). Retrieved from https://www.chronicle.com/article/How-to-Teach-About-Nature/238925.

Kardan, O., Gozdyra, P., Misic, B., Moola, F., Palmer, L. J., Paus, T., & Berman, M. G. (2015). Neighborhood greenspace and health in a large urban center. Scientific Reports, 5, 1–14.

LaDuke, W. (1999). All our relations: Native struggles for land and life. Cambridge, MA: South End Press.

Louv, R. (2008). Last child in the woods. Chapel Hill, NC: Algonquin.

Martin-Schramm, J. (2010). Climate justice: Ethics, energy, and public policy. Minneapolis, MN: Fortress Press.

Martin-Schramm, J. B., & Stivers, R. L. (2003). Christian environmental ethics: A case methods approach. Maryknoll, NY: Orbis.

McIntosh, P. (1989). White privilege: Unpacking the invisible knapsack. Peace and Freedom Magazine (July/August), 10–12.

MacNamara, M., & Moga, J. (2014). The place and consequence of animals in contemporary social work practice. In T. Ryan (Ed.), Animals in social work: Why and how they matter (pp. 151–166). London, UK: Palgrave MacMillan.

Nature Conservancy. (2014). Where do you want to play? Nature Conservancy (April/May), 20.

Orr, D. W. (2004). Earth in mind: On education, environment, and the human prospect. Washington DC: Island Press.

Park, L. S. H., & Pellow, D. N. (2011) The slums of Aspen: Immigrants vs. the environment in America's eden. New York: New York University Press.

Pope Francis. (2015). Encyclical letter Laudato Si' of the Holy Father Francis on care for our common home. Retrieved from http://w2.vatican.va/content/francesco/en/encyclicals/documents/papa-francesco_20150524_enciclica-laudato-si.html

Sanjayan, M. A. (2006). Is poverty related to conservation? Nature Conservancy, 56(2), 29.

Sanjayan, M. A. (2010). Identity politics. *Nature Conservancy, 60*(1), 8.

Segal, E. A., & Brzuzy, S. (1997). *Social welfare policy, programs, and practice.* Belmont, CA: Thomson Brooks/Cole.

Frevert, P. (2009). *Welcome: A Unitarian Universalist Primer.* Boston, MA: Skinner Hourse Books.

Williams, T. T. (2001). Red: Passion and Patience in the Desert. New York, NY: Vintage.

Wolf, D. B. (2000). Social work and speciesism. *Social Work, 45*(1), 88–93.

CHAPTER 6

Phases of Social Work Practice for Environmental Justice

There was once a city without gardens or trees or greenery of any kind. Most people spent their time indoors. As you can imagine, it was a very dreary place. —Carter Brown, no page number

How do social workers engage in environmental justice problems? The same way we engage with all human problems: we use our tried and true social work methods. The methods of social work practice lead us toward joint solutions for human and environmental problems. In working with all system sizes, from individuals to communities, the steps involved with the social work process are the same for any client system. One way to describe these steps is the phases of practice. Sometimes called the "problem-solving process," the phases of practice provide us a path for moving through and resolving environmental justice problems. In this text, we use the phases of practice as developed and explained by Locke, Garrison, and Winship (1998). The phases of practice are preferred terminology in the effort to secure environmental justice, simply because, in real life, there are not clear demarcations between practice steps. Using the word *phases* allows us to see the blending of the markers between our steps and still to feel a sense of movement in the process. Additionally, *phases* allows us to see the process as one that has shared leadership by the client and social worker; the word suggests a path we walk with the client. Avoid terminology that implies that you, as the social worker, do something to or for the client. "Helping is not a neutral act" (Lundy, 2004, p. 112). Each and every interaction with a client either reinforces the systems of privilege and oppression for our clients or empowers them. Which will you choose?

Social Work Education

Social work is a profession guided by universal understandings of the knowledge, values, and skills necessary to be an effective social worker. In our discipline these are called "social work competencies" and developed by the Council on Social Work Education. These concepts guide the education of social workers across the United States. In 2015, nine competencies were developed (Council on Social Work Education, 2015). These nine competencies provide the bedrock of education of social work practice. Ranging from understanding ethical practice to the importance of engaging diversity and difference to understanding various system sizes, these nine competencies are endorsed by our profession and guide learning as a student and as a licensed professional in practice. Each competency is further expressed through practice behaviors—statements that specifically describe what social workers do. Two of the competencies identify environmental justice as a core component of social work and are further expressed through three practice behaviors (see Box 6.1). All are integrated into field education, the signature pedagogy of the social work curriculum, assuring that social work students begin to learn about these methods of practice.

Combined, the 9 competencies assure that generalist social work practitioners are prepared to work with a range of systems, from individuals to communities, in local and global contexts. Because social workers serve at the crux of intersectionality, we are prepared for the complex problem-solving needed for human and environmental problems. Social work can be understood and described from several different views, including the methods of our practice, the problem areas we address, the population we work with, and the types of settings we work in. Imagine a lifetime of interesting work that will include all of these crosscutting ways to create solutions to human problems. In each and every one of these views of our practice, the natural environment can be conceptualized, understood, and applied as an area of practice.

Box 6.1 **More to Explore—Social Work Educational Competencies**

Competency: Advance human rights and social, economic, and environmental justice.

> Practice behavior: apply an understanding of social, economic, and environmental justice to advocate for human rights at the individual and system levels.

> Practice behavior: engage in practices that advance social, economic, and environmental justice.

Competency: Engage in policy practice

> Practice behavior: apply critical thinking to analyze, formulate, and advocate for policies that advance human rights in social, economic, and environmental justice.

Phase Model of Social Work Practice

The phase model of social work practice, as conceptualized by Locke et al. (1998), provides a process that integrates well with our foundational concepts and theories. In their textbook, *Generalist Social Work Practice: Context, Story, and Partnerships*, perhaps the first social work practice text to contextualize the natural environment explicitly, they give a full explanation of the reasoning behind using the phases of social work practice, rather than the problem-solving process. Locke et al. (p. 110) explain the rationale well:

> it appears to us that they (the problem-solving process) are worker-centered models—the social worker assesses, plans, and intervenes with clients systems. While the workers activities are important, we are persuaded that the activities of the client system are equally important, and the intent of our model is to shift the power relations in the planned change process from one dominated by the worker to one where power is respectfully shared by the client system and the social worker in partnership. This is a subtle but important shift in emphasis.

What you do as a social worker is important. We must be cognizant that the activities of social work are collaborative—and ensure the inherent dignity of all members of the process. To do so, a thoughtful and intentioned language that ensures integrity and shared power in the process rather than an allegiance to status is called for. In addition, every foundational concept of social work is present in each of these phases of practice. Every concept and every theory can be applied and lived out in each phase. "The word phase is often used to mean the way something develops or unfolds, and we think this appropriately describes the social worker and client system experiences of the planned change process" (Locke et al., 1998, p. 117). And so, the phases of practice are fitting for the work of seeking environmental justice— a justice that touches clients and social workers simultaneously. The phases are identified in Box 6.2.

Box 6.2 **Phases of Social Work Practice**

Phase 1: Telling and Exploring the Story
Phase 2: Describing a Preferred Reality
Phase 3: Making Plans and Dreams Real
Phase 4: Evaluating Outcomes and Making Transitions

Beginning the Phases of Practice

The point of entry into social work practice and environmental justice issues can be anywhere within the three levels of practice: micro, mezzo, or macro. The values, theories, and phases throughout the social work process are the same; but the skills and methods used vary at each of the levels of practice. Remember, while phases help us see a pathway forward, we must also integrate the theories, foundational concepts, and values of social work as we embark on the phases. The phases of practice provide us a pathway through a problem, allowing the real solutions to emerge in the holistic integration of social work knowledge, values, and skills to create lasting outcomes. I like the term *emancipatory* (Mulallay, 2007, p. 238) social work practice, it reminds us of our goal—real freedom from the injustices people, Earth, and other beings experience. We can begin this work with individuals, with family or group systems, even with organizations or policies. All of these system sizes begin with the first phase of practice. Before social work practice with any client system level, social workers should prepare themselves. In preparation, reflect on your own moods and outside demands. Consider ways you can open and prepare yourself to be fully present to begin to engage with the client. Be prepared to pay close attention to what the client is experiencing, sharing, and expressing verbally and in body language. Be ready to build trust as the most important component of the first and subsequent visits. Consider the similarities and differences between yourself and the client, recognizing that you can diminish privilege and build justice and equity in the relationship. Remember that clients may feel reluctant to converse about situations they find painful (Lundy, 2004), and fear of being judged or blamed for their difficulties is a very strong emotion. Doubts and fears are likely even more prevalent among members of marginalized groups who have experienced events that are alienating (Lundy, 2004).

Before beginning the phases of practice, it is important for the social worker to get to know the people, place, and culture of the family, group, community, or organizational unit. Learn their names, some of their beliefs, their history, their status, and what roles people, land, or animals hold within the family or community settings. During these introductory times, social workers have the opportunity to introduce themselves and show through their words and actions that power differentials are meant to be reduced and that the client power is highlighted. Where and how the social worker is sanctioned to work with the client should be clarified. Whether through a government or nonprofit source, the social worker can describe the roles and mission of the work he or she does as part of the engagement process. Your clients have the right to understand the mission of your agency and the reasons for the work you do.

As we move through the four phases of practice in social work, consider the environmental justice and social work matrix in Figure 6.1. Note that integration of the foundational concepts of social work practice, the environmental justice

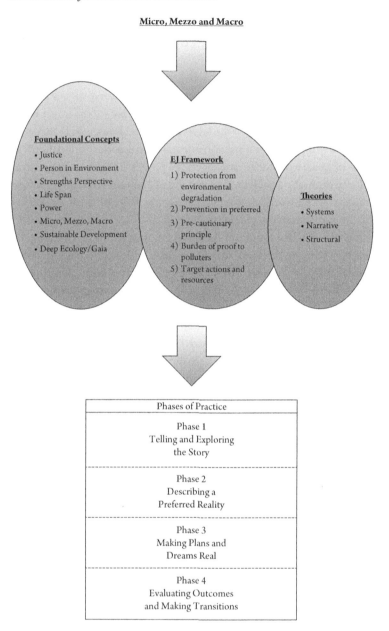

Figure 6.1 Integration of foundational concepts and phases of social work practice

framework (Bullard, 2005), and the theories we are using informs the phases of practice at all levels and stages of practice. Figure 6.1 reflects the incorporation of these perspectives, methods, and theories into the work you will conduct as you move through each of the phases of practice.

Phase One: Telling and Exploring the Story

Telling and exploring the story is the first phase of social work practice. It is the phase in which you must dedicate time and a deep willingness to explore multiple components of the story—sometimes called "the problem"—to be successful in the phases that follow. Aligned with narrative theory, telling and exploring the story requires the social worker to be a deep listener and elicit the story from the client and others involved in the story—"Respecting client systems' belief systems and inviting them to talk about what is important and life-giving to them" (Locke et al., 1998, p. 146). Seldom do people have the opportunity to really be heard without interference of questions, agendas, or specific matters to cover. When the social worker prioritizes the narrative, as the client desires to tell it, there is a newly found opportunity for expression, critical thinking, and understanding on the client's part. "Stories become the vehicles we use to define ourselves and the places we inhabit and utilize" (Finney, 2014, p. 69). Being heard is a privilege wealthy and respected people receive often—it is seldom a gift passed on to the clients of social workers. It also requires the social worker to shed personal biases—if not, the social worker threatens a full understanding of the issues. Key components to thoughtful listening at any system size are empathic responses (verbally and in body language), asking open-ended questions, and paraphrasing to assure you have understood the story. Using these three foundational skills will help the client gain trust in you and explore the story with a sense of safety and willingness, even if parts may be difficult to share. As a wise social work professor once said, when you think you are done exploring the story, explore just a little bit more to be sure. Innovative and creative questions with probes are a must in developing and exploring a full story. Some ideas for questions include the following: Who else might be interested in this story? What nonhuman influences are there? Who has power in the story? What is the view of those who do not have power, human and nonhuman? Where do the strengths reside?

One of the main goals of the first phase of practice is to build trust between the client and the social worker. This means the client understands the meaning of the work, feels respected by the social worker, and has a sense that the work ahead will be useful. Starting with a collaborative and empathic connection is necessary to begin the trust required to sustain a relationship for the four phases of practice. Using your own words, always end the exploration of the story by asking the client something like, *Is there anything else you would like to share to help me understand your concerns?* and, of course, expressing gratitude for the client's willingness to trust you with his or her story. See Box 6.3 for examples of open-ended questions that will work at all levels of practice.

Exploring the story fully leads to building the platforms that lead to phase two of practice, identifying what is a preferred reality. This is the fertile ground for developing strategies. As the understanding of the story deepens and expands,

---

Box 6.3 **More to Explore—Open-Ended Questions for Exploring a Story for Any Level of Practice, Based on Ideas of Hughes (2007)**

- Who is part of this experience? Human and nonhuman?
- Who cares about the resolution? Human and nonhuman?
- Who should be part of the decision-making?
- Who should not participate in the decision-making?
- Do we have the right kind of information to understand this fully?
- Is there specialized knowledge that can help us?
- Are there legal considerations to make?
- Are there unacceptable impacts we must avoid?
- What assumptions are we making?

---

the opportunities for new realities deepen and expand as well. Trust, respect, relationship-building, and shared understanding are the other benefits of a fully explored story.

Phase Two: Describing a Preferred Reality

In phase two of social work practice, the description of a preferred reality, a solution, begins to emerge. The skilled practitioner recognizes that client stories may flow in and out of phases one and two. Many of the same skills from phase one continue into phase two. Empathic listening, paraphrasing, and open-ended questions continue to help you explore the preferred reality. As a discipline utilizing systems theory, the key in the preferred reality stage is to not judge ideas or shut out possibilities but to encourage and nurture ideas and innovation. Oppression and marginalization steal dreams. They steal the time and opportunity to dream as people face the daily struggles of life on the margins. Oppression and marginalization steal the momentum to dream and encourage resignation to the reality one has. Building off of phase one, where clients have been deeply heard, the opportunity to imagine a preference, and actually try to achieve it, begins to become a possibility. Because the client is not oppressed or marginalized in the eyes of the social worker, he or she has found a space to dream.

Similar to planning, in this phase, the client and social worker must consider the viable options for change and what kinds of resources are needed to create the desired state. This includes the roles of the social worker and the client and a determination of who can do what in the implementation of the plan. These decisions should be based on skill, time, and resources needed. Some of the components of the preferred reality will provide a solution in a shorter time frame. Others will require the long and arduous work of building justice for the long term. Both of these components need to be part of the preferred reality, no matter their time frame. The intellectual process of understanding the long view of justice is an existential pursuit for many, and we should include clients in this effort as it gives meaning to our lives.

For clients of all system sizes, lending a vision (Locke et al., 1998) is a technique to help identify and build a new reality. When oppression and marginalization have strong footholds in the minds, hearts, and lived realities of client systems, vision can be stifled. One option for the social worker is to gently offer a vision of a reality that is possible for the client, to kindly make suggestions about what can be and encourage the client to begin to see his or her own role in the creation of that vision. It may become the client's vision—not one assigned but one he or she begins to borrow and eventually owns as his or her own. The activities outlined in Box 6.4 are options to consider as you think of ways you can begin to build a new reality.

Box 6.4 **More to Explore—Activities Social Workers or Clients Might Do to Better the Environment and Themselves**

1. Take a walk while meeting.
2. Advocate for public transit passes from your organizations.
3. Add bike-parking stations at your organization.
4. Encourage gardening at local schools.
5. Clean the area around your agency to promote walking.
6. Use energy-efficient outdoor lighting around your agency to promote safety.
7. Help clients learn about healthy home care.
8. Use water bottles.
9. Establish or participate in a community garden.
10. Establish small private gardens on balconies or in backyards.
11. Ask small grocers to carry local food options.
12. Determine how your agency can use less water, electricity, or natural gas.
13. Plant a tree at your agency, celebrate it.
14. Celebrate culture and nature combined.
15. Bring your clients to a farmers' market.
16. Share your own reduce-and-reuse stories with people you work with.
17. Appreciate biodiversity—everywhere.
18. Join the local park board or committee.
19. Identify and describe environmental concerns as human concerns.

Phase Three: Making Plans and Dreams Real

In making plans and dreams real, the work of the client and the social worker becomes complex and requires strategic action. This can be the phase of practice with the longest range of work and the deepest need to broaden your skills. Several social work skills can be very useful in this phase of practice. This phase calls on you and your client to show the grit and muster necessary to create lasting and meaningful change. Be honest with the client about the difficulty of this phase of practice, while simultaneously sharing your commitment to the process. There are several roles of a social worker that give shape to the work ahead. As you consider and implement each of these roles, the most important work of an environmentally focused social worker is to include, as an equal partner, the client in the process of making plans and dreams real. Including clients is not an exercise. It is how we practice. When we do justice work, the work, the means, and the process of getting there are the justice-making in action.

Akin to an intervention phase, action is assumed in this phase of practice. Building on the discussion from phase two, the social worker and client identify different work and steps they can complete that will lead them toward the desired goals. This phase displays the trust built in phase one as the client trusts the social worker to follow through on the identified tasks and vice versa.

SOCIAL WORK ROLES IN PHASE THREE

In utilizing the phases of practice there are several traditional roles of social work that fit most poignantly with environmental justice practice. Like all social work practice—the roles range from micro to macro practice skills—and you will be prepared to fulfill all of these roles after a generalist social work education. Prepare yourself to help clients build skills in managing problems rather than simply identifying solutions (Locke et al., 1998) that make it appear as if there is an end result that is a correct solution. This kind of thinking leads to falsehoods for our clients and possibly a distrust of social workers. Instead, aim to help clients identify ways to manage challenges over time, recognizing that life for all of us is a series of managing struggles and celebrating accomplishments.

COUNSELOR

In the counselor role of social work, you practice your skills of deep listening and intentional questioning to help the client begin to answer some of his or her own questions regarding life. It is not an advising role, though through questioning a social worker practicing good counseling can often help a client see the advice he or she could give him- or herself. In times of crisis or emergencies, the counselor role takes on one of deep care and attention, with simultaneous direction to help a person or group of people who may be in a state of shock. Consider how the natural environment can enhance your role as a counselor. Walking and talking might be helpful to a client.

BROKER AND BRIDGE BUILDER

In this role of social work practice, the momentum of the work is the connection to other people and agencies that can provide service and guidance in a specific situation. The social worker may simply be introducing a client to another agency or actively referring and creating connections for the individuals or groups. Consider how the problem the client is facing has environmental components. What might be a referral you have not previously thought of? A parks and recreation event? A food-sharing program?

MEDIATOR

This role in social work tries to help conflicting people or groups understand the other's point of view and even establish common ground among people. The skills used for this role can be amplified through specific strategies for conflict mediation and a clear commitment from both parties that moving forward is what is hoped for. As a social worker, you do not have to mediate alone. Consider how collaborative partners or agencies in the community might expand the mediation possibilities.

RESEARCHER

Be prepared to gather data about problems people are experiencing. Use your ability to access and understand research literature and identify what is important for the clients you serve, what is known about a problem, and what other people have used to solve the same or a similar problem. Be sure to consider data gathered by organizations and advocacy groups that could be useful information to share with your clients.

EDUCATOR

In the education role of social work, we provide information that people may not know about. The information can include programs and policies that may be beneficial, health or parenting information, or access to specific resources or practices, required by law, or part of a human right. Reducing toxicity in the home, or learning about a policy that can benefit them, or changing dietary habits can be important educational information for clients.

ADVOCATE

Advocacy in social work is often used to assure that clients have access to the re-sources they need or in securing the well-being of clients who may be at risk in some way. This involves speaking on behalf of the client, sharing the client's experience with another group to assure they understand the client's needs, or advocating for a change in policy on behalf of the client. You can advocate for an individual's needs or a community need. Using the power of your agency or professional status can be helpful at times.

COLLABORATOR

Collaborating with other professionals and disciplines can be an important part of environmental social work. Public health, legal services, government, and nonprofits are all potential collaborators in environmental justice issues. They may be able to provide technical or research-related information that can bring about significant change or understanding to a problem a client is facing.

There are other social work roles that you will learn about during your social work education. "Across the rich spectrum of social work roles, the best practices of the social work profession—building relationships and resources, assessment and intervention, organizing and problem-solving, celebrating diversity, and fighting oppression—can be brought to bear to advance environmental justice and healthy environments for all citizens" (Rogge, 2008, p. 5). Multiple roles are needed to address the multiple human and environmental problems we face.

> The challenge for social workers is to understand the broader political context and organization of society while responding directly to the immediate concerns and needs of those who seek help. This type of analysis focuses on the socio-economic, [environmental] or structural context of individual problems and the power arrangements and the economic forces in society that create and maintain social conditions that generate stress, illness, deprivation, discrimination, [degradation] and other forms of individual problems. (Lundy, 2004 p. 130)

Phase Four: Evaluating Outcomes and Making Transitions

In this phase of practice, the client and the social worker begin to determine how their shared work has progressed and what their next steps should be. Options can include continuing to work together, referral to another practitioner who can help in a new and different way, or discontinuing to work together. These three options should be considered as you together determine what is the next step. Sometimes, a clear additional problem has emerged that the social worker can be influential on. In these situations, continuing to work together is a good option. Other times, client problems have now become redefined, and another professional can be more helpful in the situation, such as a lawyer or medical professional. These times are good options for referral to others. In other situations, the problems are resolved in a way that is satisfactory to the client, and the social worker and client do not see an additional need to continue to work together. In these instances, closing the working relationship is the best option. However the transition unfolds, "it is important to review and acknowledge with the client system achievements in the meaning of the important work together so both the client system and the social worker can leave the change process with a clearer sense of achievement, of harmony, and of the future" (Locke et al., 1998, p. 246).

The second important role of this final phase of practice is evaluation of the social worker's work with the client. In evaluating our work as social work practitioners, one strategy is to consider the consistency of our social work process with the theories and perspectives that guide our work. New situations and dilemmas can challenge us in ways we may not have imagined. Asking evaluation-based questions can help you reflect on the success of your practice:

- Did our intervention methods fit with social work's values perspective? With the client's value perspective?
- Was our work congruent with the theoretical perspectives appropriate to practice with?
- Do the clients feel some resolution even if the problem is not ameliorated?

Answering these questions can help determine if we are on the right path toward resolution and if our outcomes are appropriate to the situation. It also helps us shape our future practice skills and refine our work.

Environmental Justice Collaborative Problem-Solving Model

The Office of Environmental Justice of the Environmental Protection Agency developed and encourages the use of the environmental justice collaborative problem-solving model (EJCPSM) "as part of its ongoing commitment to ensure environmental justice for all communities, including low-income and/or minority communities" (U.S. Environmental Protection Agency, 2008). The Environmental Protection Agency also makes clear that the purview of this environmental justice work is all members of a community, collaborating among various disciplines and professions to create change.

Situations where community residents are exposed disproportionately to environmental harms and risks require the application of science (both physical and social), environmental and civil rights law, public policy, urban planning, and other academic disciplines pertaining to community health, community development, natural resource management, and dispute resolution. These situations, more often than not, fall outside of the regulatory or programmatic responsibilities of any single governmental agency. It is virtually impossible for any single organization, institution, or sector of society, no matter how large or well established, to adequately address the environmental and/or public health problems experienced by communities. (U.S. Environmental Protection Agency, 2008, p. 1)

This model was developed with the recognition that environmental injustices have multiple stakeholders, that creating a process to help assure decision-making is done with a multitude of community voices, and that a clear vision of a pathway forward are the main components of the EJCPSM. The model should not be intimidating despite the complexity of the diagram shared in Figure 6.2. If you look closely, you will find similarities to our own phases of practice and even alignment with the social work educational competencies described earlier in this chapter.

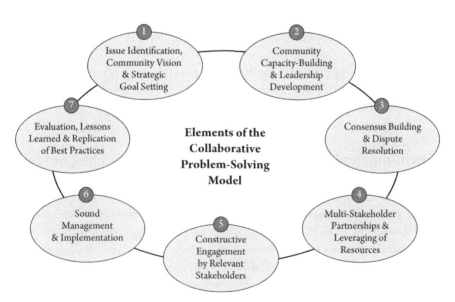

Figure 6.2 Environmental justice collaborative problem-solving model. U.S. Environmental Protection Agency (2008)

Comparing Models of Practice

You already know that we use the phases of practice (Locke et al., 1998) in this text because of the commitment to practice methods based on equality and justice. You'll see similar descriptions in other social work practice texts about the steps of working with clients in a social work process, often called the "problem-solving process" or "method." Rather than focusing on problem-saturated language, we use the phases of practice to remind us that we are not only solving problems, we are creating new opportunities and building resiliencies. The phase model of practice departs from conventional models in that it is based more on what the client system wishes for than on solving specific problems (Locke et al., 1998). This can include nurturing health, as much as diminishing poor health, for example. One cannot build on a problem, but one can continue on through a phase. When you hear other disciplines or community partners use different terminology to describe this process, you will be prepared to understand the work ahead, for the foundational components have inherent similarities. The EJCPSM fits well with social work practice as it facilitates and recognizes the important connections between stakeholders in solving community problems. To illustrate these similarities, the EJCPSM, the problem-solving process, and the Council on Social Work Education competencies are mapped to the phases of practice (Locke, et al., 1998) so that you can see the differences in language yet understand the broader concepts that are integral to each of these models or processes (see Figure 6.3).

The Balance Between Individual Problems and Social Ills

You may have strong beliefs about how problems in society should be solved. You may think people should solve their problems on their own, or you may feel social institutions like government and businesses should do more to reduce human problems. Your ideas have developed over many years, and they reflect your worldview. Your worldview is unique to you but does share commonalities with others, within a certain faith perspective, political party, or region. My goal is not to suggest a binary but to build an intellectual flexibility in which you can vacillate with the issue at hand and identify and calibrate the nuances between individuals solving a problem and the social responses required to address a problem. Nearly always, the answer lies in both areas. Finding that space, in which humans recognize their contributions to an environmental and social problem and commit to changing it, should work in tandem with a larger social response to ameliorate the issue. The phases of social work practice can work on both of these ends, the personal and the social. If we accept an ecocentric perspective, we extend the partnership of social work practice beyond that of the client and community to Earth itself. Can Earth be

Phase Model of Social Work Practice	EPA EJ Collaborative Problem Solving Model	Problem Solving Process	CSWE Competencies
Phase One: Telling and exploring the story	Issue Identification, Community Vision and Strategic Goal Setting	Engagement	Competency 6: Engage with Individuals, Families, Groups, Organizations and Communities
	Community Capacity-Building and Leadership Development	Assessment	
Phase Two: Describing a preferred reality	Consensus Building and Dispute Resolution	Planning	Competency 7: Assess with Individuals, Families, Groups, Organizations and Communities
	Multi-Stakeholder Partnerships and Leveraging of Resources		
Phase Three: Making Plans and Dreams Real	Constructive Engagement by Relevant Stakeholders Sound Management and Implementation	Implementation	Competency 8: Intervene with Individuals, Families, Groups, Organizations and Communities
Phase Four: Evaluating Outcomes and Making Transitions	Evaluation; Lessons Learned and Replications of Best Practices	Evaluation Termination	Competency 9: Evaluate with Individuals, Families, Groups, Organizations and Communities

Figure 6.3 Comparison of models of social work practice

a client in the phases of practice? Can Earth be a partner? After all, there is no environmental problem-solving without Earth's participation.

Social Change Wheel

Recognizing the connections between larger social problems and the troubles that individuals experience, the social change wheel identifies strategies and areas in which the simultaneous efforts of micro, mezzo, and macro social work are carried out. The social change wheel (Minnesota Campus Compact, 2012) is a tool to help people envision the various methods they can use to contribute to change. It gives ideas for the practice levels and practice behaviors we employ as social workers (see Figure 6.4).

The social change wheel is a way to visualize the practice of seeking environmental justice and identifying the many methods and processes we can take part in. People have different skill sets and unique ways of interacting with the world around them. As social workers, we believe these differences are our gifts and can be intentionally used to strengthen the fabric of the community we live in. With the values that we have identified, we can see through the social change wheel that there is a method for everyone to demonstrate those values. There are even multiple ways.

SOCIAL CHANGE WHEEL

All of these strategies can contribute to social change.

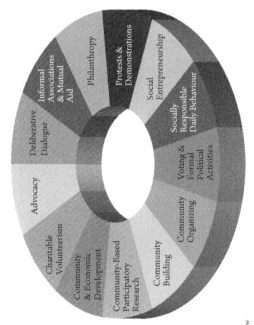

Deliberative Dialogue – exchanging and weighing different ideas, perspectives, and approaches around particular issues in a public setting
Examples:
- Organizing ongoing local discussion circles
- Using a National Issues Forums guide to prompt a group to consider multiple options on an issue

Informal Associations & Mutual Aid – unpaid, collaborative work or sharing of resources by people seeking to improve their collective quality of life
Examples:
- Starting a support group around an issue of concern
- Participating in disaster relief efforts or opening your home to a displaced person

Philanthropy – Donating money to increase the well-being of humankind or advance another social good
Examples:
- Holding a fundraiser for a nonprofit organization
- Providing cash or in-kind donations yourself

Protests & Demonstrations – expressing public disagreement with a situation or policy in a visible, non-violent way
Examples:
- Participating in rallies or marches in support of a cause
- Creating public visual or performance art intended to draw attention to an issue

Social Entrepreneurship – creating a new venture or using entrepreneurial principles to change an existing one
Examples:
- Launching a business with a clear social benefit
- Developing a new product that affordably provides clean water to people in areas without it

Socially Responsible Daily Behavior – acting on one's values and civic commitments in one's personal and professional life
Examples:
- Challenging racist or sexist words or behavior
- Buying from locally owned or socially responsible businesses

Voting & Formal Political Activities – mobilizing others to influence public policy through formal political channels – and participating yourself
Examples:
- Organizing a voter registration drive
- Running for public office or working or volunteering on another candidate's campaign

Advocacy – supporting an idea or cause through public and private communications, and collecting evidence to support one's position
Examples:
- Speaking or writing to individuals, groups, or elected officials on behalf of a cause
- Sharing a video about your cause on social media

Charitable Volunteerism – addressing immediate needs, most often through social service agencies, churches, or schools
Examples:
- Tutoring a child or an adult once a week
- Serving food or registering people at a soup kitchen or shelter

Community & Economic Development – acting to provide economic opportunities and improve social conditions in a sustainable way
Examples:
- Developing marketing plans, websites, or other supports to help small businesses grow
- Providing microloans or training to aspiring entrepreneurs

Community-Based Participatory Research – conducting research in partnership with members of a community with an intention to benefit the community
Examples:
- Defining a research agenda and implementing each aspect of research projects with local stakeholders
- Jointly publishing results to ensure they reach public as well as academic audiences

Community-Building – strengthening through interpersonal connections the capacity of local residents and associations to work together
Examples:
- Creating local history projects profiling both long-time and new residents
- Organizing neighborhood clean-ups or National Night Out activities

Community Organizing – bringing people together to act in their shared self-interest
Examples:
- Mapping the skills, interests, relationships, and other assets of residents to inform work on particular issues
- Developing an issue campaign to call for change in a troubling practice, such as the overuse of school suspensions

Figure 6.4 Social change wheel MN Campus Compact (2012)

The social change wheel is an excellent conceptual tool to identify new behaviors for people to try, to see the steps involved in those behaviors, and to practice them.

Critical Thinking Questions

1. Imagine you are meeting a client system for the first time and are explaining how you would work together. How would you explain the phases of social work practice to an individual client? A community client?
2. Imagine an environmental justice problem, such as air quality or access to green space. Develop open-ended questions you could use for phase one, to help you explore the story with your client.
3. Review Figure 6.3 comparing the problem-solving process with the phases of practice and the EJCPSM. What are the similarities? What differences can you find? If you were to develop your own model of practice, what might it look like?

Key Terms

Assessment
Ecocentric
Evaluation
Social work roles
    Educator
    Counselor
    Advocate
    Broker and bridge builder
    Mediator
    Collaborator

Additional Learning Activities

1. Use the phases of practice or the EJCPSM to develop an eco-justice analysis with a small group from your class. Choose your topic in consultation with your professor. Develop a presentation to share with your classmates.
2. Review Box 6.4, Activities Social Workers or Clients Might Do to Better the Environment and Themselves. Which could you imagine implementing at your field placement, job, or a place you volunteer? What would be the first steps in implementation?
3. Pick one of the social work roles often used in phase three of social work practice. Describe it in your own words. Have you practiced this skill before? If so,

describe the experience and how you felt, and identify the strengths you displayed in this skill. Write for 3–5 minutes.

References

Brown, P. (2009). *The curious garden*. New York, NY: Little Brown and Company.

Bullard, R. (2005). *The quest for environmental justice*. San Francisco, CA: Sierra Club Books.

Council on Social Work Education. (2015). *2015 Educational policy and accreditation standards*. Retrieved from https://www.cswe.org/getattachment/Accreditation/Accreditation-Process/2015-EPAS/2015EPAS_Web_FINAL.pdf.aspx

Finney, C. (2014). *Black faces, white spaces: Reimagining the relationship of African Americans to the great outdoors*. Chapel Hill: University of North Carolina Press.

Hughes, J. W. (2007). *Environmental problem solving: A how-to guide*. Lebanon, NH: University Press of New England.

Locke, B., Garrison, R., & Winship, J. (1998). *Generalist social work practice: Context, story, and partnerships*. New York, NY: Brooks/Cole.

Lundy, C. (2004). *Social work and social justice: A structural approach to practice*. Peterborough, ON, Canada: Broadview Press.

Minnesota Campus Compact. (2012). Social change wheel. Retrieved from: http://mncampuscompact.org/what-we-do/publications/social-change-wheel/

Mulally, R. (2007). *The new structural social work* (3rd ed.) New York, NY: Oxford University Press.

Rogge, M. (2008). Environmental justice. In T. Mizrahi & L. E. Davis (Eds.). *The encyclopedia of social work* (e-reference ed.). New York: Oxford University Press.

U.S. Environmental Protection Agency. (2008). *Environmental justice collaborative problem solving model* (EPA-300-R-06-002). Washington, DC. Retrieved from https://www.epa.gov/communityhealth/environmental-justice-collaborative-problem-solving-model

CHAPTER 7

Social Work Practice with Individuals and Families Toward Environmental Justice

We know enough of our own history by now to be aware that people explore what they have merely concluded to be of value, but they defend what they love.
—*Wendell Berry, p. 41*

Simultaneously intimate and yet socially structured, families are our most important social unit. It is here we are shaped, defended, loved, hurt, nurtured, and challenged most frequently. A very smart social worker I have known for many years says that there really is no individual social work. Every person who comes to us is holding and carrying the family experiences that molded him or her. The social, economic, and environmental forces of our lives mold us too. And so for all of the individuals and families we work with, we help them see the many layers of themselves, their own person in environment experiences.

These experiences are also strongly influenced by place: "Our preferences, phobias, and behaviors begin in the experience of a place. If those places are ugly and violent, the behavior of many raised in them will be ugly and violent. Children raised in ecologically barren settings, however affluent, are deprived of the sensory stimuli and the kind of imaginative experience that can only come from biological richness" (Orr, 2004, p. 160–161). The natural environment influences the functions of individuals and families, in many ways unseen: "Another significant aspect of the geography and environment of an area are the available natural resources and the ways in which these resources are managed and utilized to influence daily activities and lifestyles. Examples include the effects of weather, climate and terrain and the availability of water" (Locke, Garrison, & Winship, 1998, p. 74). We know that environmental injustices exacerbate individual problems, and the research addressing negative environmental factors is quite robust. For example, air pollution and asthma rates are connected, as are garbage dump locations and race. We also know that environmental benefits can mitigate individual problems. In one study on elementary school–aged children, higher levels of access to natural vegetation and open spaces nearby decreased the stressful experience of life events, while children with less access experienced greater distress (Well 2003). Throughout the lifespan, the environment impacts individuals ar Environmental social work clients are all families, not just those involve vironmental crisis or disaster.

The skills and techniques chosen for this chapter connect with the theories presented earlier in this text and present a range of practice methods. Each practice method is identified with the theory it most closely represents. Social work practitioners working in environmental justice recognize that the problems many people face are based on broad social conditions that create negative social, economic, and environmental experiences in their clients' lives. Keeping the strengths perspective in mind, this chapter is not just about alleviating environmental justice problems but also building resiliency through environmentally based interventions. Box 7.1 provides one example of the power of an outdoor experience.

Box 7.1 **People, Places, and Issues—The Power of Outdoor Experiences**

Carly, a 15-year-old girl from a working-class suburb was struggling. She was the youngest of five children, and her parents worked different shifts— allowing for a lot of freedom and not a lot of family time. She performed okay at school but had flirted with substances, felt pressure to have sex with her 17-year-old boyfriend, and couldn't quite find her place in the world.

Her family had strong connections to their faith community, and while not eagerly involved, Carly had done a few activities with youth. An upcoming summer trip was scheduled for 8 days in the Boundary Waters Canoe Area, a remote and pristine camping area on the borders of Canada and the United States. Carly decided to go, mainly because she was bored and she could get out of the same routine for a while.

Carly spent 8 days backpacking, portaging canoes, cooking over campfires, setting up camp, brushing her teeth in the woods, surviving storms and high winds, and connecting with the nine other people in her group—including the two youth counselors. One night, as they lay on a rock looking up at the amazing night sky, Carly watched the Northern Lights dance. It was awe-inspiring. She could feel herself falling in love with something way bigger than herself. Then, a shooting star, and simultaneously, she and her teenage companions grabbed hands, amazed at the beauty of nature around them.

Carly returned home, having been through a life-changing outdoor experience, a kind of nature-based intervention—one that she didn't know she was going to get. But she felt like she was discovering a place in the world, her own journey, aside from boyfriends and peer pressure for substances. Her confidence at meeting challenges had grown, and her understanding of the things she could do and the places she could go had widened.

Preparing for Practice with Individuals and Families

In preparation, social workers acknowledge the importance of nature in the life of their clients. Social workers can learn how their clients' daily behaviors are shaped in regard to nature. The effort opens the social worker to recognizing environmental influences in assessment and to using nature as a tool to improve the lives of clients.

Like building cultural competence (Cross, Bazron, Dennis, & Isaacs, 1989), we can build our environmental competence and help our clients do the same. Alongside social workers, individual and family clients also have a role to play in the development of systems that are environmentally competent. We all can advocate for nature and articulate nature's impact on our own lives. Groups of parents and communities can intentionally nurture the quality of natural spaces in their neighborhoods. "Social workers in health, mental health, schools, and other service settings can integrate basic information about pesticides, pollution, and other chemicals in homes, yards, and communities, into psychosocial and in-home assessments" (Rogge, 2008, p. 5). Our social work practice may even be the start of such changes. As always, we begin with the story.

Phase One: Telling and Exploring the Story

In phases one and two of social work practice, social workers help clients critically engage with and reconstruct a narrative that interprets their lives and environmental experiences from a strengths perspective. This use of narrative theory in practice allows the social worker and the client to discuss the social structures that have shaped the world the client lives in. It begins with the first meeting with the client. Incorporate the natural environment from the beginning (Boetto, 2016). Meeting at a park, the clients own yard, or another shared outdoor space is an option, as long as client confidentiality can be maintained. If meeting in an office, assuring that the meeting space has natural light, plants, and imagery of nature is preferable. A welcoming space that encourages calm and reflection is the goal. In addition to incorporating nature, removing blame and identifying the oppression and discrimination that shape the lives of the client are essential goals of understanding the client story. Locke et al. (1998) suggest several ways that exploring the story fully is essential for social workers: it connects the current story to a person's or family's life experience, it helps the client and social worker understand the worldview of the client, and it helps identify strengths and build the contextual understanding of the problem—reducing the chance for reductionist thinking, relying on quick fixes, and blaming people for the situation they are facing.

Box 7.2 **More to Explore—Questions for an Individual and Family Assessment Inclusive of the Natural Environment**

What do you like about the natural environment where you live?

What things don't you like about the natural environmental where you live?

Do you spend time in nature? How is this useful to you? Your family?

Do you spend time with pets? How is this useful to you? Your family?

Are their environmental factors affecting your health? Your family?

Do you have access to food that is healthy? Your family?

How do you get to places from where you live? What are the transportation options available to you?

Many social work agencies provide a protocol for understanding a client's story that you may be required to use. In practice, some of these are more amenable to environmental social work than others. I encourage you to review the protocol well before meeting with clients. Practice asking questions in ways that are genuine, and use language you are comfortable with. Consider adding questions; some examples for environmental social work are in Box 7.2. The following section provides strategies for these important conversations.

OPEN-ENDED QUESTIONS (NARRATIVE THEORY)

Questions help explore strengths and use a narrative approach in the first phase of practice. Ideally, many of the questions we ask are open-ended as we want clients to tell the story in the way they choose, in the way they currently view it. This too is fodder for practice interventions in the second phase of practice as we help clients mine and reframe the stories they have shared for the strength and beauty inside of them. Open-ended questions that are broad enough to capture the client's story and yet provide enough shape to stir thoughtful responses are most helpful. The following questions, adapted from Saleeby (2009), help focus on strengths and the power of place and environment:

- Who are the people, places, or other beings you can really count on?
- When things were going well in life, what was different?
- Where in your life do you find an opportunity for calm and clear thinking?
- What is your perspective on the current situation you face?
- What are your thoughts on how this situation can change on your behalf?
- What gives you a sense of purpose? What do you espouse as essential to your life? Who are the people, places, and other beings that give meaning to your life?

EXPLORING (NARRATIVE THEORY)

In exploring more deeply, with the questions suggested, the social worker gathers more and more information about the specific experiences of the clients. These are often expressed through unique probes given to clients based on answers to the questions posed. The questions are nonjudgmental, are information- or affect-based, and have reasoning and connection to the client's story. They are not random questions. The questions are thoughtfully constructed by a skilled practitioner who finds that more information will be helpful or senses there is more the client could share. An information-based question can sound like, *Tell me more about the empty lot next door to you. What happens there?* An affect-based exploratory question sounds like, *How do you feel about the empty lot? How does it affect you and your family?*

CLARIFYING (NARRATIVE THEORY)

In clarifying, the social worker asks questions to assure that he or she understands the story correctly. As much as possible, using the words of the client, the social worker looks for specifics, especially when it clarifies an opinion of the client. When a client expressed this opinion, "My apartment was so hot last summer, I could barely stand it," the social worker can clarify "so hot" with questions such as, "You said your apartment was hot last July. I'd like to hear more about that. Did you read the thermostat inside your apartment? If so, what temperature did it display? What did you do about that temperature? Did it help?"

PARAPHRASING (NARRATIVE THEORY)

When a social worker paraphrases, he or she verbalizes a shorter description of the conversation to assure that he or she has captured critical story elements correctly. This allows the client to confirm or clarify what he or she has said. In response to a client expressing depression, a social worker might say, "As you described the depression you are feeling, you mentioned a lack of access to your culture, 'your roots' as you said. If I understand this correctly, you want to learn more about the land and traditions that are part of your family heritage?" This gives the opportunity for the client to shape the social worker's understanding by saying what they really meant or confirming that the social worker has a good understanding of what they are describing. This can bring relief to a client, to confirm that they have been heard in the right way. Effective social workers are open to the possibility of incorrect interpretation and genuinely accept a reparaphrase from the client when offered.

SUMMARIZING (NARRATIVE THEORY)

When a social worker summarizes, he or she gives a short description of what is understood so far. This is especially useful when transitioning to a new topic. This allows for confirming a shared understanding and a chance to pivot to a new topic that may be related but is not in direct line with the previous conversation. Here is an example of a summary and a pivot: "Thanks for sharing your story on your struggles accessing healthy food. I really respect how you expressed those challenges. Eating is important to our health, and I look forward to supporting you on the changes you want to make. I would like to hear more about your health and any strengths and concerns you have. When was the last time you saw a doctor for a checkup?"

CONSCIOUSNESS-RAISING (STRUCTURAL THEORY)

It can be difficult to see the roots of our personal problems in our wider culture, especially when under stress, crisis, or even the daily demands of being a caregiver. Consciousness-raising is what a social worker does when he or she helps a client see the patterns of problems that extend beyond him- or herself. With the knowledge that problems are part of a larger context (see Box 7.3), we can see solutions there too. Being empathic is a human trait of understanding others. It is paired with a non-judgmental attitude, a caring persona, and a willingness to listen. The following dialogue gives an example of a conversation between a parent and a social worker that uses empathy as the first step for consciousness-raising, to help the client see the larger macro forces impacting the experience he or she is having on a very personal level and potential macro responses to aid them in the experience they are being facing (see Figure 7.1). The concepts are based on the work of Lundy (2004).

> PARENT: My son's asthma has gotten so bad, he keeps missing days of school. If he misses any more he could be expelled, and I might get fired. I can't take another day off to be with him.
>
> WORKER: I am sorry to hear that. It is stressful when a child must miss school for an illness.
>
> PARENT: I've been cranky at him too; my patience is wearing thin. What if he's not using his inhaler right? I can't be with him 24 hours a day.
>
> WORKER: No, you can't—and with air quality being poor, it doesn't help the situation. I heard recently that asthma is one of the leading causes of missed school days for kids. Maybe we should reach out for more information from your son's school. They may have some supports we are unaware of, and we want to avoid any suggestion that he could be expelled. I have heard of asthma-friendly schools (American Lung Association, 2017), where schools help students manage their asthma better so they don't have absences. Let me set up a meeting, and we'll talk to the school.

This simple example of consciousness-raising by the social worker lifts the problematizing off of the son and moves the solution to the adults in his life—where it belongs. These methods used in phase one of social work practice—telling and exploring the story—provide ways to learn about clients and their lives. Visual imagery can help too, and the ever-useful ecomap is an option in all kinds of social work, including environmental justice (see Figure 7.2).

Box 7.3 More to Explore—Air Pollution

Air pollution tends to impact financially poor people more than the non–financially poor. Why? The overall physical health of financially poor people is diminished, increasing the chances that they will suffer more from the effects of poor air quality (United Nations Environment Programme, 2005). Housing for financially poor people is often badly ventilated, heated by older systems that can produce indoor air pollution, and less attractive because of being located near heavy air pollution sources such as highways, industrial plants, or coal plants. This exposes them to higher levels of air pollution than others and makes air pollution a justice issue. Across our lifespan we are susceptible to the negative effects of poor air quality. Adults exposed to high levels of air pollution from major highways experience harm to the brain, including shrinkage similar to natural aging (Wilker et al., 2015). Air pollution impacts asthma severity, which is linked to school absenteeism in youth (Moonie, Sterling, Figgs, & Castro, 2006). Children are particularly vulnerable due to their physiology and the amount of exposure they have while attending school, playing outside, and participating in sporting events. Worldwide, approximately 300 million children live in areas where air pollution is at toxic levels (UNICEF, 2016). The micro to macro concept helps us identify intervention options for addressing air pollution and respiratory problems, from the individual to the global. Figure 7.1 gives examples for each of these levels.

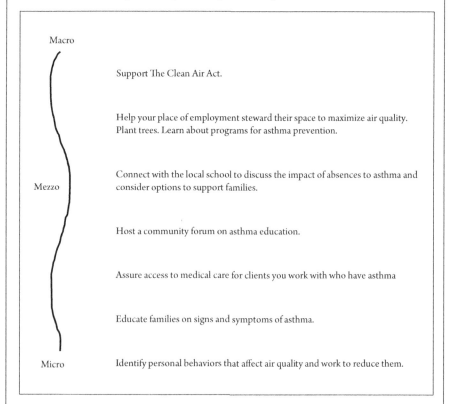

Macro

Support The Clean Air Act.

Help your place of employment steward their space to maximize air quality. Plant trees. Learn about programs for asthma prevention.

Connect with the local school to discuss the impact of absences to asthma and consider options to support families.

Mezzo

Host a community forum on asthma education.

Assure access to medical care for clients you work with who have asthma

Educate families on signs and symptoms of asthma.

Micro

Identify personal behaviors that affect air quality and work to reduce them.

Figure 7.1 Air Pollution and Asthma Macro to Micro practice skills

ECOMAP (SYSTEMS THEORY)

The ecomap is an essential tool in this first phase of the practice process. Ecomaps provide a pictorial view of the lives of clients—and tend to remove blame from any one component in relation to the problem. It is putting systems theory on paper. An ecomap displays the variables that frame the experience of the people you are working with. Providing this visual tool helps people see the story they are telling and is an aid in returning to the story and making modifications as needed. Pictures can help all of us think through multiple components and give a prioritization to what is most pressing for the problem at hand.

To develop an ecomap, one needs something to write on. Having blank paper, pencils, and crayons (both utensils create very little garbage compared to pens and markers) is useful in any setting. These are essential tools for working with individuals and families. While there are no hard and fast rules for drawing ecomaps, there are general guidelines social workers follow; and you can develop your own as needed. Feel free to develop your own symbols depending on the nature of the work you are doing and the influence of the clients you are with. The only requirement is to include a key so that readers of the ecomap can understand the relationships represented. Ecomaps are useful, precisely because they are so flexible.

In this ecomap (see Figure 7.2) you see common elements of a family structure in relation to the community around them, a visual example of people in their environment. In this family, we can get a quick depiction of the environmental and social variables most important and influential in their life, as well as the relationship they have with that social construct. We can see in this family that the grandparents are an important unit in their life as they are close to the center circle and have a very strong line drawn from the family unit to the grandparents. We can see that housing quality is an area of concern for the family. We can also see that while food access is not necessarily negative, the thin line connecting the family to food access suggests that the family sees room for improvement in this area.

Guidelines for ecomap creation:

- The center circle is the client you are working with.
- The circles around the center circle reflect the components of the story.
- The size of the circle reflects its predominance in the story.
- The distance of the circle from the center circle reflects the importance to the client.
- The lines between the circles reflect the relationships. Examples could be
  - Positive relationship
  - Negative or conflicting relationship
  - Distant relationship
  - Cut off relationship

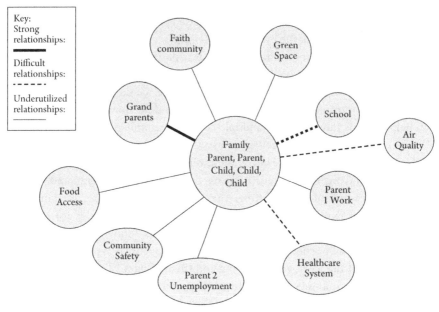

Figure 7.2 Ecomap

The ecomap in Figure 7.2 is for the family in the case study in Box 7.4. Compare the narrative in the case study to the ecomap created. You will be able to see how the pictorial view of the family is a quick representation of the case study.

Mapping the components of the story and the relationship between the components helps a social work practitioner see what may be able to be restored, where advocacy can help, what relationships could be bolstered, and where it may be time to let go and move on. Power and strategy are part of the ecomap pictogram. The similarities between using an ecomap with an individual or family as well as a group or community are many. Power is part of all human relationships, whether recognized or not, and the ecomap helps elucidate these connections. I like to add timelines to some of my ecomaps because, in some stories, history reigns prominent. Timelines help the historical components of the story emerge (see Figure 7.3). An ecomap is a snapshot of a moment in time; a timeline is a long view, stretching back in history and projecting forward if one wishes. Both of these tools are powerful and flexible and can be adapted by the social worker and the client to meet the needs of the client system. The ecomap and timeline can also expand and contract as the need allows.

The ecomap and timeline are a long-standing tradition in social work. One area seldom included is the natural environment and other nonhuman species. As you can see, a timeline can be useful to include any important elements of the story.

Box 7.4 **Family Case Study**

Trevor is a 7-year-old boy in the first grade. He lives in an urban area, in a lower–socioeconomic status neighborhood. His parents have been together for 10 years, and he has a younger brother. Trevor is having trouble concentrating at school. In first grade, he got in trouble a few times for distracting other children during learning times. It was addressed by the teacher and his parents, and they chalked the behaviors up to a typical developmental stage and getting used to the transition to school. He had a normal summer at home, though his parents found him struggling to follow directions and misbehaving quite frequently. It is now the fall of his second-grade year, and things do not seem to have improved. In fact, rather than maturing and getting more used to school, Trevor seems even more distracted and easily agitated and finds it difficult to concentrate on learning material, even for short periods. This year, the teacher makes a referral to the school social worker.

Isaac is a school social worker and has been working in urban settings for the past 8 years. He is new to school settings. When he gets the referral for Trevor, he finds that it is not out of the ordinary. Young boys often get referred for this kind of behavior, sometimes for far worse activities. Isaac first meets with Trevor and finds he is a pleasant young boy who does not understand why he is having such trouble concentrating on school. He seems a bit despondent. After a phone call home to Trevor's dad, Isaac sets up a meeting at school to discuss options with the parents and teacher. At this meeting, they discuss behavioral modifications with the teacher and shared language and visual cues the parents can use at home to provide Trevor consistency. Because Isaac was trained in the person in environment perspective, he knows he needs to consider the environment of the classroom and home. He asks when Trevor's last doctor's visit was and learns it was before kindergarten. He suggests that the parents see their pediatrician and request a blood test for lead levels and an attention deficit hyperactivity disorder assessment. He is also aware of the importance of play, exercise, and the freedom to explore nature and the outdoors and discusses with Trevor's parents the opportunities and strategies needed to give Trevor more outdoor playtime after school. He also confirms with Trevor's teachers that he is participating in recess during the school day.

Isaac checks in with Trevor's parents 2 weeks later. They visited the doctor and discovered lead levels in Trevor's blood that were too high, a likely explanation for Trevor's difficulty concentrating and his misbehaviors. It was in the 1970s that research identified the relationship between lead levels in kids and negative school outcomes, including difficulty concentrating and behavioral changes (Needleman, 2004). Isaac begins a conversation with the family on their housing. They live in and own a 100-year-old house in which lead is present. Updates are expensive, and Isaac begins working with the community housing program to learn about their lead abatement options and funding sources for the family. He knows it is imperative for Trevor and his younger brother's health that the lead is removed from the home. He looked up www.leadfreekids.org, part of the Environmental Protection Agency, to begin to provide education to the parents. Because of the geographic area the school is in, there are many older homes. Isaac begins to plan a public education effort via the school's communication channels to alert other parents and provide them guidance and information on concerns for exposure to lead.

Having a fully explored story is the springboard for phase two of practice—defining how the client would like reality to be.

Phase Two: Describing a Preferred Reality

NORMALIZING THE PROBLEM AND CONNECTING TO OTHERS (NARRATIVE THEORY)

One of the most common responses for individuals or families experiencing problems is to pull inward and try to shelter their heart and reputation from the harm of other's knowing their troubles. This can be a very powerful motivator, especially for parents wanting to protect their children; but all individuals and family members can likely relate to this impulse. One of the most powerful facts about environmental justice social work is that individual private troubles are rarely, if ever, unique to the individual or the family. Often, many people within a geographic area or lifespan stage are affected in similar ways. If kids don't have a place to play in an outdoor setting to build community and exercise their bodies, behavior problems

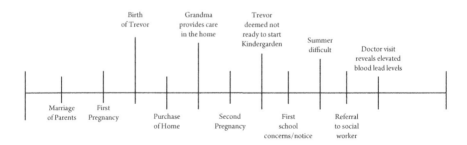

Figure 7.3 Timeline

may emerge which parents may feel shame about. Recognizing that several parents on the block are having the same experiences can be relieving. Normalizing human problems has been a long-standing practice technique for social workers. One of the ways normalizing occurs in environmental justice issues is by connecting people to others in their community who are experiencing the same or similar troubles. One story people or families may have told about themselves is that their problems are their fault. Because shame is a powerful component in people keeping their troubles private, recognizing that one is not alone in one's troubles creates an immediate sense of relief and community for the individuals living with the problem.

Utilizing the practice of narrative theory, problems become normalized as they are shared with others and as other stories are heard in turn. This storytelling, hearing of shared difficulties, helps clients realize that their story, or at least parts of their story, are normal human problems that can be solved in a collective process rather than solely in the privacy of their home. Social workers are connectors in the community, and because they have a broad awareness of experiences of multiple families within a community setting, they may be the first person to identify similarities among problems. Without revealing confidential information, social workers can begin to connect people to each other to explore and potentially resist the environmental injustices and the impacts individuals and families are experiencing.

RECOGNIZING AND BUILDING RESILIENCY (NARRATIVE THEORY)

Being resilient refers to a process in which individuals and families not only endure hardships but create lives that are meaningful to them and contribute to those around them (Van Hook, 2014). Beyond coping with problems, resiliency suggests an ability to find meaning even in dark and difficult times. Resiliency is considered a process rather than an outcome. Access to the natural environment can provide a protective factor (Van Hook, 2014), such as access to green space for play and recreation, beautiful views that inspire, or appreciation and joy for gardening and growing food.

Environmental problems can also be additive factors on stress levels, meaning that they increase the distress when the individual or family is often experiencing other issues (Van Hook, 2014). The distress that families experience often occurs around typical life cycle issues, such as the birth or adoption of a child, the loss or beginning of a job, school demands, or struggles with finances or social relationships. Families frequently experience several difficult life experiences at one time. The addition of an environmental problem can be layered upon these existing individual and family stressors. Overarching these are problems of discrimination, oppression and violence. Van Hook (2014, p. 85) suggests several probes to help explore additive problems, and they are amended here to include the natural environment:

- Have you had your hands full with other problems?
- Is anything else happening in your family, neighborhood, environment, or community that has made this more difficult to cope with?
- Are there other worries you have that are making this problem worse?
- Has anything been happening in your family, neighborhood, or community that could improve your ability to handle this problem?

Recognizing and naming these additive factors can bring relief and perspective to the client and allow for some recognition of the scope of the issues being addressed. One technique for building community resiliency has been community gardening. Box 7.5 describes some of the realities of this community resiliency activity.

Box 7.5 **People, Places, and Issues—Whose Garden Is It Anyway?**

Community gardens are promoted as a two-pronged strategy: build community and improve the local environment. But a community is also a prerequisite to start a community garden. Individuals in a block group organization in St. Louis, Missouri, had known each other for years. When an opportunity to start a community garden came along, it was possible because of their collective effort. The social resource was essential to develop the environmental resource. Local community organizations play an important role by providing necessary materials and volunteer groups. Once people start working together, the nature of their relationship changes. One garden leader noted that previously they used to meet around a table and discuss neighborhood issues. Now, they are out in the garden helping each other. The garden provides a space to foster deeper relationships. People cultivate both land and relationships. It is not only gardeners who come to the garden. Other residents in the neighborhood stop by to talk and enjoy the garden space. The availability of green space can be a catalyst in strengthening existing social cohesion through interactions among neighbors.

The twentieth century saw U.S. cities go through a pattern of growth, stagnation, and decline. St. Louis, Missouri, embodies this story. In 1904 St. Louis hosted the first summer Olympics outside of Europe, and in 1950 it was the eighth most populous city. Suburbanization and construction of highways provided the catalyst for the rapid population decline. Based on the 2010 Census, the city's population had declined by 62% compared to 1950. As people left, the number of vacant properties soared. Dilapidated houses and unpaid taxes led the city to create the Land Reutilization Authority (LRA) in 1971. It was tasked with maintaining the properties and selling them for redevelopment. The LRA currently holds nearly 11,000 parcels costing more than a million dollars for maintenance. The vacant lots were an eyesore with growing weeds and vines but also attracted deviant behavior, especially drug use. The neighborhoods were trapped in a vicious cycle where vacant lots and buildings reduced the attractiveness of the neighborhood, which further reinforced the decline.

The social and the environmental were interconnected; as one deteriorated, so did the other. Individuals and neighborhood block groups were worried about the stability of their neighborhoods. They started beautification projects, working collaboratively with other residents for the upkeep of the neighborhood. As a part of this movement, block groups started establishing community gardens in vacant lots. Some of the garden leaders pointed out that they grew up on a farm in the south. Growing food was part of their lifestyle. They knew how to garden and enjoyed it. It made sense to turn vacant lots into community gardens, especially when the LRA was leasing these lots for a dollar per year for 5-year terms.

Although the opportunity to lease land for a dollar per year to start a community garden is enticing, the community gardeners seem like a means to an end. First of all, the land is owned by the LRA, which is tasked to sell the plots to developers. In the meantime, managing the land is costly, so a garden is a good alternative. The gardeners work to beautify the land without any cost to the city, but when a developer shows interest, the plot will be sold—without the gardeners' input. Community gardeners don't pay any taxes, but a business or an apartment building will. From an environmental justice perspective, the community had to bear the brunt of negative impacts of decline and pay a price to beautify and keep up the properties through their collective effort. But as revitalization occurs, the land will be lost, and the people who helped to stabilize the neighborhood through beautification projects may not be able to afford to continue living there. Land stewardship is underrecognized in a society where paying the highest possible price for land is the claim to ownership.

Contributed by Nishesh Chalise, PhD, MSW

SHARING A VIEW (NARRATIVE THEORY)

When a social worker shares his or her own personal view with a client, it must be done for the benefit of the client and the process of critical analysis that can illuminate the causes of suffering. We do not share our personal views to try to sway our clients one way or another. We do not share them to validate our own struggles. We share them to express ideas and experiences that can reduce the power differential between client and social worker and expand the view of the client. Sharing a view, also called *self-disclosure*, is a tool that, when used with discretion, shows your humanness to your clients, lets them know they are not alone in their feelings or their struggles, and builds a shared equality (Lundy, 2004). Sharing genuine feelings and experiences can be points of strength for the client and social worker to connect. The stress relief and healing power of nature is one view social workers can share. Taking a walk outside provides opportunity for a literal change of view too.

BUILDING HOPE (NARRATIVE THEORY)

Building on the answers to questions from phase one, begin to formulate with your client the possibilities of what can become real for him or her. This is a hopeful process and one in which the social worker must be prepared to find the opportunities within the difficulties, especially if the client cannot. This is not a false hope of overrated positivity but a hope that endures and recognizes that change can come in time. Again, calling on the concepts and methods in narrative theory, bring this to your clients through personal stories of your own or anonymous stories of other clients you have worked with. In this way, you help clients see that step by step progress and change are possible. Narrative interventions work to transform problem-saturated stories into stories of resilience and possibility. Narrative social work believes that language shapes thinking in experiences and that the stories people construct shape their life events in the future and shape their understanding of their past. Narrative social work re-creates the stories people tell so that they include factors of resiliency and change and capacity to contend with the problems of life. Such an interpretation of the story of life helps promote a person's or families' capacity and sense of power over life, potentially liberating them from perspectives that may limit their life. Narrative intervention questions that attempt to challenge problem-saturated stories can help (Van Hook, 2014, p. 87):

- What have you told yourself about this event?
- What has been your interpretation of this event? What is another interpretation?
- Have you ever asked why this happened?
- Is there a storyline that does not yet have an ending?
- What are your thoughts on ways to help the situation?
- Who or what do you know in life that is always resilient? Always bounces back?

Begin to translate client stories from suffering to survival, from coping to influencing, noting the points in their stories when they may not realize they have already done so. This is the foothold of the changes they and you are about to embark on as you enter phase three of practice, making plans and dreams real. Nature provides an amazing metaphor: it always expresses resiliency.

Phase Three: Making Plans and Dreams Real

DEFENSE OF THE CLIENT (STRUCTURAL THEORY)

Problems experienced by clients are often associated with macro inequities built into the social structure: access, time constraints, lack of information, and other factors that lie beyond the individual's control (Moreau & Leonard, 1989). Social workers help clients claim and identify rights and entitlements (Lundy, 2004). Social workers help clients identify what those rights might be and navigate a complex public and private welfare system to assure access to those rights and entitlements. This work requires and includes the following:

1. education and information
2. access to benefits
3. help to communicate with authority, verbally or in writing
4. accompanying clients to meetings and helping them vocalize the ways in which their entitlements are not being fulfilled.

Defense of the client, closely related to advocacy, requires the social worker to have knowledge of the rights and entitlements within the community in which he or she lives, bringing awareness of these rights and entitlements to the client, and using the methods of social work to assure that these rights and entitlements are being provided. These rights often include access to healthcare, monetary benefits, and education. But they also include drinkable water, a safe community, food access, information for natural disaster preparedness, and other environmental issues. Box 7.6 highlights some of the issues to consider in the rights to food access.

INCREASING CLIENT'S POWER (STRUCTURAL THEORY)

Social workers enter the helping relationship with power granted to them through status, education, and the agency with which they are affiliated. Clients are often in positions that feel powerless. Reducing this power differential over time is integral to the helping relationship, which is based on a value of equity. Environmental justice is the great equalizer as we share the air in the communities we work in, drink the same water, and respond to the same natural disasters. To enhance client power, Lundy, (2004) suggests structural social work requires us to:

- Maintain respect for the client's dignity
- Ensure client autonomy
- Identify strengths in the client and in the environment
- Clarify the limits of the social worker's professional role, and expand the limits of the client's role

Box 7.6 People, Places, and Issues—Food Access

Lack of food access and food deserts have become a recognized problem in the last decade. Called "food security," this issue of finding a healthy meal for a family is not new to social workers. Social workers have been working on the issues of securing healthy meals for individuals and families since the start of our profession. Social workers were on the forefront of supporting food banks and public programs that supplement the nutritional needs of low-income families or families at risk such as the Women, Infants, and Children program, known as WIC, or what has commonly been called food stamps, the Supplemental Nutritional Assistance Program, or SNAP. Another important food-security program that social workers advocate and enroll clients for is the free and reduced lunch program that is offered within the school system. For social work practice, feeding the hungry is evolving into ensuring food security for individuals within the community. There is a growing understanding that a meal alone is not enough for quality health. There are connections between nutrition, physical and mental health, and maintaining culture and a thriving economy. Industrialized food systems are partly to blame for gaps. "Two generations ago, most of our tribal communities in the north produced our food locally. Today, we buy food shipped to us from far away. . . . This means that our food security is now tied to industrial food systems and oil. We are feeling the consequences of that relationship. Food is costing more and more, not just in dollars but also environmentally and in terms of our physical and cultural health" (LaDuke, 2008, p. 5).

Without access to healthy meals, it can be difficult for adults to participate in the economy through a job; and it can be difficult for a young person to participate in his or her educational life. The stress of finding and maintaining food can also take a toll on the well-being of individuals and lead to loss of culture or relationships. Some of the roles social workers play in ensuring food security are helping clients enroll for WIC or SNAP benefits, assuring that young people are registered to receive free and reduced lunch if they are eligible, and linking older adults to Meals on Wheels, and seeing that food banks, often called food markets now, have food that reflects the community. Ensuring that policymakers understand the importance of food-security programs as well as that all community members who are eligible are enrolled and have access to these programs are important linking roles of professional social workers in responding to environmental justice. In addition to assuring that these programs stay in place, social workers can advocate for fewer processed foods as part of these programs and that more local, organic, and fresh produce be included in these food choices. If we are working toward health for our clients, we will do our best to assure they have local, organic, healthy, and culturally fitting food in their homes.

- Share in decision-making about the rationale for interventions that are chosen
- Give equal credence to intervention ideas proposed by the client.
- Share the evidence about why certain interventions could be successful
- Enhance a client's power outside of the social work relationship

NATURE AS INTERVENTION (SYSTEMS THEORY)

There is a long-standing area of work, especially with youth, that includes environmental spaces and experiences as the main mode of intervention for youth.

From experiences as benign as the summer camp and all it has to offer a developing young person to intensive and arduous physical exploration programs that attempt to change the behaviors of people involved in drug abuse to therapeutic recreational experiences combining yoga or farming, nearly every person can identify the therapeutic benefits of returning to nature—even if it simply includes rest, relaxation, and a new view. Harnessing the intensity of potential therapeutic change is hard to overstate and hard to clearly identify. From experiencing a sense of awe and wonder to challenging our sense of self, nature has a way of providing what possibly nothing else in the universe can. Nature can be the source of intervention in a more clinical practice too. Box 7.7 explores one potential way clinical social workers can integrate nature and the environment to inspire and change behaviors.

Phase Four: Evaluating Outcomes and Making Transitions

In this final phase of practice, determinations are made about continuing to work together, making plans for maintenance of capacities, and/or referral to another professional. This is an optimal time for the environmental social worker to review efforts at increasing access to nature; conversing about the strengths found in people, places, and nonhuman animals in the clients life; and assuring that the client has built skills in narrative theory, especially around reframing and building hope and resiliency.

REVIEWING THE PROGRESS MADE (NARRATIVE THEORY)

This is your opportunity to reify the new story of hope, competency, and resiliency you have created with the client. Do not shy away from sharing what you saw in the story. Be brave in your word choice, beginning with the phrase "I see how far you have come" and continuing with affirming the narrative of accomplishment that the client has begun and can continue beyond your work together. Count the accomplishments across micro to macro levels of practice, identifying what has improved for the individual, family, and community.

Box 7.7 **More to Explore—Green Space Interventions:**
Psychoeducationally Based

The basic human needs of our clients have not changed over many years. What has changed are ways of supporting the growth and healing of clients. Environmental social work is an opportunity for addressing and meeting such changes. I encourage you to be in nature with your clients, to nurture growth and healing while holistically meeting the client where the client is. Such an integrative social work approach as this, held within open green spaces, is a viable and valuable contribution to clients and community. I call these approaches *green space interventions.* There are four primary principles that guide my own green space interventions:

1. Nature settings within our local environments are a profoundly appropriate metaphor and useful resource for supporting holistic growth and healing.
2. Direct experiences with nature can sprout benefits that translate into the client's daily life. These benefits continue to unfold, rekindle, and foster growth and healing even after the client has left the natural environment.
3. Clients can experience a therapeutic outcome where accessible nature exists: backyards, national parks, forests, bodies of water, open fields, shared common green areas, etc.
4. We can create growth-enhancing opportunities with which clients take goal-oriented steps.

Here is an example of a green space intervention that I call "life's circles and cycles." It is founded on the idea that as in the world of nature, so it is within ourselves. For example, there are circular and cyclical patterns around us and inside us. These patterns inform and help us experience interrelationships. Examples are movement patterns of the sun and moon, seasonal changes, ocean tides, the rounded form of bird nests, the circumference of tree trunks and limbs. In ourselves, patterns are the regular rhythm of breathing in and out, the seasons of our lives, states of sleep and wake, the rounded shape and circumference of our limbs.

The invitation is for clients and families to gather with us in an open green space. We ask them to concentrate on the following question: *What circles and cycles in this green space can you identify?* It is amazing how many similarities, overlapping patterns, and recurring dynamics of circles and cycles occur between humans and nature. Whatever sense of control and power we think we might have, related to many aspects of our lives, the circles and cycles continue. What we choose to do with them will make all the difference, and it seems that a perspective full of persistence, positivity, and permissiveness can help us embrace hope while we endure daily challenges.

Because we are growing alongside the dynamics of circles and cycles, we can rest in the idea that if we are patient, there is always going to be growth, change, and new opportunities for us in relation to all parts of our lives. For example, growth and change can speak to the idea of release (or shedding) of something about us that doesn't serve well (like a dog shedding hair in the spring).

In order for clinical social workers to consistently provide competent and quality support to clients with green space interventions, we need the following: willing participants, accessible natural environments, sufficient administrative/financial resources, creativity, and reliance on principles which are effectively sound, practical, and malleable enough to evolve as the profession does. Together with the right combination of these elements, our clients can find what does and does not make natural sense for themselves and for their families.

Contributed by Jeffry Jeanetta-Wark, MA, LICSW

CONNECTIONS TO LOCAL GROUPS OR OTHER PROFESSIONALS (SYSTEMS THEORY)

Sometimes a referral for continued growth and change is needed for the individual or family. Some of these referrals might be to continue building relationships with nature, though it may also be for legal or medical help or a specialized social worker. As clients learn to manage problems, they often build connections to lots of institutions in society: schools, activist groups, clinics, faith communities, and community agencies. These connections could be long-lasting or short-lived. The key is an experience of accessing resources, utilizing them, and extending that knowledge of how to do that to the next coping process.

Universal Human Needs

Very often, social workers are called to work with families experiencing a problem related to a human need common to us all. For years we have been aware of food, shelter, clothing, and access to education. And now we turn our gaze to include safe drinking water, clean air quality, and access to nature and green space. For years we have attended to the need for a loving family and social relationships, and now we include loving nature and other species in our work. We often attempt to find work for our clients that is respectful, dignified, and meaningful—and now we include sustainable. We have worked to assure our clients can be safe and free from violence—and now we include free from toxic chemicals. We always hope for opportunities for self-actualization, and now we see the connections between the rhythms and cycles of nature and its ability to nurture our own self-growth. Environmental social work has many applications to our work with families and individuals. As we move forward, we continue our exploration into the mezzo and macro phases of social work practice.

Critical Thinking Questions

1. Think about your own community. What phenomena in the natural or human-made environment might have an impact on human behaviors? If these behaviors are negative, how might they be ameliorated? If the behaviors are positive, how might they be nurtured to grow?
2. Think about your job, a place where you volunteer, or your field placement. Which of the assessment questions from Box 7.2 could you add at your work? Write at least three of them down, and share them with a classmate, explaining how they could be helpful.
3. Review the case study on lead. Identify a micro, a mezzo, and a macro practice skill that Isaac used in his job as a school social worker.

Key Terms

Ecomap
Food access
Food security
Green space
Normalizing
Resilience
Timeline

Additional Learning Activities

1. Review the website www.leadfreekids.org. Write down three points that are new to you about lead. Then, write down one way each of these points will be useful to you as a social worker.
2. Divide your class into small groups. What environmental activities do you think would be important to incorporate into the lives of people your age, where you live? Why? Defend your answers with your classmates. Where do you find commonalities with your classmates?
3. What food security issues do you see in your community? Identify local organizations trying to ameliorate this insecurity. What are their tactics? Give the pros and cons of the tactics they employ.

References

American Lung Association. (2017). Asthma-friendly schools initiative. Retrieved from http://www.lung.org/lung-health-and-diseases/lung-disease-lookup/asthma/asthma-education-advocacy/asthma-friendly-schools-initiative/?referrer=https://www.google.com/

Berry, W. (2000). *Life is a Miracle: An essay against modern superstition.* New York: Counterpoint.

Boetto, H. (2016). Developing ecological social work for micro-level practice. In J. McKinnon & M. Alston (Eds.). *Ecological social work towards sustainability* (pp. 59–77). London, UK: Palgrave.

Cross, T., Bazron, B., Dennis, K. W., & Isaacs, M. R. (1989). *Towards a culturally competent system of care: A monograph on effective services for minority children who are severely emotionally disturbed.* Washington DC: Georgetown University Child Development Center.

LaDuke, W. (2008). *Launching a green economy for brown people: Building a good future for our communities and coming generations.* Minneapolis, MN: Honor the Earth.

Locke, B., Garrison, R., & Winship, J. (1998). *Generalist social work practice: Context, story and partnerships.* Boston, MA: Brooks/Cole.

Lundy, C. (2004). *Social work and social justice: A structural approach to practice.* Peterborough, ON, Canada: Broadview Press.

Moonie, S. A., Sterling, D. A., Figgs, L., & Castro, M. (2006). Asthma status and severity affects missed school days. *Journal of School Health, 76*, 18–24.

Moreau, M., & Leonard, L. (1989). *Empowerment through a structural approach to social work.* Montreal: Ecole de Service Sociale, Université de Montréal and Carleton University School of Social Work.

Needleman, H. (2004). Lead poisoning. *Annual Review of Medicine, 55*, 209–222.

Orr, D. (2004). *Earth in mind: On education, environment, and the human prospect.* Washington DC: Island Press.

Rogge, M. (2008). Environmental justice. In T. Mizrahi & L. E. Davis (Eds.). *Encyclopedia of Social Work* (e-reference ed.). New York, NY: Oxford University Press.

Saleeby, D. (2009). *The strengths perspective in social work practice* (5th ed.). Boston, MA: Allyn & Bacon.

UNICEF. (2016). *Clean the air for children: The impact of air pollution on children.* Retrieved from https://www.unicef.org/publications/index_92957.html

United Nations Environment Programme. (2005). *Urban air quality management toolbook.* Retrieved from http://staging.unep.org/urban_environment/PDFs/toolkit.pdf.

Van Hook, M. P. (2004). *Social work practice with families: A resiliency based approach.* Chicago, IL: Lyceum.

Wells, N. M., & Evans, G. W. (2003). Nearby nature: A buffer of life stress among rural children. *Environment and Behavior, 35*(3), 311–330.

Wilker, E. H., Preis, S. R., Beiser, A. S., Wolf, P. A., Au, R., Kloog, I., Li, W., Schwartz, J., Koutrakis, P., DeCarli, C., Seshadri, S., & Mittleman, M. A. (2015). Long-term exposure to fine particulate matter, residential proximity to major roads and measures of brain structure. *Stroke, 46*(5), 1161–1166.

CHAPTER 8

Social Work Practice with Groups and Communities Toward Environmental Justice

There is opportunity amid this peril—a chance to change the way we do business, plan our cities, fuel our homes and factories, and move our goods and ourselves. A low-carbon path beckons—a path that can create jobs and improve public health while safeguarding the environment. —Ban Ki-moon (2013)

As we move into the larger system sizes in social work practice, we still count on our phases of practice to guide our work with groups and communities. Your challenge is to expand person in environment to include groups and communities in their environment and recognize how interactions shape culture and how social, political, environmental, and economic influences shape a group and community. Also, maintain your commitment to the four phases of practice, your theoretical bases, and our foundational concepts. You will learn different skills and methods, but the theories and foundational concepts remain integral to your work. As we move through the phases I have again identified the theory that most closely relates to each practice skill. As you read through the interventions, identify how it relates to the theory, and you'll begin to strengthen your own conceptual thinking muscles.

Groups and communities are so powerful; they have the power to make us feel central to our human community or shun us in ways that are painful and cruel. There is one crucial element for environmental justice that must be addressed up front: the real and inequitable marginalization of some groups in efforts toward environmental justice. Part of the reason for the current environmental degradations has been the deeply accepted marginalization of voices of entire groups and communities. This accepted marginalization is so endemic that it manifests as policy, culture, access to decision-making bodies, unquestioned business practices, and the media spotlights on those with economic prowess and social media starlight. The narrow range of voices heard has created such a fog of dissonance that efforts to have these marginalized voices heard have been forced to become protest—further marginalizing the message as it decenters the messenger from a typical platform in our community.

The 2016 nonviolent action and encampment at Standing Rock Sioux Reservation in North Dakota in an effort to halt the Dakota Access pipeline provides a startling example of the hegemony of a business practice to assume rights to cross other people's lands. Despite thousands of protestors and requests for the respect of clean water, the power of business interests was indomitable. The aversive tactics used to quiet the voices of the nonviolent protestors, including hosing and military intervention, were frightening examples of infringement on the rights of people to organize. The mainstream media did not make this story central to their news coverage, again diminishing the voice of American Indian and water rights activists. Surprisingly, the Flint, Michigan, water crisis, just a year before the fight to maintain clean water at Standing Rock, did not appear to influence decision-making bodies, despite the recent flashpoint of access to clean water being a human right. The Dakota Access pipeline isn't the only fight against the "black snake" of oil, and Flint is likely not the only city experiencing tainted water systems.

In a report on the "invisible crisis," Jones and Moulton (2016) describe the unaffordability of water for many families in the United States. They note rising water costs, by as much as 40%, in a 5-year period (p. 3), making water unaffordable for many low-income families. Rural areas have been hit the hardest. For years, social workers have been serving families who experience water shutoffs from the municipality in which they live. "Currently, there is no national, enforceable, affordability standard for water in the United States" (p. 6). As water costs rise, the most vulnerable families are those who are financially poor. Water is necessary for hygiene, health, avoiding dehydration, and cooking. Reduction in any of these areas reduces one's ability to participate in community, parent adequately, earn a livable wage in the economy, and care for elders. In the worst-case scenario, lack of access to water can be considered neglect, and children have been removed from homes due to lack of water. The experience in Flint made public the injustices of water quality. However, Flint, Michigan, is not alone. There are rural areas in the United States and around the world where water and sewage systems are still not available to all homes. Social workers often have direct access to these families and advocate for their water bills to be reduced, forgiven, or paid for by a charitable source. Social workers help families maintain their homes and stay unified when lack of water access threatens their family life.

When environmental justice, for even our most basic human rights such as water, is forced to be addressed from the sidelines of our regular social decision-making process, it diminishes and negates the centrality and importance of clean water and human health. Protesting at Standing Rock for clean water should be a top national concern, and the inability of poor people to pay rising water bills is an opportunity to advance human rights. Until care of Earth's resources is of mainstream concern, there will continue to be disparities, burdens, and suffering.

Preparing for Practice with Groups and Communities

As you develop a relationship with a group or community, note that it will be dependent on the attitude with which you engage it. The first step is to consider your motives before you reach out to the community group. Ask yourself, *What are my intentions?* Identify your own interest in the issue the community you're hoping to help is facing—you likely have a shared struggle. Environmental justice and environmental issues are pervasive enough for all of us. This can help you identify how you can contribute to the overall goals and interests of the group or community, setting the stage for a mutually empowering and liberating experience (Reitman & Ewall, 2007).

Phase One: Telling and Exploring the Story

Communities and groups are formed in a myriad of ways. In this section we will explore groups and communities based on location, identity, and personal experience (Fellin, 2000). In environmental justice social work, it is not uncommon for these communities to be formed by geographic location. Communities of a locality are often based on clear physical boundaries that may include city signs or markings, neighborhood affiliations, or boundaries of natural elements such as mountains, rivers, or tree lines. These communities and the institutions that are part of them shape and are shaped by the behaviors of the people and natural environment of that locality. Examples can be towns, tribal lands, ranches, farms, and neighborhoods.

Another way communities are formed is through identity, by people with a common interest, problem, or identity. These communities may have no connection to geography but may be based on shared history, ethnicity, or issue. While these communities may not have physical proximity to each other, their engagement and commitment can be powerful. Technology has made communities of identity more available and possibly more important in contemporary times. Examples of these groups include members of environmental or social justice organizations, groups formed from shared personal experiences, social identities and groups based on interest areas.

Personal communities are amalgamations of an individual's multiple communities. A personal community consists of local and identity groups. This constellation of personal communities makes up the community of an individual. While unique to every person, these personal communities are powerful in the ways that they shape and support the lives of our clients and their experiences. It is a common practice within social work to help clients expand or contract their personal communities when these are viewed as shallow by the client or unhealthy in some way.

COLLECTIVIZATION (STRUCTURAL THEORY)

The goal of collectivization is to help clients inform each other about their shared difficulties and to reduce isolation, self-blame, and alienation (Lundy, 2004). This method of normalizing the problem is an important part of working in groups and communities. "The personal dimensions of clients' difficulties can be recast with them taking into account the role of institutional inadequacies and the role of oppressive social structures" (Moreau & Leonard, 1989, p. 123). Collectivization often occurs in groups with a commonality, such as location or problem. Collectivization does not have to occur in person. It can be done using social media as people and organized groups connect with each other over common shared interests, pursuits, and goals. Social media pages are ways to collectivize with people you may never have an opportunity to meet in person. A group that shares its stories can build mutual aid. While the stories in a mutual aid group are of the individual, there is enough crossover for a shared story to emerge, one each member can feel a part of. This sharing of a story can be shifted to include a transformation of the shared story to one of hope, resilience, and opportunity for change. Not only is mutual aid a relief for many to find they are not alone; it can be a source of social transformation and energy for change.

FACILITATING COMMUNICATION IN GROUPS (NARRATIVE AND STRUCTURAL THEORIES)

Environmental justice issues can often cause controversy or conflict. Preparing in advance to address difficult issues is imperative. Identifying general guidelines for communication can be helpful for any group of people seeking solutions. Rather than calling these "group rules," I use what I learned with friends in Mexico, "how to talk about how to talk." The people you are with will always have some of their own ideas about respectful dialogue. Mine the people you are with to come up with these guidelines on talking. The group will develop norms that are culturally appropriate methods for group discussions. Be ready to join them in what they develop. We can also learn a lot from the social justice dialogues that have preceded us, such as race and gender. Here are some basic guidelines to get groups started, but remember to use your strongest asset, the people you are working with. These are adapted from Weber Cannon (1990), and I have adapted these to include the environment.

- We know that discrimination exists in many forms. Any critical understanding of discrimination and oppression means that we need to recognize that we have been taught misinformation about our own groups, as well as about members of other groups, species, places, and nature.
- Based on these assumptions then, let's agree that we cannot be blamed for the misinformation we have learned, but we should take personal responsibility for repeating misinformation after we have learned otherwise.

Box 8.1 **More to Explore—Questions to Explore a Story with a Group or Community**

- What are the physical characteristics of the locality? What are the characteristics of the group?
- Who lives in the locality? Who is a member of the group?
- What is the relationship between natural resources and economic opportunities?
- How does weather shape life in this locality?
- What special meanings do members have for the locality? For the group?
- How is the meaning of community expressed?
- How are the community and locality perceived by outsiders?
- How do insiders of the community and locality perceive themselves?
- Historically, how were the community and locality perceived by others?

Based on the work of Locke et al. (1998).

- Assume that people and environments are always doing the best they can.
- We can talk about ideas with respect for each other as human beings. We each have an obligation to actively combat the myths and stereotypes about our own groups and other groups, species, places, and nature.

As you speak with your groups and learn more about them, there are questions that are worth exploring that can bring about a richer understanding of the experience the group or community is having. Consider the questions in Box 8.1 as you build your conversations and narratives with the groups and communities you work with.

FRAMING THE PROBLEM (NARRATIVE THEORY)

Sometimes, communities or other entities are so deeply disregarded that their ability to mobilize action is limited. Sometimes this looks like race, class, or gender oppression; other times it is environmental degradation. When framing a problem, expanding the understanding of who experiences and faces the ills of the problem can bring attention to the issue at hand. Another way to frame a problem is through the use of experts, those who can speak about the problem and be heard due to the "legitimacy" of their perspective. Members of the professional class, including social workers, can count as people who can bring legitimacy to a problem. When framing the problem, consider the consistency, the empirical credibility, and the credibility of the claims-makers (Simpson, 2002). Our clients may be poor and lack education or status. These factors compromise their ability to make claims, so social workers and the organizations we represent may need to be claims-makers with or on behalf of our clients.

HELPING A COMMUNITY IDENTIFY A PROBLEM (STRUCTURAL THEORY)

Sometimes environmental or human problems feel like they are occurring in isolation. The reality is that the experience may be more broadly shared but is as yet unknown to a group of people with a shared experience. Social workers who spend time in communities, talking with people and learning about them, often begin to see patterns. But without a mechanism for tracking these patterns, the connection between the people and the issues may never be made.

By logging the identified issue, a group of social workers within a community has a broad view of the community in which they serve. Imagine five community social workers visiting families in a geographic locality. Over time, and with careful logging, they may be able to identify an asthma cluster or a lead exposure problem or a lack of access to recycling. Many health-related environmental problems have been identified this way, a simple identification of who is experiencing what and where. Once identified, more sophisticated exploratory methods can be used to track symptoms, experiences, behaviors, and habits, to begin to determine potential connections for causation and solutions. Moreover, the community that is built in this process is the foundation of a social change movement. As you work with communities, consider the opportunity to build both primary and secondary leadership roles (Gamble, 2010) by helping identify natural leadership in the community and considering ways succession can occur so that efforts can be maintained. Consider the template in Box 8.2, and modify it to fit your community. This could be useful to a community social worker who may be encountering various problems in the community and wanting to know the relevance of the issue to others. Sometimes a pattern requires a documentation process to see. Maps and other geographic systems, such as Google Earth, can help a social worker see what else may be in the community that members are unaware of that affect their shared experiences.

IDENTIFYING EXISTING RESILIENCIES (NARRATIVE THEORY)

When communities are facing difficult environmental problems, members of the community are already responding to the problems in ways that are possible for that community. Often, these existing problem-solving initiatives go unnoticed to a professional set of eyes (Denborough et al., 2006). While these efforts may not

Box 8.2 **Community Issue Identification**

Date	Location	Issue Description	Name	Contact Info

be enough to ameliorate a problem, they are significant in the lives of the people who are members of that community and have maintained or resisted further problems. Identifying, documenting, and celebrating these existing responses can be a powerful method of support and likely an inspiration for others to join in (Denborough et al., 2006). One way to identify these initiatives is to allow for intentional listening and to document the methods of problem-solving the community already uses. Then, using the language of the community members, combine the stories of struggle and perseverance, pain and progress, in a shared format, possibly organizing by values or themes (Denborough et al., 2006), and share them back with the community so that they can hear their own capacity for strength.

Highlighting and sharing existing initiatives requires multiple methods of communication and can be a resource and time-laden activity. Be prepared to actively participate within the community. Do they need help with their community website? With a newsletter? When doing the work of justice-making, it can sometimes be hard to find the time to communicate the strategies, opportunities, and victories. Do this communication on the forefront. Be prepared to jump in and help out in these situations, focusing on the skills and abilities of the group or community. Be clear who you are communicating on behalf of, and use language that is inclusive and invitational to additional participation if you need it.

Phase Two: Describing a Preferred Reality

STRUCTURING GROUPS FOR SOLIDARITY (NARRATIVE THEORY)

One of the important tasks in facilitating groups is to nurture the cohesion already budding among the group members. I suggest that the most powerful group experiences any of us have ever had have been in a group that combines getting things done with deep emotional commitment. Without this, it becomes hard to build the passion and commitment that provide the thrust of the work of groups. Building cohesion creates a sense of "we-ness" (Yalom, 2007). This kind of cohesion and solidarity increases attendance at groups, improves satisfaction with the group, and increases a sense of accomplishment (Yalom, 2007). Consider how people's personal experiences, pleasure at being together, can be enhanced even as you work on the tasks the group hopes to accomplish.

STRUCTURING GROUPS FOR ACTION (SYSTEMS, STRUCTURAL, AND NARRATIVE THEORIES)

One of the most important ways in which social work practice is accomplished is through task groups or a task force. Task groups are groups of professionals, constituents, clients, or citizens, who wish to address a certain need within the community or the organization. The initiation of a task force can come from a variety of sources. Task groups form out of client needs or advocacy, out of staff or personnel policy discussions, or by a leader in the community who may identify that a problem will be best solved through the methods of a task force. However it is formed, the social worker should be prepared to initiate, facilitate, and lead (Toseland & Rivas, 2012). In therapeutic groups, the social work role is to facilitate, assure, invite participation, maintain group boundaries, and link issues and ideas (Birkenmaier, Berg-Weger, & Dewees, 2011). Good task group facilitators take these therapeutic skills with them into the task group. In task groups, the social worker role is to set the agenda, maintain the group's focus, and provide documentation of the agenda and meeting minutes (Birkenmaier et al., 2011). With solidarity in mind, keep cohesion and facilitation at the foreground.

There are many titles for the different kinds of groups social workers facilitate. For example, a social worker may facilitate an ad hoc group; this is a group focused on a specific issue, often with time-limited efforts to address a certain problem. Social workers may also be part of committees or cabinets. These task groups often are continuous in nature. They do not have a specific ending time and often address policies, programs, or issues that need continuous attention. Social workers may be part of coalitions or collaborative groups that involve multiple stakeholders from different areas. Social workers also facilitate educational groups about specific topics of interest, from parenting to stress reduction. Support groups are another type of group common to social work practice.

The first job of creating any group is to identify purpose and membership. The source, or the reasoning, for the group often determines who should be part of the task group. Membership of the task group should be broad enough to include a multiplicity of stakeholders. Membership in the group should also be diverse enough to include multiple perspectives on the problem. When developing a task group for environmental justice issues, social workers advocate for the participation of those who have less power in the decision-making process or who may not initially be considered for the group. This may include women, youth voices, people who are economically poor, and others who may not be initially invited to participate in the group.

Clarity in the group's purpose is reassuring for the members and the facilitator. Identify the purpose clearly, and you often get information on who should be in the group and how long it should stay in action. The purpose is an important element to consider. If the purpose of the group is identified solely by those who have power, the goals of the group will reflect the current dominant power structure. As the purpose of the group is established, social workers assure that voices of those who do not have power are included in the purpose. Sometimes the purpose of a group can have multiple components. This works as long as the values in the purposes are in concert with each other.

STRUCTURE GROUPS FOR PARTNERSHIP ACROSS OPPRESSIONS (STRUCTURAL THEORY)

Often, groups who are experiencing an environmental injustice are also experiencing another injustice based on another social experience or social identity. Groups oppressed in one way, for example, economically, can work in solidarity with a group oppressed environmentally as they identify their shared interests and stakes in the issues. Box 8.3 describes one organization's effort to bridge such a divide.

Phase Three: Making Plans and Dreams Real

The most powerful element of the group experience is the potential collaboration and connections made among and between group members—this is the essence of the difference from social work practice with individuals. This source of networking and connecting among group members provides the "social soup" of engagement and

Box 8.3 **Organizations in Action—Green for All**

Green for All is a national advocacy organization (www.greenforall.org), aiming to build an economy that is inclusive, sustainable, and strong enough to "lift people out of poverty." They share practices, shape conversations, and work to inspire action in the private sector and government to create jobs. Efforts to reduce the unemployment rates for working-age Americans and for those who are traditionally underemployed, including those who are living in an urban area where previous employment opportunities have faded, have been combined with the environmental movement to create an environmental justice movement called "green collar jobs" or "green collar economy." These jobs and economic sectors focus on creating environmentally sustainable products and services that can employ individuals in need of livable-wage jobs and provide opportunities to reduce the carbon output of our communities and increase sustainability and affordability. Jobs included in the green economic movement include the technicians to build, install, and maintain solar arrays; expanded recycling methods; green space maintenance; environmentally friendly manufacturing; and home construction and remodeling that utilizes green building practices, including weather stripping, insulation, and complex heating and cooling systems. Building demand for this economic sector will also build demand for trained employees, and training is focused on underemployed communities—all efforts to boost a local economy, employ people with livable and fair wages, and steward environmental resources.

Founder and author Van Jones writes (2008, p. 106–107),

> I have been trying to bridge this divide for nearly a decade. And I have learned a few things along the way. What I have found is that leaders from impoverished areas . . . tended to focus on three areas: social justice, political solutions, and social change. They cared primarily about "the people." They focus their efforts on fixing schools, improving healthcare, defending civil rights, and reducing the prison population. Their studies centered on "social change" work like lobbying, campaigning, and protesting. They were wary of business; instead, they turned to the political system and government to help solve the problems of the community.
>
> The leaders I met from affluent places . . . had what seemed to be the opposite approach. Their three focus areas were ecology, business solutions, and inner change. They were champions of the environment who cared primarily about "the planet." They worked to save the rain forests and important species like whales and polar bears. Also, they were usually dedicated to "inner change", including meditation and yoga. And they put a great deal of stress on making wise, Earth-honoring consumer choices. . . .

Every effort I made to get the two groups together initially was a disaster—sometimes ending in tears, anger, and slammed doors. Trying to make sense of the differences, I wrote out three binaries on a napkin:

1. Ecology versus social justice
2. Business solutions (entrepreneurship) versus political solutions (activism)
3. Spiritual/inner change versus social/outer change

... I thought to myself: what would we have if we replaced those versus symbols with plus signs? What if we built a movement at the intersection of the social justice and ecology movement, of entrepreneurship and activism, of inner-change and social change? What if we didn't have hybrid cars—what if we had a hybrid movement?

energy far beyond that of a single social worker. Using narrative theory, build these connections through the stories of the members. Let them weave their own narrative, with the social worker providing the space. This reconstruction of the narrative of the problem can provide a strong and powerful basis for shared problem-solving in environmental justice issues. The social worker is the professional nurturer and facilitator of this powerful group process, and natural leaders will emerge from within the group. Rather than managing the group experience, the social worker identifies strengths and ameliorates barriers to this new construction of the understanding of the problem.

ANTI-OPPRESSIVE GROUP PRACTICE (STRUCTURAL THEORY)

Anti-oppressive group practice should be integral to the group and community work conducted by social workers. To help ensure that your work is anti-oppressive, consider the following questions (Reitman & Ewall, 2007, p. 19) (see also Box 8.4).

- Who is in our group? Do we look like the constituency we claim to represent (race, class, gender, sexuality, ability, age, neighborhood, etc.)? If not, how come?
- Why are we interested in this issue(s)? Could we change or reframe our current focus, to make the group more inclusive, forward-looking, and justice-oriented?
- Are we doing something that will negatively affect another community, species, or nature? How can we stop?
- Are we following the principles of environmental justice? Do we have copies of documents like this on hand for people to see and use on a regular basis?
- Are we getting at the root of problems, or are we just perpetuating oppressive systems?

Box 8.4 **A Checklist for Evaluation and Action**

The questions in this checklist will help you evaluate and prepare for action. The answers to these questions will guide your work and increase the likelihood of your success. Check back frequently as the answers to these questions may change over time.

- From whom do we want to get a response? A large company, the government, a local organization? Community members?
- What response do we hope to get? Do we have any concessions?
- What actions are most likely to lead to that response? Who can join us in these actions?
- What might this action lead to next?
- Do our actions fit our outcomes? Are they ethical to people, nature, and other living beings?
- How do we assess the effectiveness of our efforts?
- Would the people who have come before us approve?
- Will the people, nature, and other living beings that come after us agree?

Adapted from Homan (2016).

Once you've answered these questions, you may have identified new members, new goals, or strategies, as well as more clarity for your group's work.

MATERIALIZATION (STRUCTURAL THEORY)

Analysis of the tangible resources and the material conditions under which clients live along with a consciousness-raising about how these conditions impact their lives, their perceptions of their lives, and the problems they experience is an essential practice skill in environmental social work. We call this work *materialization* (Lundy, 2004; Moreau & Leonard, 1989). Imagine a parent angrily discouraged and expecting his or her child to perform well in school, without an analysis of the harm due to poor air quality, lead in the home, lack of outdoor activity, or excessive noise and light pollution that disrupts the child's sleep. A full assessment of a client's situation is necessary to see the potential variables within the environment that could be impacting the life of that child. Our understanding of who we are is rooted in a transactional analysis of understanding ourselves, the environment around us, and our perceptions. This is related to the material conditions of where we live. If we live near garbage dumps, we may feel like garbage. As we help clients with this material analysis, with contextualizing their lives, they will begin to see the connections between their experiences and their worldview and have their consciousness raised.

BEARING WITNESS (NARRATIVE THEORY)

One of the methods communities use when they come together to work for justice is to uplift the voices of those seldom or never heard. Bearing witness is an act of storytelling, in which the voices of those who seldom get the opportunity to stand at the pulpit are given that opportunity at community gatherings, forums, meetings, and protests.

Bearing witness is not an easy task, and the work of the social worker is to identify and support the people who are ready and prepared to share intimate emotional experiences that help others understand the depths of the wounds they are experiencing. As a method of building understanding and strengthening knowledge for those on the outside of the oppression, it serves a powerful purpose: "Let us not rush to the language of healing, before understanding the fullness of the dignity and the depth of the wound" (Pierce, 2014). Bearing witness is the strength to share the sad and aching parts of oneself, on behalf of a shared problem. In that one story, multiple stories within a community are heard—because the story of that witness connects to others experiencing the pain of the oppression and injustice.

Bearing witness requires the strength of people we often call our clients. In reality, they are our partners in the shared work of justice-making. In our roles working with community members, we as social workers can be prepared to identify witness-bearers we know in the community and provide the coaching and assistance they may need to complete the witnessing. Social work roles in working with witness-bearers include the following:

- Witness-bearers do not need experience in public speaking; some of the best stories are from those who have little to no experience.
- Be prepared to coach a witness-bearer who feels unsure of his or her role. You can sit with the person; help him or her identify key points of his or her story, elements that are most salient; and identify the beginnings and endings to help the story maintain its coherence.
- Remember that witness-bearers are often victims of injustices; they need support and encouragement to stay strong.
- Help the community share its gratitude for the gift of the witness-bearer.
- Hold the story with a sense of the sacred.
- Identify ways witness-bearing can be shared more broadly to expand the impact of the message: social media, transcripts as parts of the letter to the editor, or letters to politicians.

Witness-bearing is a powerful tool for advocacy, outreach, and cohesion-building toward changing an environmental justice problem. The people experiencing the environmental injustice can share, from their perspective, how the problem is experienced.

PROXIES (NARRATIVE THEORY)

A *proxy* is someone who speaks on behalf of one who cannot. He or she gives the opinions and perspective of whomever or whatever is voiceless. Nonhuman entities are considered voiceless, as are future generations and those who are deeply marginalized and unable to participate in the process (Schlossberg, 2007). The point of a proxy is to give the power of persuasion, advocacy, and even a vote to someone or something who cannot be present. Being a proxy requires one to extend one's thinking into what one is representing, imagining the responses from and impacts on that which one is providing a proxy for. While it does not give perfect representation, it does provide an extension of the possibilities into a wider purview and a broader and deeper understanding of the problem being deliberated. Any group, making decisions on a variety of topics, can identify who and what is voiceless that is impacted in the decision-making process and appoint a person to represent the interests of the voiceless through the proxy process. For example, animal species, water, and air are all potential clients of a proxy. Imagine social workers giving voice to the land when their organization is building a new building or giving voice to water quality as a community makes decisions on shared green spaces (see Box 8.5).

Phase Four: Evaluating Outcomes and Making Transitions

In phase four of practice, we evaluate our shared work and create transitions as they are needed. There are multiple ways to create transitions and many options for evaluation. Keep in mind the overarching goals of this phase of practice: providing the client what he or she needs in regard to continued services, acknowledging accomplishments made, and evaluating practice skills of the social worker.

TRACKING PROGRESS (NARRATIVE THEORY)

For social workers working with groups and communities, one of the best ways to facilitate evaluation and transitions needed is to track a community group's movement toward a goal (Locke, Garrison, & Winship, 1998). Sometimes progress is not always clear when you are in the thick of the work. In this method the social worker, identifying tangible gains made, even when subtle, shares the progress in such a way as to empower the group. For example, a social worker had engaged with a local community on getting safer playground equipment and a clearly marked pedestrian pathway to get to the park. The project took 3 years. Tracking progress made at 6-month intervals, even with long stretches of limited progress, kept the progress tangible. New and safe park equipment was eventually installed, and a community celebration was the capstone to the tracking progress.

Box 8.5 **People, Places, and Issues—Urban Heat Islands**

Urban heat islands are created when urban areas heat more quickly during the day and do not cool off at night. They are caused by large building structures that create heat, the loss of vegetation and their natural cooling effect, and the proximity of buildings to each other that traps heat. A phenomenon of urban areas, urban heat islands can lead to heat stress and heat-related emergencies, especially for children, older adults, and others without access to cooling systems (Hamilton & Erickson, 2012). Infants and small children have underregulated physical systems to respond to extreme heat, and this makes them vulnerable to heat-related illnesses. Children often have something older adults do not—someone watching over them. In recent heatwaves, 45% of heat-related deaths were older adults (Centers for Disease Control and Prevention, 2003). Poverty is another major indicator of loss of life in a heatwave (Klinenberg, 1999). Roles for social workers outlined by Hamilton and Erickson (2012) include organizing and partnering to mitigate urban heat islands by planting trees and increasing vegetation in urban areas. Adding these natural coolants to the urban heat island brings aesthetic appeal as well as natural cooling effects. Social workers can also educate individuals, especially those living in high-rises with limited income and few family or friends to check on them, to understand the threats of heatwaves and what they can do about it. Social workers can also set up cool zones in public places such as libraries, keep these public places open longer, and organize door-to-door community checks to be sure people have water, have air circulation in their homes, and are aware of the public cool zones as options to reduce heat stress, illness, and death.

CELEBRATIONS, RITUALS, AND ACKNOWLEDGMENT (NARRATIVE THEORY)

One of the best ways to end the social worker–client relationship is to celebrate the accomplishments that have been made and simultaneously acknowledge the strides and ability to overcome hardship. When the endings are shared in a public way, such as with family, friends, or community, it provides another access point for additional resources to be part of the client's life and help maintain the change. It also provides an opportunity for celebration at a time when celebration and good news may be limited. In this story of the struggle for 3 years to get park equipment installed, a community celebration was warranted. This gave the social worker a chance to publicly acknowledge the hard work of community members, including giving awards such as "Strength in Leadership," "Commitment to the Kids," and "Healthy Community Leader" to the tireless community members who helped bring about the improved green space.

SOCIAL WORKER EVALUATION (NARRATIVE THEORY)

In supervision or in consultation, social workers can evaluate their work with groups and communities. This can often be in the form of dialogue. It can build from the tracking of progress the group or community has made. How did the social worker help facilitate these gains? Did the social worker impede the changes in any way? Have skills or competencies increased for the social worker? Reflecting on and assessing our own social work practice builds the skill set for the next client encounter.

Finding and Using Quantitative Data

Social workers use data gathered by researchers to help explore the story of environmental justice problems. Data help us explore the story deeper in our first phase of practice, set realistic goals in phase two, know where interventions can be found for phase three, and evaluate outcomes in our final phase of practice. Using data effectively is a very important social work skill that requires the social worker to know what data are available and to understand how to read the data and frame them to fit the problem within the community. Sources of data are important, especially in a time when all kinds of information can be found on the Internet and the conflagration of incorrect information can be common. Moreover, some information can seem alarming, so it is important to trust the accuracy and integrity of the resources you use to collect data. Examples of reliable and accurate sources of data available on the Internet for environmental justice issues are shown in Box 8.6.

Finding and Using Qualitative Data

While data driven by numbers and facts are deeply useful, it is important to see and hear the qualitative elements of a story. This fits with our theoretical and social work foundational concepts. When gathering data, Homan (2016) gives the following good advice.

> First, get the perspectives of people who feel the need as well as those who could potentially feel the need. Second, have a night to the future. Gather information from people whose support you will need down the road as you respond to the issues you identified. Collect information in a way that strengthens the likelihood of their future involvement. Two sets of people are important for future contacts. One set includes the people who will decide on the course of action in response to the recognition of these community conditions, including those with influence on these decision-makers. The second set includes those people who will implement the action. (p. 153)

Box 8.6 **More to Explore—Sources of Data**

CDC: Centers for Disease Control and Prevention, in the United States
https://www.cdc.gov/

County and city data books, in the United States
https://archive.org/details/countycitydatabo1956unit

County Health Rankings and Roadmaps, in the United States
http://www.countyhealthrankings.org/

EJSCREEN: Environmental Justice Screening and Mapping Tool, in the United States
https://www.epa.gov/ejscreen

EPA: U.S. Environmental Protection Agency
https://www.epa.gov

International Union for the Conservation of Nature
https://www.iucn.org

National Center for Health Statistics—Centers for Disease Control and Prevention
https://www.cdc.gov/nchs/

Union of Concerned Scientists
http://www.ucsusa.org/

United Nations
http://www.un.org/en/index.html

U.S. Census Bureau
https://www.census.gov/

WHO: World Health Organization
http://www.who.int/en/

World Bank
http://data.worldbank.org/topic/environment

Worldwatch Institute
http://www.worldwatch.org/

Three useful methods for collecting qualitative data are key informants, focus groups, and a community dialogue or forum.

KEY INFORMANT INTERVIEWS

In key informant interviews people who may have a special understanding of a situation are interviewed to gather their perspective or expertise. Key informant interviews can be useful with a variety of individuals and provide an opportunity to gather data that cannot be found anywhere else. Key informants are chosen because of their specialized experience or expertise. Weaknesses of such interviews are that key informants have a particular perspective and may not have the same values or interests of the social worker. However, understanding the issue faced from another perspective is seldom useless.

FOCUS GROUPS

Focus groups are small groups of individuals who are interviewed. Focus groups are useful in gathering ideas and generating shared perspectives from multiple stakeholders. The shared conversation that can ensue can drive further understanding and imagination on the part of the participants. While gathering information from a focus group is useful, a limitation can be a focus group with a dominant participant or with members who may not have felt equally able to participate, skewing the information learned. Focus groups can be invitation-only or open-invite. One community, working to address crime in its open spaces including parks and empty lots, held open focus groups at the parks and invited anyone to join in. This gave narrative and context to a problem that until then was only understood through police reports.

COMMUNITY DIALOGUE OR FORUM

Community dialogues or forums can be very useful in gathering information from large groups of people. It is important to have the right tools for such large groups. Methods for gathering data from large groups of people are possible, and several options exist. The Community ToolBox (ctb.ku.edu/en) is one such place that strategies can be found. The World Café is another strategy and website that offers tips on garnering useful information from large groups of people in ways that assure voices are heard (www.theworldcafe.com). When leading a community forum or dialogue, you want to strengthen the initiative rather than reduce feelings of agency or positive energy. Consider the tactics for losing outlined in Box 8.7 and the potential consequences before you implement any strategies that empower experts over community or clients.

Uneven Ecological Systems Between Communities

One of the important facets of community work is to recognize the competition for and disparities in resources that occur in neighborhoods, cities, and communities. Often, these disparities show up in land use that translates into differing access to parks, community centers, schools, recreation facilities, public transportation, healthcare facilities, faith communities, and others. These community arrangements

Box 8.7 **More to Explore—Recipe for Losing**

You may think that the best way for a group to win an environmental justice issue is to hire lawyers and let them fight the battle for you, but this is a perfect recipe for how groups lose! Here's the recipe for how to lose. Many groups have tried this. Most have lost.

Step 1: Group forms around an issue. People get involved.

Step 2: Group decides they need to hire a lawyer (and/or other experts such as hydrogeologists or toxicologists) to work on permits, zoning, etc. Experts cost a lot of money, even at discounted charity rates.

Step 3: Group members start to assume they aren't needed much anymore since the experts must fight the battle and they don't think of themselves as experts. Meeting involvement and attendance dwindles.

Step 4: Since it's legal to pollute, the battles revolve around narrow technical issues. The experts try many things, and the fight lasts a long time. The group becomes little more than a fundraising operation for their experts, sometimes raising tens of thousands of dollars or more. The group is then surprised when the strategy fails because it was politically untenable or because of a technicality.

The point is that it's politics and economics, not science, that bring about community change. It's imperative that communities work on a local, political level. While using an expert can be a great tactic if done properly, making the fight technical and legal brings it out of the hands of the people and takes it to courtrooms, hearing boards, and other technical forums where winning becomes a technicality rather than a community initiative.

Reitman and Ewall (2007, p.14).

are not accidental but are a representation of the power and economic resource stores that some communities have access to. Reasons for these community dynamics can be found in the history of the community; the community setting; the physical setting; and social, racial, and other demographics of the community and the economic system. This may also include interactions between communities or a lack of interaction, representing the potential for segregation and separation. The fifth element of the environmental justice framework (Bullard, 2005) requires us to target resources to ameliorate disparities. Resources needed to ameliorate these uneven ecological systems include tax dollars, natural resources, policy change, and community commitments.

As we advance toward equity in our ecological systems, we know that empowering clients to participate in the process of seeking and creating environmental justice is a key strategy and method in structural social work. To assure that community members' voices are not lost in the process of social change, emphasis on community members' knowledge and skills must be endorsed along with their equitable participation (Lundy, 2004). Consider the degree of participation you seek (Lundy, 2004), and build toward the kind of participation you want and need in the community you are working with. At the highest level of participation, the community identifies the problems and generates the solutions to ameliorate them. The effective practitioner adjusts his or her work to empower participation as much as possible. The process in which we seek environmental justice is as important as our final outcome. All of the methods to produce individual, family, or community change begin with relationships built on equity and participation. Participation is a formidable task for the social worker to attend to but worthy of our time.

Critical Thinking Questions

1. Identify a group marginalized in environmental decision-making. What is the impact of this marginalization?
2. Think forward to the future, what role will a new generation of social workers play in making environmental justice meaningful?
3. Have a courageous conversation with people in your class about race, socioeconomic status, privilege, and the environment. Rather than focusing on others, focus on your words, your body language, and your emotions. What did you learn about yourself? How can you improve your skills by participating in such conversations? Where will you practice next?

Key Terms

Cohesion
Collectivization
Community
Group
Materialization
Qualitative data
Quantitative data
Stakeholders

Additional Learning Activities

1. Check out the U.S. Environmental Protection Agency's EJSCREEN: Environmental Justice Screening and Mapping Tool (http://www.epa.gov/ ejscreen). Directions on using the tool are on the website. Look up your community. What do you learn?

2. Choose a community in another part of the country. Write down your assumptions about this community. Review their profile on the EJSCREEN. Were there overlaps between your assumptions and what you learned? Did you have misinformation as part of your assumptions?

3. Identify an environmental issue being addressed by a group in your community. Attend a meeting. What do you observe about this task group? How were human relationship skills important? Was it clear how decisions were made? Did you understand the format of the meeting?

4. Explore the relationships between a person's individual health and the environmental, social, and economic forces that contribute to that health. How is individual health mirrored by the community in which a person lives? What are the connections?

References

Ban Ki Moon. (2013, September 24). Ban Ki Moon invites world leaders to climate summit in 2014. Retrieved from http://www.un.org/climatechange/blog/2013/09/ban-ki-moon-invites-world-leaders-to-a-climate-summit-in-2014/

Birkenmaier, J., Berg-Weger, M., & Dewees, M. (2011). *The practice of generalist social work* (2nd ed.). New York, NY: Routledge.

Bullard, R. (2005). *The quest for environmental justice*. San Francisco, CA: Sierra Club Books.

Centers for Disease Control and Prevention. (2003). Heat-related deaths—Chicago, Illinois, 1996–2001, and United States, 1979–1999. *Morbidity and Mortality Weekly Report, 52*, 610–613.

Denborough, D., Kookmatrie, C., Mununnggirritj, D., Djuwalpi, M., Dhurrkay, W., & Yunupingu, M. (2006). Linking stories and initiatives: A narrative approach to working with the skills and knowledge of communities. *International Journal of Narrative Therapy and Community Work, 2*, 19–51.

Fellin, P. (2000). *The community and the social worker* (3rd ed.). Belmont, CA: Brooks/Cole.

Gamble, D. N. (2010). *Community practice skills: Local to global perspectives*. New York, NY: Columbia University Press.

Hamilton, B., & Erickson, C. L. (2012). Urban heat islands and social work: Opportunities for intervention. *Advances in Social Work 13*(2), 420–430.

Homan, M. (2016). *Promoting community change: Making it happen in the real world* (6th ed.). Boston, MA: Cengage.

Jones, P. A., & Moulton, A. (2016). *The invisible crisis: Water unaffordability in the United States*. Unitarian Universalist Service Committee. Retrieved from http://www.uusc.org/sites/default/files/the_invisible_crisis_web.pdf

Jones, V. (2008). *The green collar economy: How one solution can fix our two biggest problems*. New York, NY: Harper One.

Klinenberg, E. (1999). Denaturalizing disaster: A social autopsy of the 1995 Chicago heat wave. *Theory and Society, 28*, 239–295.

Locke, B., Garrison, R., & Winship, J. (1998). *Generalist social work practice: Context, story, and partnerships*. Boston, MA: Brooks/Cole.

Lundy, C. (2004). *Social work and social justice: A structural approach to practice*. Peterborough, ON, Canada: Broadview Press.

Moreau, M., & Leonard, L. (1989). *Empowerment through a structural approach to social work.* Montreal: Ecole de Service Sociale, Université de Montréal and Carleton University School of Social Work.

Pierce, Y. (2014). A litany for those who aren't ready for healing. Retrieved from http://yolandapierce.blogspot.com/2014/11/a-litany-for-those-who-arent-ready-for.html

Reitman, M., & Ewall, M. (2007). *Campus-community organizing guide: Building power for lasting change in the youth movement for clean energy.* Energy Justice Network. Retrieved from http://www.energyjustice.net/files/campus/ccog.pdf

Schlossberg, D. (2007). *Defining environmental justice: Theories, movements, and nature.* New York, NY: Oxford University Press.

Simpson, A. (2002). Who hears their cry? African American women and the fight for environmental justice in Memphis Tennessee. In J. Adamson, M. M. Evans, & R. Stein (Eds.), *The environmental justice reader: Politics, poetics, and pedagogy* (pp. 82–104). Tucson: University of Arizona Press.

Toseland, R. W., & Rivas, R. F. (2012). *An introduction to group work practice* (7th ed.). Boston, MA: Allyn and Bacon.

Weber Cannon, L. (1990). Fostering positive class, race, and gender dynamics in the classroom. *Women's Studies Quarterly, 18*(1/2), 126–134.

Yalom, I., & Lesczc, M. (2007). *The theory and practice of group psychotherapy.* New York, NY: Basic Books.

CHAPTER 9

Social Work Practice with Policies and Organizations Toward Environmental Justice

Our environment is the base upon which all other institutions are built; thus, our polity, our economy, and our social systems must reflect the principles of sustainability. They must value human life and the lives of all species; they must promote fairness and equality, as well as economic and social justice; they must support decision-making that involves participation in partnership rather than domination, and they must protect our Mother Earth. —Nancy L. Mary, Social Work in a Sustainable World, p. 153

As we move through the continuum of micro to macro practice, we end our section of practice chapters with macro social work focused on organizations and policies. While the techniques and methods you will learn in this chapter will be new, I hope you will be able to see the threads and connections that bring the elements of micro to macro practice together. Effective social work spans this artificial divide in micro to macro work, recognizing that systems theory tells us that changes in one level of the system produce outcomes in other levels. To make the content in this chapter more digestible, I have separated the two sections. We'll begin with policy and proceed to organizations—recognizing that policies are an important factor in organizational practice—a link I hope you will see.

Policies as Environmental Justice Practice

Policies are written statements that tell us what actions are appropriate to take to guide our work and decision-making. Policies often enforce specific behaviors of people, how resources are allocated to people or programs, and who can or cannot participate in opportunities. Policies shape the way equity and justice are applied within a nation, a city, a community, or an agency. National policies set rules for government programs and agency policies to provide guidelines for organizational practice. Because of our commitment to the triple bottom line of equity, economy, and environmental; policy and organizational work should be developed with intersectionality in mind. Improving environmental conditions is linked with improving economic and social conditions. Racial justice programs can be developed to include environmental justice. Patriarchy can be dismantled along with ending environmental degradation. "Policy practice and analysis for environmental justice engages social workers in finding common ground as advocates and condition-builders with citizens, environmental engineers, industrial planners, labor unions, and environmental activists to press for greater institutional integration of social, economic, and environmental policies that will protect, benefit, and amplify the political voice of disenfranchised populations" (Rogge, 2008, p. 5).

Because of the power of a written policy, how it is implemented, and its influence on the life of programs, services, and resources, policy practice is an integral part of social work. It is often an area in which justice can be clarified and made into practice strategies. Policy practice includes developing new policies, modifying existing policies, and defeating or relinquishing poor policies in order to achieve goals of environmental, economic, and social justice (see Box 9.1). In any of these ways, the phases of practice continue.

Policy practice for social work includes the opposition to oppressive policies and the creation and support of policies that extend freedoms and opportunities. Human experiences that occur because of policy are reflections of values and ethics, not just a movement of goods or an implementation of services. If we strip morality from policy and the experiences that occur, we will leave people vulnerable (Titmuss, 1968). If we truly understand that all exchanges resulting from policy have a social and environmental dimension, we know they either support or erode equity and sustainability.

Phase One: Telling and Exploring the Story

RECOGNIZE AND NAME CONNECTIONS (SYSTEMS THEORY)

All policy is considered to have social implications and impacts on humans' lived experience. I extend that concept and suggest that all policy has an environmental impact—natural resources are always impacted in some way. All policies suggest the use of resources that impact the lives of people and communities. One policy in the United States has been providing access to healthy food to women and children through WIC, the Women, Infants, and Children program established in 1972. This policy—with a focus on the health of developing children and their caregivers—has environmental implications as it identifies accepted food sources, where that food came from and how it was grown. This government subsidy pays for food that

Box 9.1 **People, Places, and Issues—Climate Change**

Climate change, or climate disruption, will affect all communities. Like other environmental justice issues, climate change will affect those who are disproportionately poor more severely than those who live in more affluent areas. One serious effect of climate change is poor air quality. For 18 years the American Lung Association has been collecting and reporting data on air quality in the US, called the State of the Air report. They found that more than 18 million people live in counties that received the lowest possible score on air quality on 3 different measures (American Lung Association, 2017).

Scientific evidence has shown that the Earth is warming and that the main activities increasing this warming are human-made. The efforts to halt climate change must also be human-made. In 2014, under then president Barack Obama, the United States enacted the President's Climate Action Plan implemented by the Environmental Protection Agency, focusing on renewable energy, energy efficiency, climate resilience, and other areas (https://www.c2es.org/federal/obama-climate-plan-resources). The goal of the clean power plan is to reduce carbon pollution from power plants by 30% by 2030 from 2005 levels. The plan requires each state to act independently to reduce carbon emissions. Because each state has a unique array of energy usage, each must develop its own reduction plan. The policy includes governments, businesses, and individual homes, with efforts to reduce energy at each level. Investments in energy-efficient technologies and programs are part of this process as energy efficiency encourages a reduction in carbon emissions without reducing standards of comfort for people. In addition, the American Lung Association (2017) states that at least 230,000 deaths and $2 trillion annually will be saved when the Clean Air Act is supported.

Climate change will also impact our weather patterns, creating what is now termed *superstorms*, severe storms that cause flooding, drought, high winds, and hurricanes, such as Hurricane Katrina. These weather patterns will impact agricultural practices, changing production and distribution with economic fallout as well as furthering disparities in food access.

Education is one of the key practice roles for social workers. Begin with sharing how climate change is affecting the part of the world where the client lives and works. Since climate change is universal, speaking in terms of solidarity, such as "we" and "our community," is a helpful place to begin. If you live in the United States, check out the National Climate Assessment (www.globalchange.gov) and specify the region you live in. This will describe, in reader-friendly terms, the impacts of climate change in your area. Consider the following elements of the conversation:

1. If the summers are getting warmer, consider a plan to address a heatwave.
2. Share information on heat impacts that can be dangerous, especially for children and older adults, and what first responses are.
3. Discuss air quality and its impacts, especially if you are in an urban area.
4. Inform your clients on local emergency programs for disaster preparedness.

One must wait for the right time and not expect climate change to be front and center in the concerns of all clients. Explain that on Earth Day in 2016, 195 countries signed the Paris Agreement to reduce greenhouse gas emissions, slow climate change, and switch to renewable energies which have a far smaller pollution output. This was a hopeful step. Every country has its own methods of reducing greenhouse gasses. The Climate Action Plan enacted by President Obama is likely to be dismantled under new presidential leadership. Resistance to that dismantling continues. You can check out the current state of this issue at www.climaterealityproject.org.

has a cultural identity, is grown and processed and then shared with young families. As you can see, WIC is not just a nutrition policy; its implementation has environmental consequences, and its distribution has social meaning on what is good, healthy, or preferable. Identifying and naming connections like these is the first step to telling an accurate story.

UNIVERSALIZE AN ENVIRONMENTAL ETHIC OF CARE (NARRATIVE THEORY)

Most people around the world live in urban areas. If human behavior change and innovation are required to restore Earth's resources, then we must begin to touch people who live in urban areas and help them reclaim, identify, and revere the natural places in their urban settings. We must build a resurgence of nature in the urban core. To do so requires creating an ethic of care (Cummins, Byers, & Pedrick, 2011) for nature in all of the of places we find it. For years, conservation policy was about saving expansive natural places that seldom saw human interference. While that is one important part of the environmental story, another important aspect requires conservation where people live and interact on a daily basis, connecting them to the relevance of Earth's health to our wellness. The easiest places to begin are our city policies, identifying their impacts on the rivers that trespass our cities as well as the opportunity to create city forests, considering the ways people move and enjoy outdoor spaces. Every policy in every municipality—no matter the size— needs to consider nature (see Box 9.2).

Box 9.2 **More to Explore—City Policy**

San Francisco is a city known for progressive environmental policy. Since 2006 the city has required restaurants to use recyclable carryout containers. It banned plastic bags in 2007 and began a foam ban in 2017 (*Har,* 2016, from Associated Press). Banning these three elements alone will greatly reduce solid waste. Often, policies implemented in one city spread to other cities and are sometimes the catalyst for even larger movements.

ANALYZE POLICIES WITH ENVIRONMENTAL RESOURCES IN MIND (SYSTEMS THEORY)

For many years, as part of our modernist structure, policy analysis was based on the story of financial efficiency and outcomes toward goals. Social workers do want to measure these variables, but we also insist on measurements of equity and access, carbon footprint, unintended policy consequences, and impacts on stakeholders—including Earth. This multidimensional approach is inclusive of the foundational concepts of social work. Especially important are the three components of sustainable development, the triple bottom line: equity, environment, and economy. When completing a policy analysis, useful questions can include the following:

> What resources are required to implement this policy?
> Have micro and macro issues been considered?
> Can the resources to implement the policy be accessed ethically and responsibly?
> Are there environmental justice implications to the policy enactment or accessing the required resources?
> How does the policy affect people across the lifespan?
> Is power shared? Have a range of people been consulted?
> Can sustainability be achieved?

Phase Two: Describing a Preferred Reality

Describing a new reality is the backbone of policy development. Policies void of feedback and collaboration are often weak. Remember that a lack of equity limits relationships, and lack of participation limits idea generation as well as who is responsible for and who is a recipient of policy implementation.

INSTITUTIONALIZED ENVIRONMENTAL POLICIES (STRUCTURAL THEORY)

The concepts of residual and institutional social policy (Wilensky & Lebeaux, 1965) are guides to understand and label the kinds of policies social workers work with and to bring clarity to the kinds of policies social workers want to develop. As a profession, we are committed to the prevention of problems in the lives of people. The environmental justice framework calls us to prevent harm before it occurs (Bullard, 2005). Institutional policy development is one way to do that. Institutional environmental policy calls us to see the policy implemented as part of a "normal function of society" (Segal, 2010, p. 7). An institutionalized environmental policy would make caring for nature around us a normal part of our human endeavor, and the preventive efforts to assure reduced harm to Earth due to human activities would become standard in the policy and programs created.

This is contrasted with residual policy programs in which policy responses are developed only after all other options have become unavailable, the problem has become well known, and it cannot be solved through other means of human intervention. This approach is visible in current environmental concerns on climate change. Earth has already warmed so quickly that natural adaptations by species are threatened. The residual approach is dangerous because many of the problems humans and the environment experience can take more than one lifetime to correct.

CONNECTING POLICIES TO PROGRAMS (SYSTEMS AND NARRATIVE THEORIES)

Once policy change is enacted, it often is reflected in new programs or ways of providing programs (Segal, 2010). As we learned about quantitative and qualitative data in Chapter 8, you can see how data can be used to support or resist the enactment of policy. However, quantitative data are seldom enough for people to deeply understand the impact of policy and how a program can help people in their personal situation. Telling a story of the experience, or providing context to the data, is an influential way to connect a policy to implementation—which brings the policy to fruition. The problem of lead is one good example of this connection of problem to policy to program. Box 9.3 provides a summary of these connections.

Phase Three: Making Plans and Dreams Real

IMPLEMENTING NEW POLICY (STRUCTURAL AND NARRATIVE THEORIES)

One of the best ways to reach the triple bottom line is to implement new policy. Imagine, the Clean Air Act (1963), the Fair Labor Standards Act and the 40-hour workweek (1938), the Clean Water Act (1972), and the Civil Rights Act (1964) were all once brand new policies put forth by brave individuals and groups. New policies are still needed today—and they should address the triple bottom line of economy, equity, and environment. Policy decisions that are environmentally

> ### Box 9.3 People, Places, and Issues—Lead Abatement
>
> The story of lead and its abatement is a successful story of identification of an environmental hazard that spurred new policy enactment and provided programs to improve the health and well-being of children.
>
> One of the most effective environmental policies enacted was the banning of lead in 1978. Informed by good scientific data, lead was determined to be unsafe to humans at any level. Researchers have documented the ill effects of lead exposure, including developmental disorders (Banks, Ferretti & Shucard, 1997), and attention deficit hyperactivity disorder (Braun, Kahn, Froehlich, Auinger, Lanphear, 2006). Childhood exposure has even been shown to increase aggressive behaviors and crime as the child has aged (Nevin, 2007; Reyes, 2015). Like all contemporary injustices, people of color, those living in poverty and substandard housing, and those who are recent immigrants have higher levels of exposure (Cleveland, Minter, Cobb, Scott & German, 2008), mostly due to living in older homes that may not be well maintained and in areas with high traffic where lead may have settled in the soil.
>
> When lead was banned from gasoline and commercial products, new products emerged such as unleaded gasoline and lead-free paints. Because lead had already been used in so many products over time, lead abatement programs developed, to reduce lead's harmful effects on health, especially in relation to children. Lead abatement programs provided new paint and window components to homes built before lead was banned. As of 2016, 44 U.S. states have laws to address lead hazards in paint and/or dust (County Health Rankings and Roadmaps, 2017) and some U.S. states and cities have lead abatement or lead hazard reduction programs. The reduction of lead in our environment is a successful example of how data can inform policy, which creates programs at state, county, and city levels. The case study of Trevor in Chapter 5 provides the narrative that makes the story personal to a family, providing understanding of the policy in the lives of citizens. To find out about lead levels in your state, visit the Centers for Disease Control website at https://www.cdc.gov/nceh/lead/data/state.htm.

friendly often find conflict with other aims to increase business, jobs, and economic growth. This tension between economic interests and environmental interests manifests itself in big and small ways. Education, outreach, and the support of alternatives to the common behavioral practices must accompany successful policy changes. Developing new policy is akin to writing a new story or redefining what the outcome can be. This work can be done at the local, state, or federal level—and social workers have held these executive policymaking roles. Structural theory gives us the bases of considering what our policies should be, and narrative theory provides us the persuasive capacity to reimagine our collective story.

EMBRACING CONFLICT (STRUCTURAL THEORY)

Policies always involve conflict. There are not always enough resources or enough agreement on how the limited resources should be spent. Embracing and moving through these conflicts to find the best responses for the well-being of society is the goal of policymaking. Difficult questions are part of this process. Can a business care for the natural resources and community culture in the process and still make enough money to pay all of its employees a livable wage? Social workers have long worked to address disparities in the social welfare system, and now we must expand that work to the environmental welfare system as we learn how deeply connected these two systems are.

ADVOCACY AND PERSUASION (STRUCTURAL THEORY)

Advocacy is the important act of speaking with or on behalf of or validating another person, group, institution, or being, to reinforce specific needs and issues. Advocacy and persuasion encourage others to build awareness and understanding about an issue. If you are frustrated and angry about a problem affecting the people you work with, don't leave your anger and frustration behind. Bring it with you, shape it into passion, use it thoughtfully in your conversations, and channel it so that it brings even more persuasion. Persuasion can be influential and allows for a new partnership where previously there may not have been a relationship at all.

Advocacy comes in many forms within social work practice. This is a time when using your own power as a professional will be very useful to you. Your own comfort in this work will go a long way. Rather than being selfless, this has been called "self-full"—a full sense of confidence and a full sense of how to use your legitimized power for positive influence (Wood & Middleman, 1991). Your spheres of influence include your colleagues, your community members, and even the profession itself, in an effort to expand your range of impact. You and your clients can participate in many activities related to advocacy: email and letter-writing, professional use of social media, lobbying, phone-calling, in-person meetings, and community meetings. One area requiring advocacy is the "reduction of risk from and exposure to pesticides and other chemicals for vulnerable age groups" (National Association of Social Workers, 2014, p. 10). Young people are vulnerable because of their smaller bodies and frequency of exposure as a result of outdoor play and hand-to-mouth behaviors. Older adults are vulnerable due to the accumulation of their lifetime of exposure. Social workers can work to advocate for policy change and join in partnership with influential groups, such as the Environmental Working Group (www.ewg.org), to advocate with additional influence and persuasion.

RESISTING POLICY INJUSTICES (STRUCTURAL THEORY)

The loss of land, people, cultures, and biodiversity is directly related to the constant and grinding pursuit of a seldom-questioned belief in economic expansion as the singular goal of a thriving community. This leads to economic interests as the paramount and overriding factor in policy development and decision-making, excluding the other two elements of the triple bottom line, environment and equity. These unquestioned assumptions are fodder for social workers. There lies the space for questioning, rationalizing, and then resisting—often in the form of nonviolent action. There are still indigenous lands, in which the caretaking of place, without the spoils of economic gain, continues. In North Dakota and other places around the world, American Indians, indigenous peoples, and their allies have resisted implementation of oil pipelines in the hope of keeping their land and water free from the threat of pollution. Resisting in solidarity can be a powerful way to change policy or policy implementation. One of the reasons resistance to reliance on oil is so important is its connection to the burning of fossil fuels, which is accelerating climate change.

EDUCATION AS A SOCIAL WORK ROLE (SYSTEMS THEORY)

Policies can be accepted and voted on, changes made in documents and materials; but that does not mean the policy change will be felt by individuals. This is an area in which social workers can have expanded influence. "Social workers also have an important role to play in increasing public awareness of the human impacts of environmental change" (Kemp & Palinkas, 2015, p. 15). There are always limitations in the reach of policy. Despite a policy change or development, individuals may be unaware of the policy. Social workers can provide education and outreach to groups, especially helpful when translated into impacts on the daily lives of clients. It can take years for this outreach to saturate and change a community—or it can take months. The Internet and social media have changed the length of time for information to spread.

GREEN FEES AS SUSTAINABLE PRACTICE (STRUCTURAL THEORY)

Green fees or green assessments (Jones, 2008) are essentially voluntary taxes to pay for greening efforts or retrofits on a campus or in a community, neighborhood, city, or state. Green fees are often small and voluntary monetary commitments and are focused on specific environmental and human issues. For example, in the state of Minnesota, people who own cars can purchase a special license plate that costs more. The additional fees help preserve state parks. This voluntary option is meant to increase funds for land preservation but also to encourage use of public land— the land all residents share.

Colleges also use the green tax as a way to fund sustainability efforts on their campuses. Does your school institute a green fee? Check your tuition statement. If your college doesn't have one, you could request that your student government initiate one. Green fees provide a continuous basis for collecting money for environmental sustainability initiatives and assure attention to the issue as long as the fees are enacted.

Phase Four: Evaluating Outcomes and Making Transitions

Evaluating policies and the programs they initiate is an important part of social work. Evaluation is used to determine program effectiveness and modifications needed. Unfortunately, the success of social policy is rarely shared. Often, it is the next problem we face rather than the success of the last effort that receives the most attention. There are several methods we can use in phase four of policy work, and we highlight four of them here.

THEORIES OF CHANGE (NARRATIVE THEORY)

A theory of change is a narrative, developed by stakeholders, that clarifies how and why the policy created the desired change. The theory of change that is developed also articulates the implementation and functions of the change (Callahan, DeShazo, & Kenyon, 2012). Often in the form of a paper or statement, it attempts to explicate the why and how of the policy changes, taking multiple perspectives into consideration. The theory of change can help create an understanding of the intermediary steps needed to reach a long-term outcome. Quantitative and qualitative data, as described in Chapter 8, can be helpful in developing the theory of change. The data are useful for either continued improvement, transitioning to a modification in the policy, or to celebrate shared work.

EVALUATION TO DETERMINE EFFECTIVENESS

Measuring changes made by policy is crucial in helping determine next steps— often for policy improvement. Policy can be delivered unevenly across populations or with limited efficiency among some groups. Evaluations of methods can help determine better ways to implement the policy and any gaps that are discovered. Generating this knowledge shows "if desired outcomes have been met" (Callahan et al., 2012, p. 6) and is the best method to determine appropriate next steps for a continuing policy. Formative evaluations are concerned with the service delivery of the policy, summative evaluations are concerned with the results of the policy implementation, and a cost/benefit evaluation attempts to determine if the outcome is worth the expense of implementing the policy (Cummins et al., 2011).

HOLD APPROPRIATE GROUPS ACCOUNTABLE FOR PROGRESS AND IMPROVEMENT (STRUCTURAL, SYSTEMS, AND NARRATIVE THEORIES)

Without data, there is no way to know if the resources used for policy implementation are being used wisely and if the implementation plans are in need of improved response. Data can help hold agencies accountable for the policies they should be implementing (Callahan et al., 2012). Groups, agencies, and task forces can undergo an audit or review to determine the success of their initiatives and room for change. These audits and reviews can be completed internally or by an outside group. Making the information public, along with strategies for improvement, is one way to help a group hold itself accountable. Holding people accountable is not about getting people in trouble—it is about improvement. Awareness of the "spin" of the story is important. The combination of progress, safety, transparency, and a willingness to be vulnerable to identifying weaknesses is a brave and difficult stance for many groups to take.

Policy and Organizational Practice

Policies regarding food, energy, healthcare, taxes, and education all have implications on the natural world. Systems theory tells us that all is connected—we cannot separate our political or organizational practice from the natural world. Policy within the structures of government, as well as policy within an organizational context, has environmental impacts. Both kinds of policies can be influenced and shaped by social work practitioners. We turn now to organizational practice, which has some overlaps with policy practice.

Organizations

Organizations can be clients of social workers too. As employees of a social service organization, we have a responsibility to shape the culture and programs provided by organizations to assure that they reflect the values of our profession and the call of justice we adhere to. This creates our organizational culture, the expression of how work is done in the organization. Organizational leaders, which many social workers are called to become, are also people who shape and influence the culture of an organization, often in conjunction with policy practice. "Cultural practices indirectly affect organizational behavior by creating a climate that gives primacy to particular values and behaviors" (Mattaini & Holtschneider, 2016, p. 215). The importance of this influence cannot be overstated. Most social service agencies are organized to conform with the larger institutional systems that perpetuate the environmental and human degradation that has been built over time, often called *hegemony* or *privilege*. Resisting, on an organizational level, the structures, privileges, and powers of these unquestioned systems is the call of leadership. These very institutions often embody the values and oppressions we are trying to resist. To do so, we must intentionally engage with the agencies as our clients. Even good organizational cultures need strategy to maintain a commitment to environment, equity, and economy. This section provides concrete ideas for creating organizations responsive to the natural environment around them. While an organization includes multiple subsystems, the entire organization can be engaged in the phases of social work practice. A social worker can engage an organization because he or she is an employee of that organization, as an interested citizen, a leader, a volunteer, or a member of the organization in some other way.

Phase One: Telling and Exploring the Story

Organizational assessment can be complex due to the multiple subsystems that exist within the organization's boundaries. Picture a modern-day settlement house with multiple programs across the lifespan of people in the community. Each program itself has a story to tell. A few options for understanding the organizational story are particularly relevant for environmental justice practice.

PLACE AND STRUCTURE (NARRATIVE AND SYSTEMS THEORY)

An organization can tell a story of its place and structure. Learning about the building history and its grounds; the amount of energy needed to heat, cool, and power the building; the history of the land and neighborhood are all part of the story. Consider who first lived on the land, what is native to the area, and what culture and languages are predominant near the agency. An assessment of structure and place can include an audit of the use of cleaners, trash and recycling, care of the land, composting, the number of truck deliveries, accessibility, and other topics. Similar to getting to know any client, note what is important to the agency and investigate the story.

ORGANIZATIONAL CULTURE (NARRATIVE AND SYSTEMS THEORIES)

An assessment of an organization can include organizational culture and behavioral patterns within that culture. This includes a variety of ways in which people do the work of the organization with impact on the environment. Culture is expressed in what meetings are held and for what issues, who speaks at meetings, where and how decisions are made and communicated, what committees are formed, how people speak to each other in the workplace, and how joys are celebrated and stresses are handled. Shifting culture is either the purview of leadership and/or a committee sanctioned with power. A green team or committee is a good option to penetrate and change culture on caring for the environment.

ENVIRONMENTALLY COMPETENT ORGANIZATIONS (SYSTEMS THEORY)

Creating environmental competence can be a goal for organizations, programs, and the policies that support them. Decades ago the literature on cultural competence led the way to creating organizations welcoming and responsive to human diversity. Using a developmental approach, cultural competence became integral to systems of care (Cross, Bazron, Dennis, & Isaacs, 1989). Like cultural competence, the environment can be imagined on a continuum that ranges from environmental destructiveness to environmental proficiency. Adapted from cultural competence (Cross et al., 1989), I have identified four essential elements that contribute to an environmentally competent organizational system:

1. Value diversity in nature and humans
2. Practice self-assessment of the organization's influence and impact on the environment
3. Institutionalize environmental knowledge for all members of the organization
4. Develop adaptations to enhance the natural environment and steward natural and human resources

Environmental competence can be present at all levels and subsystems within a given organization. For example, policies that affect the entire organization, behaviors of individuals on a day-to-day basis, as well as the structure of the organization are all areas in which environmental competence can be created. From the front-line social workers to the administrators and leaders, congruence among these levels creates the greatest potential for effectiveness in environmental competence. An environmentally competent organization acknowledges and incorporates the importance of environmental knowledge and experience, assessment of the relationship to nature, vigilance toward the injustices that result from environmental degradation, and adaptation of programs to meet environmental sustainability goals. Like cultural competence, organizations without a clear commitment to environmental competence or cultural competence weaken their impact on the social change they seek. Environmental sustainability and cultural sustainability are important partners in the justice equation. This becomes even more clear as we begin to develop our preferred reality.

Phase Two: Describing a Preferred Reality

CREATE ENVIRONMENTAL COMPETENCE (SYSTEMS THEORY)

You will find plenty of opportunities to work toward environmental change within your agency or organization. Environmental competence builds on and borrows from the work of cultural competence. Organizations that are environmentally competent display the following characteristics (adapted from Cross et al., 1989):

- Respect the unique needs of the geographic locality
- Acknowledge seasons, topography, and weather as predominant forces in shaping behaviors, values, and institutions
- View natural environmental systems, such as plants, animals, weather, and topography, as a mechanism of support
- Acknowledge that people need access to the natural environment
- Believe that diversity within nature is as important as diversity within humans
- Function with the awareness that the dignity of the person is not guaranteed unless the dignity of Earth and the person's neighborhood is preserved
- Acknowledge and accept that natural environmental burdens and privileges exist and have an impact on clients' lives
- Advocate for effective services on the basis that the absence of environmental competence in any part of the organization compromises the environmental competence of the entire organization
- Respect nature as indispensable to understanding the individual because the natural environment provides the context within which the person functions
- Respect preferences that value process rather than product and harmony or balance within one's life rather than achievement
- Acknowledge that when working with clients at all system levels, process is as important as product
- Understand that some behaviors are the expression of adjustments to living in a toxic world
- Identify when values of environmental competency are in conflict with dominant values of economic gain

These same authors developed a continuum of culturally competent practice that I borrow and adapt for environmental competence. The continuum is identified in Box 9.4 and provides a definition of each of these levels (Cross, Bazron et al., 1989).

Box 9.4 **More to Explore—Environmental Competence Continuum**

Environmental destructiveness—Attitudes, policies, and practices that are destructive to the environment, the most extreme examples including the purposeful destruction of the environment.

Environmental incapacity—When organizations do not seek to be environmentally destructive but lack the capacity to ameliorate the environmental destructiveness of their work.

Environmental blindness—Denial reigns. When organizations ignore environmental strengths and encourage status quo resource depletion with the perspective that nature is problematic.

Environmental precompetence—The environmentally precognitive organization recognizes its weaknesses in including the natural environment and attempts to improve some aspect of this area. It may be working on one part of environmental sustainability but stop there.

Environmental competence—When organizations are characterized by respect for nature, continuing self-assessment regarding nature, attention to the dynamics of environmental injustices, and continuous expansion of environmental knowledge and resources.

Environmental proficiency—When an organization is characterized by holding nature in high esteem, developing new approaches based on the environment, and sharing the results of its efforts at including nature in its systems.

AIM TO PROGRESS ALONG THE ENVIRONMENTAL COMPETENCE CONTINUUM (STRUCTURAL THEORY)

Attitudes, policies, and practices are major areas where development can occur. Positive movement along the continuum occurs because of many decisions made to enhance the practices of the system. Systems, organizations, programs, and social workers do not start out being environmentally competent. Like any kind of competence, it is developed over time with practice, education, and evaluation. Like all change, it occurs in the complex interplay between the levels of the system, the attitudes of the people within the system, the policies developed, and the leadership and structure of the organization (see Box 9.5). Funding can be used as an incentive for programs and organizations to develop environmental progress along this continuum. Agencies such as the United Way, private foundations, and government can encourage the development of environmental competence by placing requirements on recipients of their funding.

Box 9.5 **People, Places, and Issues—Case Study**

LaTonya and Omar are completing their social work field placement at a community youth center. With supervision from their field instructor, Hong, they develop after-school programming for kids in the nearby immigrant community. They are learning about kids aged 7 to 12, activities that are engaging to the youth, partnering with the neighborhood school to support academic achievement to reduce educational disparities, and providing enrichment activities for neighborhood youth with the larger goals of reducing crime, building community, and helping the kids adjust to a life in the United States that is very unfamiliar to their parents. Part of the mission of the organization is to "help youth create a life of health, happiness, and community involvement for the betterment of themselves and the community around them." LaTonya and Omar really like their field placement, the kids they work with, and Hong, their field instructor. They spend a lot of time focusing on improving the kids' grades, developing and implementing community-building activities, and purchasing healthy snacks for the program. They convinced the agency to start reusing a lot of the items that were often tossed away, such as forks, cups, and art supplies, in favor of reusable items. The agency agreed once it considered the cost savings. Now, LaTonya and Omar are talking about the agency's exterior and the land around it. It's not used well and is mostly dirt from heavy foot traffic and lack of care. It can get really littered at times, and it's not clear who's in charge of it at the agency. The agency can't afford a grounds crew. It contracts out for basic landscape services, but the services are limited to keep the cost low so that expenses can be used toward the mission of the agency.

LaTonya and Omar start wondering what the empty land could be used for. They decide to broach the subject with Hong. Applying the environmental competence continuum, they begin a conversation with Hong about using the land more carefully. Hong is intrigued and suggests that a conversation with a larger audience should be pursued—the executive committee of the agency. LaTonya and Omar are excited and nervous but begin preparing their presentation about the land the agency rests on as a beginning point to their presentation to the executive committee. They hope for idea generation, support, and maybe a chance to bring their presentation to the broader community, including the kids and elders.

Phase Three: Making Plans and Dreams Real

Organizational policies affect the day-to-day operations at countless agencies in which social workers are employed, from nonprofits and government agencies to schools, community agencies, prisons, and healthcare systems. Because everyone in society is impacted by organizations within the community, the role of organizational social work practice is as important as individual practice. Good programs and good organizations begin with good design. Good sustainability design is attuned to the weather, the land, the people, the customs, the rituals that bring health and vitality to that area. "Good design promotes human competence instead of addiction and dependence, efficient and frugal use of resources, sound regional economies, and social resilience" (Orr, 2004, p. 105). When we design programs and organizations for people and places in ways that promote this we optimize the capacity for human and natural goods to flow from these experiences. Remember the power of local and connected solutions. Neighborhood- or community-based services can be more easily adapted to community cultural preferences. In all of the suggested techniques of this section, consistently recognize the strengths and culture of the community, the espoused values of the people served, and the natural resources and strengths endemic to the community and area in which the organization is located. Keep values out front—especially those of equity and relevant participation. Make the connections to people and the environment transparent, and consider the following specific methods to build organizational environmental competence and make the plans and dreams real.

DEVELOP COMMUNITY PARTNERSHIPS (SYSTEMS THEORY)

Imagine a social justice and social service agency in intentional partnership with an environmental organization. Imagine the possibilities of overlap and connection and new areas of practice convergence. Creating formal or informal agreements between your organization and a well-established environmental agency within the community can help to assure that progress will be made. These organizational relationships can facilitate growth for both groups; environmental organizations benefit when learning about the impacts on community members in their area and organizations that serve people can benefit by understanding the environment in which they reside. Consider developing shared local initiatives with social, economic, business, for-profit, and nonprofit sectors within your local community. Develop shared decision-making strategies based on equity, economy, and environment. One community created a transit partnership as many organizations were along a well-used transit corridor for social services, medical services, and government organizations. Together, they crafted policy that enabled people to access transit to their area more easily. This includes shared bike racks, a bike-share system, transit passes, and accessible walking paths.

HIRE LOCAL (STRUCTURAL THEORY)

Members of the community who work in the organization and care for the infrastructure of the agency can have a positive impact due to their local connections. While the best person for the job is the most important element of hiring, posting open positions and recruiting locally should always be a priority. When community members are part of the organization as employees, you assure that you have another connection to be culturally competent to humans and nature within that community system. Their level of care may be higher and the ripple effect stronger.

ENVIRONMENTAL LANGUAGE IN THE AGENCY MISSION STATEMENT (NARRATIVE THEORY)

An organization's mission statement tells a story of the organization in one quick snapshot. The mission statement can be reviewed to assess its commitment to environmental justice in its actions as an organization and in its programmatic structure. Adaptation of the mission statement to include a commitment to environmental sustainability as an organization or environmental justice in its practices is one way organizations can institutionalize environmental competence. Environmental justice, sustainability, sustainable practices, stewarding of natural resources, reduction in the carbon footprint, attention to the impact of place—there are a myriad of ways to incorporate your care and concern for place and nature in your organization's mission statement. The language must be culturally relevant to the people and an addition that the whole agency can pursue.

ENVIRONMENTAL JUSTICE ADVISORY BOARD (SYSTEMS THEORY)

Create and institutionalize an advisory board to oversee environmental competence practices at your organization, a group that can view the entire ecosystem of the agency. Formalizing a structure to review environmental experiences within the organization can be pivotal in creating environmental competence practices at the organizational level. These formal groups can expand awareness to all of the employees within the organization. Because these advisory boards hold oversight power, they have the capacity to encourage staff within the organization to work toward environmental competence. When advisory boards are filled with people within the organization or who are served by the organization, they can build legitimacy and influence. Include a diversity of the agency hierarchy when forming the Board.

AUDITING FORMAL POLICIES AND PROCEDURES (STRUCTURAL THEORY)

Institutionalize, through formal policies and procedures, environmental competence. Institutionalizing changes within an organization typically requires working within the existing power structures such as the organization's governance and committee structure. One example of a formal institutional change an organization can make is to examine and audit the employee handbook to modify and add appropriate practices that enhance environmental sustainability. For example, there may be a section in the employee handbook on staff travel. This section may only include a reimbursement protocol for those who drive their car. Additional language could be added to the employee handbook to encourage public transportation or a bike-share program to make home visits or attend meetings.

MARKET EFFORTS (NARRATIVE THEORY)

Be prepared to show progress in your annual report, commitment to your mission, and your ability to measure and evaluate your impact on the environment. Marketing the success of an organization's environmental competence has proven to be beneficial in the for-profit and nonprofit sectors. There are many community members who care about the impact on the natural world around them. It is likely that sharing your story of attempts and successes toward environmental competence will be viewed favorably by the community, grant-funding agencies, and the clients you serve.

FUNDING (STRUCTURAL THEORY)

Seek to fund environmental justice initiatives or be prepared to incorporate environmental competence initiatives into your existing grant-seeking efforts. There are funds available for greening organizations or creating sustainable environmental practices. It is possible that an organization could seek out funding to enhance its environmental justice mission or its environmental competence practices. However, it is important not to be caught up in the idea that funding is required for changes at the organizational level. The commitment to environmental justice can be implemented by modifying existing practices within the organization at no cost, and sometimes with a cost savings. Nonetheless, it can be helpful to be prepared for potential grant-seeking opportunities to cultivate environmental sustainability within an organization, and it may be favorable to report on environmental efforts to existing funding bodies.

BUDGET (STRUCTURAL THEORY)

Assure that the budget matches the agency and social work values of social, economic, and environmental justice. Aim for the triple bottom line in the way your program and organizational budgets are implemented. Question the balance between funds used for people, planet, and profit. Does it reflect an allocation of resources that matches the mission statement you have created? Make sure you can identify ways that all three values are supported in the budgetary line items. If not, identify ways to create balance over time. Consider building a sustainability line-item into your budgets, as a spring board for your efforts.

Phase Four: Evaluating Outcomes and Making Transitions

In organizational practice too, we attend to the outcomes and the transitions in our social work practice. There are often multiple stakeholders interested in the accomplishments or failings of organizations. These can be community members, funders, staff, and, of course, clients. A few methods to use in this phase of practice are shared here.

LOGIC MODELS (SYSTEMS THEORY)

For organizations and the programs that are part of them, outcomes have become very important as they help funders identify if the program and organization are meeting their intended goals (Westerfelt & Dietz, 2010). When complex organizational components and multiple stakeholders and client groups are part of this process, it can be difficult to discern what should be measured and when. And more importantly, it can be difficult to see big changes in short periods of time. Some things need time before being measured. An outcomes-based logic model can help determine what can be measured in the short term, in the intermediary, and what needs the long term for tangible outcomes to show (Westerfelt & Dietz, 2010). Logic models begin with the end in mind and help those planning to identify the steps needed to reach their goals.

CASE STUDIES (NARRATIVE THEORY)

The organizational case study analysis can be an informative tool in evaluating organizational change. The *Harvard Business Review* has been using cases as a teaching tool in the field of business for a number of years. Common in social work, especially with individuals and families, case descriptions can be very useful at the organizational level as well. It is a tool that can identify the unique stakeholders, cultural context, and a power analysis that can be descriptive in ways that other measures simply are not. Like the importance of the lifespan of the individual person, the lifespan of the organization—its historical context—has a bearing on the outcomes of today. A case study is one way to capture historically important and contemporary data and provide context to understanding and using it. A collaboratively written case study provides assurance that the multiple perspectives needed for a quality case study are included.

Values-Driven Macro Practice

Relationships are paramount in organizational practice. Relationships among the community members served, between staff at the agency, and with funders and other organizations are all equally important. No harm to relationships should be tolerated. Develop programs based on building competency and empowerment rather than on delivering a service. View environmental justice problems as a means for communities to "gain a greater sense of their own capacities and competencies" (Locke, Garrison, & Winship, 1998). Remember, when inviting community members "to the table," that the table need not be set by white middle-class participants There are lots of tables, and rather than inviting groups to the dominant table, we should offer to attend theirs. Using the ideas explored in this chapter, begin to converse with your colleagues about how policies and agencies can be influential and transparent in their efforts to nurture environmental and cultural sustainability. One step at a time, you can influence these macro contexts in all different kinds of organizations.

Critical Thinking Questions

1. Discuss an environmental organizational strategy you think could work in an agency where you intern or work. How might it occur?
2. Rate an organization you are familiar with on the environmental competence continuum. Explain your rating.
3. Identify policies from the city you live in or the campus community you are a part of that impact the environment. How many can you name? Do you know who mandated them?

Key Terms

Audit
Institutional policies
Institutionalize
Organizational change
Organizational structure
Policies
Residual policies

Additional Learning Activities

1. Get in small groups with fellow classmates. Discuss the environmental impact of the campus community you are part of. Are there organizational practices that support the environment? Write them down. Discuss how these practices are maintained and communicated on your campus.
2. Using the Internet, explore a national policy on water or air quality. Now, find a nonprofit organization working on this issue. Can you identify similar goals between the stated policies of the nonprofit and the government policy?
3. Find a policy at an organization you work or internship for. Review the employee or volunteer handbook if you need ideas. In what ways does this policy have an environmental influence at the organization? Make suggestions for improvement.

References

American Lung Association (2017). Air Quality Facts. Retrieved from http://www.lung.org/our-initiatives/healthy-air/sota/air-quality-facts

Banks, E.C. Ferretti, L.E. & Shucard, D.W. (1997). Effects of low level lead exposure on cognitive function in children: a review of behaviora, neuropsychological and biological evidence. *Neurotoxicology 18*(1), p. 237-281.

Braun, J.M., Kahn, R.S., Froehlich, T., Auinger, P. & Lanphear, B.P. (2006). Exposures to Environmental Toxicants and Attentention Deficit Hyperactivity Disorder in U.S. Children. *Environmental Health Perspectives, 114*(12), 1904-1909.

Bullard, R. (2005). *The quest for environment justice: Human rights and the politics of pollution.* San Francisco, CA: Sierra Club Books.

Callahan, C., DeShazo, J. R., & Kenyon, C. (2012). *Pathways to environmental justice: Advancing a framework for evaluation.* Los Angeles, CA: UCLA Luskin School of Public Affairs, Luskin Center for Innovation. Retrieved from http://luskin.ucla.edu/sites/default/files/Pathways%20to%20Environmental%20Justice.pdf

Cleveland, L.M., Minter, M.L., Cobb, K.A., Scott, A.A., & German, V.F. (2008). Lead Hazards for Pregnant Women and Children, Part 1: Immigrants and the poor shoulder most of the burden of lead exposure in this country. *American Journal of Nursing 108*(10), p.40-49.

County Health Rankings and Roadmaps. (2017). Lead paint abatement programs. Retrieved from http://www.countyhealthrankings.org/policies/lead-paint-abatement-programs

Cross, T., Bazron, B., Dennis, K. W., & Isaacs, M. R. (1989). *Towards a culturally competent system of care: A monograph on effective services for minority children who are severely emotionally disturbed.* Washington DC: Georgetown University Child Development Center.

Cummins, L. K., Byers, K. V., & Pedrick, L. (2011). *Policy practice for social workers: New strategies for a new era.* Boston, MA: Pearson.

Har, J. (2016, July 10). San Francisco enacts a broad ban on foam items. Star Tribune,

Jones, V. (2008). *The green collar economy: How one solution can fix our two biggest problems.* New York, NY: Harper One.

Kemp, S. P., & Palinkas, L. A. (with Wong, M., Wagner, K., Reyes Mason, L., Chi, I., & Rechkemmer, A.). (2015). Strengthening the social response to the human impacts of environmental change. (Grand Challenges for Social Work Initiative Working Paper No. 5) Cleveland, OH: American Academy of Social Work and Social Welfare.

Locke, B., Garrison, R., & Winship, J. (1998). *Generalist social work practice: Context, story, and partnerships.* New York: Brooks/Cole.

Mattaini, M. A., & Holtschneider, C. (with Lowery, C. T.). (2016). *Foundations of social work practice: A graduate text* (5th ed.). Washington DC: NASW Press.

Mary, N.L. (2008). Social Work in a Sustainable World. Chicago: Lyceum.

National Association of Social Workers. (2014). Environment policy. In *Social work speaks* (10th ed.). Washington DC: NASW Press.

Nevin, R. (2007). Understanding International Crime Trends: The legacy of preschool lead exposure. *Environmental Research 104*(3), 315–336.

Orr, D. W. (2004). *Earth in mind: On education, environment, and the human prospect.* Washington DC: Island Press.

Rogge, M. (2008). Environmental justice. In T. Mizrahi & L. E. Davis (Eds.). *Encyclopedia of Social Work* (e-reference ed.). New York, NY: Oxford University Press.

Segal, E. A. (2010). *Social welfare policy and social programs: A values perspective.* Belmont, CA: Brooks/Cole.

Titmuss, R. M. (1968). *Commitment to welfare.* New York, NY: Pantheon.

Westerfelt A. & Dietz, T.J. (2010) *Planning and Conducting Agency Based Research.* (4th ed.) Boston: Allyn and Bacon.

Wilensky, H. I., & Lebeaux, C. N. (1965). *Industrial society and social welfare.* New York, NY: Free Press.

Reyes, J.W. (2015). Lead Exposure and Behavior: Effectson Antisocial and Risky Behavior Among Children and Adolescents. *Economic Inquiry, 53*(3), p. 1580-1605.

Wood, G.G., & Middleman, R.R. (1991). Advocacy and social action: Key elements in the structural approach to direct practice in social work. *Social Action in Group Work, 53-63.*

CHAPTER 10

Holistic Practice

STEWARDING PEOPLE AND THE ENVIRONMENT

Anything we love can be saved. —*Alice Walker, p. 45*

Because what we do matters, we might want to wake up to more than
the mere routines of the day. —*James J. Ferrell, p. 31*

By now, you have an understanding of the primacy of nature in human life and the
promise of environmental justice as a social work practice arena. You also know
that the knowledge and skills social workers have been developing for decades provide cogent connections to aiding people and the environment. I hope you are convinced that working toward environmental justice is within the domain of social
work practice.

Well-honed social work practitioners are fluid in their work in such a way that
one cannot even tell they are practicing social work. Their practice has become
holistic, incorporating the foundational concepts of social work, theories that res-
onate with their practice skills and the community they work with, and practice
methods that have become natural to them. The connection between micro and
macro social work is vibrant and transparent. In doing this work, we cannot think
discretely between problem sets but must see the wholeness in the problems we
face. In this holistic practice, stewarding people and the environment is simultaneous and symbiotic. As we move forward in our environmental justice practice,
we round out understanding of these concepts by considering a few more ideas
related to wholeness.

Shared Problems

Environmental justice is rarely a stand-alone problem. Where there are environmental injustices, human injustices reside. *Intersectionality* is the word to describe

the complexity of the concept that where there are environmental problems there are often social ills: "skewed landscapes overflowing with the excesses of industrial society—too much pollution, too much poverty, too much unemployment, too much disheartenment. Moreover, they are landscapes starved by a scarcity of other elements—too few trees and green spaces, too little artwork, too few good jobs, too little hope" (Di Chiro, 2002, pp. 285–286).

Social workers have been working in communities such as these for years, and including the natural environment as part of this practice brings intentional alignment to these intersections. Rather than creating a hierarchy of social ills, or injustices, the shared problem approach allows solution development that solves more than one problem at a time and takes the natural environment into account, knowing it is paramount to human health and the amelioration of other social ills.

A New Economy

The challenge we face as we work to build communities that provide adequate healthcare, comfortable and safe homes to create family life, workplaces that give meaning and livable wages, transportation infrastructures to travel to those we love and move products we need, and inclusive educational institutions is daunting. Decades of work by many people have focused on elevating the living conditions of the world's poor. These goals cannot be suppressed. However, the natural resources needed for the demands of this expansive infrastructure must be considered along with the needs of Earth for health and sustainability. "Extinction of species and cultures is driven by globalization, the pursuit of progress through resource extraction and economic expansion" (Hawken, 2007, p. 102). Beyond what is necessary and needed, what about those humans who simply ask for too much? Where does human need for safety and comfort become lost in greed and hubris? The psyche of industrialized countries must confront the voracious consumption mentality and the waste it creates. From the most micro of human interactions to the most macro of global economies, the ever-hungry machine of economic growth and capitalism must be reigned in. "In order to do that we must close the circle. The linear nature of industrial production itself, in which labor and technology turn natural wealth into consumer products and wastes, must be transformed into a cyclical system. In the best scenario, natural resources must be reused or not used at all, and waste production cut to a mere trickle" (LaDuke, 1999, p. 197).

In their book *The Upcycle*, McDonough and Braungart (2013) bravely suggest that abundance is what we are after in our social transformation. "The goal of the upcycle is a delightfully diverse, safe, healthy, and just world with clean, air, water, soil, and power—economically, equitably, ecologically, and elegantly enjoyed." Creating abundant economies built on renewable and reusable energies and items is at the heart of feeling we have enough, without decimating Earth. Rather than devising methods to reduce waste and pollution, these same authors suggest new designs in human products that don't contribute to waste at all.

The only economic model that has been tried is the intensive extraction of Earth's resources. This model of growth cannot be sustained. So we must determine new measures of success, new personal human standards for what is acceptable, and new ways of creating what is needed without pillaging natural resources. There are statements of principles of building and maintaining an "eco-nomy." Box 10.1 provides the principles for a green economy, submitted to the United Nations, with sustainable development as its focus.

Box 10.1 More to Explore—Principles for a Green Economy

Submitted to the United Nations Conference on Sustainable Development—2012

1. Equitable Distribution of Wealth—Promote the equitable distribution of wealth within nations and among nations, to reduce disparities between rich and poor, and achieve social and economic justice, within a sustainable and fair share of the world's resources and leaving sufficient space for wildlife and wilderness.

2. Economic Equity and Fairness—Guided by the principle of common but differentiated responsibilities, create economic partnerships that would transfer substantial financial and technological assistance to less developed countries, to help minimize the gap between the developed and developing world and support the environmental sustainability of both.

3. Intergenerational Equity—Environmental resources and ecosystems must be carefully managed and safeguarded so as to enhance the value of environmental assets for future generations, thereby equitably meeting their needs and allowing them to flourish.

4. Precautionary Approach—Science should be utilized to enhance social and environmental outcomes, through the identification of environmental risk. Scientific uncertainty of environmental impacts shall not lead to avoidance of measures to prevent environmental degradation. The "burden of proof" should lie with those claiming that there will not be significant environmental impacts.

5. The Right to Development—Human development in harmony with the environment is fundamental to the achievement of sustainable development so that individuals and societies are empowered to achieve positive social and environmental outcomes.

6. Internalization of Externalities—Building true social and environmental value should be the central goal of policy. To this end, market prices must

reflect real social and environmental costs and benefits so that that the polluter bears the cost of pollution. Tax regimes and regulatory frameworks should be used to "tilt the playing field," making "good" things cheap and "bad" things very expensive.

7. International Cooperation—The application of environmental standards within nation states must be undertaken in a cooperative manner with the international community, based on an understanding of the possible impact on the development potential of other states. Environmental measures relating to trade should avoid unfair protectionism but overall should ensure that trade supports sustainable resource use, environmental protection, and progressive labor standards, promoting a "race to the top" rather than the bottom.

8. International Liability—Acknowledging that actions within national boundaries can cause environmental impacts beyond national jurisdictions, requiring cooperation in the development of international law that allows for independent judicial remedies in such cases.

9. Information, Participation, and Accountability—All citizens should have access to information concerning the environment, as well as the opportunity to participate in decision-making processes. To ensure that environmental issues are handled with the participation of all concerned citizens, institutions at all levels (national and international) must be democratic and accountable and make use of tools that enable civil society to hold them to account. In this regard, the access to justice by citizens for redress and remedy in environmental matters is a cornerstone of enhancing accountability.

10. Sustainable Consumption and Production—Introduce sustainable production and consumption with sustainable and equitable resource use. Reduce and eliminate unsustainable patterns of production and consumption (i.e., reduce, reuse, and recycle the materials used), acknowledge the scarcity of the Earth's resources and implement activities accordingly.

11. Strategic, Coordinated, and Integrated Planning—To deliver sustainable development, the green economy, and poverty alleviation, an integrated approach must be adopted at all levels to expedite the achievement of socioeconomic and environmental sustainability through strategic planning with civil society and stakeholders and across all relevant government departments.

12. Just Transition—There will be costs in making the transition to a low-carbon, green economy in the pursuit of sustainable development. Some states and actors are better able to bear those costs than others and are more resilient to transitional changes. In the process of change, the most

vulnerable must be supported and protected—developing countries must have access to appropriate financial and technical assistance; citizens and communities must also have access to new skills and jobs.

13. Redefine Well-being—Gross domestic product (GDP) is an inadequate tool for measuring social well-being and environmental integrity. Many socially and environmentally damaging activities enhance GDP—such as fossil fuel exploitation and financial speculation. Human well-being and quality of life and environmental health should be the guiding objectives of economic development.

14. Gender Equality—Gender equality and equity are prerequisites to the transition to a green economy and the achievement of sustainable development. Women have a vital role to play as agents of change for environmental management and development—their actions must be rewarded accordingly and their skills enhanced.

15. Safeguard Biodiversity and Prevent Pollution of Any Part of the Environment—Protect and restore biodiversity and natural habitats as integral to development and human well-being, and develop a system of governance that protects the resilience of ecosystems to prevent irreversible damage.

Stoddart, Riddlestone & Vilela, (n.d.)

Working with, Sharing Power, and Sharing Governance

In working toward environmental justice, helping professionals cannot see themselves as working on behalf of others but should see the shared benefits of our work. "A shared power perspective recognizes that all actions by the social worker, client, and other actors in the case either contribute to or damage the interconnected reality within which all are embedded" (Mattaini & Holtschneider, 2016, p. 32). This is true with environmental justice issues, such as climate justice, which are pervasive and will eventually impact us all with some level of universality. To see ourselves as partners is the most effective way to engage and provide the space for others to participate with equity. Mulally (2007) calls this a dialogical relationship, one in which "all participants in the dialogue are equals" (p. 317). In this way, client and worker learn from each other, and equivalent wisdom is expected and strategy-building equally shared.

Shared power is growing in acceptance in professional circles. Different from our expert knowledge or expert power, in shared power everyone is recognized for their elements of expertise; and while the expertise is different, the expertise is equally respected. In social work, we have a long-standing ethic to recognize and empower our clients as the experts in their own lives, culture, dreams, and goals.

In working toward environmental justice, we work with professional groups that have different understandings about the role of shared power and its usefulness in solving human problems. Our job, as social workers and keepers of empowerment practice, is to ensure that power is shared as much as possible among the groups working to solve environmental justice problems. When shared power is not part of the problem-solving process, marginalization and stigma are nearly certain.

Shared power is a goal and a process. Moment-by-moment activities and actions bring this dynamic concept to life. It is never completed and always nuanced into greater and greater levels of shared power. Combined with "a critical awareness of one's situation and an increased capacity to act on that awareness" (Lundy, 2004, p. 129), we develop adeptness for personal and social change. Without such awareness, one identifies personal struggles only as they are defined by the dominant structures in society. This creates a sense of internalized oppression. This creates and sustains feelings of powerlessness and stress and degradation, with social and health consequences.

When we imagine ourselves as people who choose to "give," we situate ourselves in a standpoint of power, one in which we have something to give and the people we work with only are recipients. In an equitable and far more powerful method, we can stand with and share learning, giving, and receiving. For example, over the last few decades, what are called "developed" countries have cast a critical gaze upon human communities living in environmental spaces in which it can be very difficult to live—with limited water supplies, harsh agricultural climates, and limited food and economic resources. Developed countries may assume these countries need assistance to improve their standard of life. And yet, what would occur if we turned this critical assessment onto ourselves? How might we critique our middle-class and upper middle-class lives? And what if we changed the language of this discourse to critique the lives of developed countries, living on the margins of full community, yoked to the idea of economic growth? How might the critical gaze change? How might changing the language of economically privileged people actually improve the experiences of poor and marginalized people? What would occur if we studied "the colonizers rather than the colonized, the culture of power rather than the culture of the powerless, the culture of affluence rather than the culture of poverty" (Nader, 1972, p. 284).

Moving beyond diversity and inclusion, we must begin to forge equity and participation in our work. The metaphor for diversity and inclusion has long been to "bring others to the table." The problem is, the table is still set, and placed, and positioned by those who have more power in society. Rather than bringing others to a single table, equity and participation calls on everyone, including those with privilege, to attend other tables as they are equally valid. Certain demonstrable behaviors help establish a culture in which we can share power. Lowery and Mattaini (1999) suggest that mutual recognition of positive actions, low levels of aversive exchanges (like microaggressions), active pursuit of an alternative perspective, and high levels of authenticity are some of the ways we can demonstrate and build a movement toward shared power and governance. We must also recognize the self-healing qualities of all living things—including our clients. They do not need repairs done by us but a place in which to be nurtured into their own natural process of self-healing.

Simultaneous Social Change Practice at All Levels

In this book the phases of practice are written as discrete and specific stages of a process the social worker engages in with clients. While the new practitioner should be very cognizant of these discrete steps—because each of them is important— a mature social work practitioner moves in and between the phases. The social worker may be investigating potential interventions with the phrasing of assessment questions and even evaluating potential outcomes based on what is heard in the beginning interviews. It takes time to develop the confidence to practice with this sophistication.

In addition to interweaving all of the phases of practice in a seamless and sophisticated way, social workers recognize that individuals and policies, families and community, are all areas that are connected. As they work on one area, they can simultaneously work on another area. In describing the crosscutting movement and the potential that lies before us, Hawken (2007) writes,

> a movement cultivating innovative, sometimes brilliant, social technologies that would accomplish just that reversal by returning people to the heart of the world and of life. It comprises design as much as action, imagination as much as innovation with a focus on everyday life: the demands and pleasures of learning, taking care of others, preparing food, raising children, taking journeys and doing meaningful work. These timeless ways of being human are threatened by global forces that do not consider people's deepest longings. (pp. 14–15)

The United Nations' sustainable development goals, announced and supported by world leaders, models this holism in practice and the recognition that macro forces and the micro experiences of our days impact our lives. The "17 Goals to Transform Our World" highlight efforts considering the needs of Earth while aiming for social, economic, and environmental sustainability. The goals aim to "end poverty, protect the planet and ensure prosperity for all" (United Nations, 2016). To do so, they get specific. Social workers can integrate each of these goals into their own agencies, programs, and personal practice. The 17 goals are stated simply (United Nations, 2016):

1. No poverty
2. Zero hunger

3. Good health and well-being
4. Quality education
5. Gender equality
6. Clean water and sanitation
7. Affordable and clean energy
8. Decent work and economic growth
9. Industry innovation and infrastructure
10. Reduced inequalities
11. Sustainable cities and communities
12. Responsible consumption and production
13. Climate action
14. Life below water
15. Life on land
16. Peace, justice, and strong institutions
17. Partnerships for the goals

The sustainable development goals need supporters worldwide, and an acceleration in the interest to achieve them (United Nations, 2017). Efforts and successes remain uneven (United Nations, 2017). Social work values fit well with these goals.

Use of Self and Application to Our Lives

Good social workers have mastered the art of using their toolbox, their personal self, as a catalyst for change. Social workers are required to reflect on their thoughts, feelings, and actions to match their behaviors with the knowledge values and skills of social work. This is no easy task. An important aspect of our use of self is to maintain openness within ourselves for change and transformation to occur within and on behalf of our clients. Brenee Brown (2012), a social work researcher on vulnerability, offers social workers language to assist in the process of engaging with vulnerability to provide the opportunity to find solutions in a purposeful way. Brown's suggestions for language to incorporate as part of our personal toolbox builds bridges between people, rather than walls (pp. 210–211). Some examples from Brown's list follow:

I'd like to give it a try.
It's important to me.
Here's what I need.
Here's what I feel.
Can you teach me how to do this?
That means a lot to me.

I accept responsibility for that.
It didn't work, but I learned a lot.

Social workers can apply these practices and principles to their own lives in ways that benefit their own mental, physical, familial, and community health. One of the greatest benefits of having the knowledge and skills of advanced social work practice is being able to apply them in our own life. The foundational theories of this book—systems, narrative, and structural—as well as the foundational concepts are as applicable to our lives as they are to those of our clients. Using the knowledge, skills, and values of social work and reflecting on our lives will improve our own living conditions, which, as we know, are connected to the community and people around us.

Part of self-care in environmental justice work is claiming and owning our place at the environmental issues table. "It is difficult to consider the potential problems that may occur if environmental degradation is not addressed. Social workers roles may become even more stressful and complex if we choose not to address environmental problems" (Erickson, 2011, p. 188). For many years environmental issues were left to the realms of natural science and technology. Connections to other academic disciplines, were nonexistent due to a lack of recognition of the importance of interdisciplinarity in resolving environmental issues. This segmented thinking grew out of specific disciplinary knowledge being claimed but not necessarily shared. As we move toward understanding "wicked problems," we have realized that we must respond with wicked answers, the kind that come from a multiplicity of human experience, knowledge, and skill. Without this kind of complex response, the future of human life on Earth could become very difficult. Social workers have a place in this conversation. Our understanding of our foundational concepts, theories, and values is essential to resolving environmental problems and issues. Social workers are part of the environmental justice solution.

The social institutions that we participate in, such as schools, churches, and workplaces, have a large impact on the natural environment. Working closely with these institutions, we can have a significant impact on the production, consumption, and pollution produced by them. Consider the college campus environmental audit. It provides an opportunity to look closely at particular components that have an impact on the natural environment in many campus communities. However, don't be afraid to adapt this audit for your field placement or a smaller organization which you may be a part of. Simply review and identify which questions are salient for the organization which you are auditing. Then, gather with a few of your peers, colleagues, or friends to consider how together you can create an audit of your organization. Answering these questions may give you new and interesting fodder for a continued greening of the organization. Box 10.2 provides a framework for a campus audit.

Box 10.2 **More to Explore—College Campus Environmental Audit**

General campus information
1. Number of students on campus?
2. Number of employees on campus?
3. Name of the environmental organizations on campus?
4. Is the college a member or partner of environmental organizations?
5. Is sustainability or environmental care part of the college mission, vision, or values statements?

Food
1. Who operates the food service? What is available on campus? Who decides what is offered? Does it meet the cultural needs of the student body?
2. To what extent does the food service purchase from regional growers and food processors?
3. Does the food service purchase organically grown produce, meat, and dairy products?
4. Have any classes, student groups, or events taken place on campus highlighting the connection between food and the environment?
5. Are the utensils and plates reusable?
6. Does the student dining area use trays? Are these necessary?

Solid waste
1. How much solid waste does your campus generate annually? What are the costs?
2. Does the college have a recycling program? What materials are recycled? Is it widely used? Can it be expanded? Are there gaps in accessibility on campus?
3. Does the college have a composting program? What materials are composted? Is it widely used? Can it be expanded? Are there gaps in accessibility on campus?
4. Has the college implemented programs that promote source reduction, such as a reusable mug program, switching from disposable to washable dishes, reduction in deliveries, or others?

Hazardous substances
1. What kind of chemicals are used for cleaning and lawn care?
2. Are safety and nontoxicity considered in making these purchases? Are there other options?

Energy
1. What are the college's energy sources for heat and electricity? Are clean options available?
2. Does the campus encourage alternative transportation options?

Procurement policies

1. How many reams or tons of paper does the college purchase annually? What is the associated cost?
2. Does the college have a policy of preferentially buying products made from recycled materials?
3. What programs and policies have been established to promote purchasing environmentally friendly products?

Environmental education and literacy

1. What environmentally focused courses are offered? Are they assessed or measured in regard to student learning? Are they connected to social and economic justice?
2. Are their co-curricular opportunities for students related to environmental sustainability? Social sustainability?
3. Is there support for faculty curriculum development in regard to environmental stewardship, ethics, or sustainability in relation to their curricula?

What else is important to add to your environmental campus audit? Review the United Nations' sustainable development goals. Consider your campus culture, your student body, your geographic location, and any other special considerations that make your campus unique for ideas.

Collaborative Partners in Environmental Justice Efforts

The environmental crisis is not an issue we face alone. We are partners in working toward building resiliencies, and our partners will be found in many places. One partner in the current effort is business and employers. Their role is to help build livable wages, addressing the need for respectful and meaningful work for humans (Jones, 2008) that are local and promote sustainability. When labor is a partner, working-class, unemployed, and underemployed people will benefit from efforts to care for Earth and get their individual and family needs met by bringing a paycheck home that they can feel good about.

A second partner is social justice activists and organizations (Jones, 2008). Social justice activists already have structured agencies and groups that have built skill and recognition in working toward justice in social relationships in society. While their work is far from done, their efforts are not so different from those of environmentalists. We share many similar values, issues, and strategies. Women's rights, interfaith movements, racial justice, LGBTQ rights, disability rights, and other causes can join the opportunity to push for environmental rights as part of a shared agenda. We all need a clean and healthy environment.

Another partner for us is environmental organizations. Many long-standing environmental organizations have an interest in the human aspects of environmental degradation—in its harm to humans as well as its potential for solutions for Earth. In this text I have introduced you to several, but there are many more. What environmental organizations are available in your community? Look them up and start a conversation on shared goals and values. Often the work will emerge.

In reality, the potential partners for dealing with environmental injustices are limitless. Environmental problems are, in the end, completely universal. Our client stories become a shared story—a "superstory" (Locke, Garrison, & Winship, 1998). A superstory links an individual's story to that of others, the nation, and even the world. The superstory contains the myths, the facts, and certainly the beliefs of the people. What is our superstory on climate change? On the degradation of nature? Let's make it a superstory of partnerships, solutions, and creation of a healthy Earth.

Environmental Justice, Ecological Justice, and Intergenerational Justice

As we have seen throughout this text, social work has a place in the work of environmental justice. We have a discipline grounded in creating justice networks, and the expansion to include environmental justice is now an imperative, even mandatory, as the Council on Social Work Education competencies now assures that all social work students include environmental justice alongside social and economic justice in their learning. In 2016, the International Federation of Social Workers celebrated World Social Work Day with the motto "Promoting Community and Environmental Sustainability." Social work is ready to claim and share our strategies toward these efforts. See Box 10.3.

This is the way forward, and working toward environmental justice in practical and applied ways is the aim of this book. But there is one further extension that all of humanity will need to make. That is toward ecological justice. Ecological justice is the recognition that all living things supported by Earth are relevant and worthy of inclusion in the justice perspective. This calls people to become advocates for an ecocentric justice, one that "gives equal moral standing" (Besthorn, 2013, p. 37) to all natural systems and all beings in that system. Environmental justice is a human-centered perspective, and ecological justice is a living being–oriented perspective. This brings us back to the very beginning of this book. The history of environmental justice—which began with indigenous views of nature and human relationships and continues with intergenerational justice—the opportunities, resources, and burdens one generation leaves for the next (Cournoyer, 2014).

Box 10.3 **Organizations in Action—Arbor Day Foundation**

A conservation and education nonprofit, the Arbor Day Foundation (www. arborday.org) works to support trees, plant trees, and make the planet "cleaner and greener" in the process. Trees do remove air pollution and improve air quality, and this translates into public health savings, valued at $6.8 billion dollars (Nowak, Hirabayashi, Bodine, & Greenfield, 2014). To help support the planting and care of trees, the Arbor Day Foundation partners with corporations, governments, and institutions to care for and manage tree canopy. Tree City USA and Tree Campus USA are two of its major programs in the care of urban forestry. The Arbor Day Foundation cites research that says trees reduce crime, reduce energy consumption, increase property values, reduce the effects of climate change, and even help students succeed in school. Their message is specific, connects people to their environment, and aims to bring the benefits of trees to any and all communities.

Biophilia—We End with Love

The term *biophilia*, a desire to affiliate with living things, was coined by Edward O. Wilson in 1984 to describe our subconscious desire to seek connection with the rest of life and that this desire is innate. "We are not likely to fight to save what we do not love" (Orr, 2004, p. 46). To save Earth and all of the beautiful beings that inhabit it means we may have to recognize and identify our need, our want, for love of living things. Love does matter. Love motivates us to do better, and identifying our love of living things can motivate us to find new ways to live on and with Earth. Joining our discipline of social work—connecting it to our love of Earth and all life forms—can bring about this needed change, this embrace of biophilia. "It would be the worst kind of anthropocentrism to dismiss such accounts in the belief that the capacity for biophilia and awe is a human monopoly" (Orr, 2004, p. 139). Other living things likely experience biophilia too. While biophilia is considered innate, writers have pondered its ability to be stunted, destroyed, twisted, or simply lost. Current degradation and exploitation of Earth and its resources point to violence, lack of care, and a thwarting of our natural biophilic qualities. With so many human and environmental problems to choose from, you may find it difficult to determine where to put your energies. Begin where you exude love. Encourage your clients to do the same. With a holistic understanding, we are assured that our work connects social, economic, and environmental justice. Our future is bright, onward!

Critical Thinking Questions

1. What does holistic practice mean to you? What might this look like when you are a social work practitioner?
2. Are you courageous enough to act on your knowledge of environmental injustices? Explain.
3. What have you gained from a relationship with an animal? What about this relationship appears universal?

Key Terms

Anthropocentrism
Biophilia
Ecocentrism
Holistic
Leadership
Shared governance
Universal

Additional Learning Activities

1. Look up the website of the Environmental Working Group. How might this information help clients you work with? The community you work in? Your own life?
2. Identify one of the current environmental problems in your area. What are the micro to macro components you see? How is the human spirit affected?
3. Develop an eco-map and a timeline for yourself. What are the important elements of the system? Draw it out and share it with a small group of peers. As you analyze your eco-map and timeline, identify two revelations you learned during the process.

References

Besthorn, F. (2013). Radical equalitarian ecological justice: A social work call to action. In M. Gray, J. Coates, and T. Heatherington (Eds.). *Environmental social work* (pp. 31–45). New York, NY: Routledge.

Brown, B. (2012). *Daring greatly: How the courage to be vulnerable transforms the way we live, love, parent, and lead.* New York, NY: Gotham.

Cournoyer, B. R. (2014). *The social work skills workbook.* Belmont, CA: Brooks/Cole.

Di Chiro, G. (2002). Sustaining the "urban forest" and creating landscapes of hope. In J. Adamson, M. Evans, & R. Stein (Eds.). *The environmental justice reader: Politics, poetics, and pedagogy* (pp. 284–310). Tucson: University of Arizona Press.

Erickson, C. L. (2011). Environmental degradation and preservation. In L. M. Healy & R. J. Link (Eds.) *Handbook of international social work: Human rights, development and the global profession* (pp. 184–189). New York, NY: Oxford University Press.

Farrell, J. J. (2010). *The Nature of College: How a new understanding of campus life can change the world*. Minneapolis, MN: Milkweed.

Hawken, P. (2007). *Blessed unrest: How the largest social movement is restoring grace, justice, and beauty to the world*. New York, NY: Penguin.

Jones, V. (2008). *The green collar economy: How one solution can fix our two biggest problems*. New York, NY: Harper One.

LaDuke, W. (1999). *All our relations: Native struggles for land and life*. Cambridge, MA: South End Press.

Locke, B., Garrison, R., & Winship, J. (1998). *Generalist social work practice: Context, story, and partnerships*. New York, NY: Brooks/Cole.

Lowery, C. T., & Mattaini, M. A. (1999). The science of sharing power: Native American thought and behavior analysis. *Behavior and Social Issues, 9*(1/2), 3–23.

Lundy, M. (2004). *Social work and social justice: A structural approach to practice*. Peterboroush, ON, Canada: Broadview Press.

Mattaini, M. A., & Holtschneider, C. (with Lowery, C. T.). (2016). *Foundations of social work practice: A graduate text* (5th ed.). Washington DC: NASW Press.

McDonough, W., & Braungart, M. (2013). *The upcycle: Beyond sustainability—Designing for abundance*. New York, NY: North Point Press.

Mulally, R. (2007). *The new structural social work* (3rd ed.) New York, NY: Oxford University Press.

Nader, L. (1972). Up the anthropologist: Perspectives gained from studying up. In D. Hymes (Ed.). *Reinventing anthropology* (pp. 284–311). New York, NY: Vintage.

Nowak, D. J., Hirabayashi, S., Bodine, A., & Greenfield, E. (2014). Tree and forest effects on air quality and human health in the United States. *Environmental Pollution, 193*, 119–129.

Orr, D. (2004). *Earth in mind: On education, environment and the human prospect*. Washington DC: Island Press.

Stoddart, H., Riddlestone, S., & Vilela, M. (n.d.) Principles for the green economy: A collection of principles for the green economy in the context of sustainable development and poverty eradication. Retrieved from http://www.stakeholderforum.org/fileadmin/files/Principles%20FINAL%20LAYOUT.pdf

United Nations. (2016). Sustainable development goals: 17 goals to transform our world Retrieved from http://www.un.org/sustainabledevelopment/sustainable-development-goals/

United Nations. (2017). *The Sustainable Development Goals Report 2017*. Retrieved from http://www.un.org/sustainabledevelopment/blog/2017/07/pace-of-progress-must-accelerate-to-achieve-the-sdgs-finds-latest-un-progress-report/

Walker, A. (1997). *Anything we love can besaved: A writers activism*. New York: Random House.

Wilson, E. O. (1984). *Biophilia*. Cambridge, MA: Harvard University Press.

INDEX

Page references for figures are indicated by *f*, for tables by *t*, and for boxes by *b*.

Made in United States
North Haven, CT
25 May 2023

36978978R00122